CONTEXT AND MEANING IN PROVERBS 25-27

SOCIETY OF BIBLICAL LITERATURE

DISSERTATION SERIES
J. J. M. Roberts, Old Testament Editor
Charles Talbert, New Testament Editor

Number 96
CONTEXT AND MEANING IN PROVERBS 25-27
by
Raymond C. Van Leeuwen

Raymond C. Van Leeuwen

CONTEXT AND MEANING IN PROVERBS 25-27

Scholars Press
Atlanta, Georgia

CONTEXT AND MEANING IN PROVERBS 25-27

Raymond C. Van Leeuwen

Ph.D., 1984
University of St. Michael's College

Advisor:
Paul E. Dion

© 1988
Society of Biblical Literature

Library of Congress Cataloging-in-Publication Data

Van Leeuwen, Raymond C., 1948–
  Context and meaning in Proverbs 25-27.

  (Dissertation series / Society of Biblical
Literature ; no. 96)
  Originally presented as the author's thesis
(Ph.D.–University of St. Michael's College,
1984).
  Bibliography: p.
  1. Bible. O.T. Proverbs XXV-XXVII–Criticism,
interpretation, etc. I. Title. II. Series:
Dissertation series (Society of Biblical Literature) ;
no. 96.
BS1465.2.V36 1988   220.6'6   86-29830
  ISBN 1-55540-004-3 (alk. paper)
  ISBN 1-55540-005-1 (pbk. : alk. paper)

Printed in the United States of America

To the Memory of Cornelis Van Leeuwen (1913-1984)

CONTENTS

Acknowledgments ix
Abbreviations x
Sigla and Technical Terms xi
Introduction: The Problem 1

1. The Problem Pursued: Twentieth Century Research 5

2. The Problem in Proverbs 25: The Work of G. E. Bryce 21

3. Heuristic Assumptions 29

4. Methods: Structural, Poetic, Semantic 39

5. Proverbs 25:2-27 57
   Translation 57
   Structures 61
   Poetics 70
   Sense 72

6. Proverbs 26:1-12 87
   Translation 87
   Structures 88
   Poetics 95
   Sense 99

7. Proverbs 26:13-16 107

8. Proverbs 26:17-28 111
   Translation 111
   Structures 113
   Poetics 116
   Sense 119

CONTENTS

9. Proverbs 27:1-22 123
   Translation 123
   Structures 126
   Poetics 127
   Sense 129

10. Proverbs 27:23-27 131
    Translation 131
    Structures 135
    Poetics 136
    Sense 136

11. Recapitulations and Reflections 143

Bibliography 147

Index 163

Acknowledgments

Several people and institutions deserve thanks and credit for assistance given in the course of this work. Preeminent among these is Professor Paul E. Dion to whose encouragement, meticulous comments, and kind criticism I owe a debt which cannot be repaid. *Qui bene amat, bene castigat.* My readers, Anthony R. Ceresko, William H. Irwin, R. A. F. McKenzie, and especially Ronald J. Williams, have spared me many a slip and made a number of suggestions to improve this study. My colleagues at Calvin College, William Vander Kopple and Clarence Walhour, were kind enough to read sections of the work and discuss linguistics and literary criticism with me. Religion colleague Henry Vander Goot gave me help with Swedish. Among librarians Mrs. Lynn Hopkins and Mr. Conrad J. Bolt are especially to be praised. My wife, Mary, produced two books to my one and, with Dirk and Neil, we maintained both sanity and love.

For financial assistance I owe thanks to the Government of Ontario for an Ontario Graduate Scholarship in 1979-80, and to the Social Sciences and Humanities Research Council of Canada for a Doctoral Fellowship in 1980-81. Since leaving the nurturant ambience of St. Michael's, Calvin College and Seminary have provided a place, a library, and a bit of the *communio sanctorum* in which to pursue my work. For that too I am grateful. Psalm 103.

Abbreviations

For abbreviations not here listed, see *The Catholic Biblical Quarterly* 46 (1984) 401–408.

AEL	*Ancient Egyptian Literature*, Lichtheim
AI	*Ancient Israel*, de Vaux
APA	*The Aramaic Proverbs of Ahiqar*, Lindenberger
ASI	*Die ältesten Spruchsammlungen in Israel*, Skladny
IW	*Israelite Wisdom*, Gammie et al.
RR	*Vom rechten Reden und Schweigen*, Bühlmann
SAL	*Studien zu altägyptischen Lebenslehren*, Hornung and Keel
SAIW	*Studies in Ancient Israelite Wisdom*, Crenshaw
SAT	*La Sagesse de l'Ancien Testament*, Gilbert
SIPW	*Studies in Israelite Poetry and Wisdom*, Skehan
SIS	*Studien zur israelitischen Spruchweisheit*, Hermisson
SPOA	*Les Sagesses du Proche-Orient Ancien*
WGW	*Wesen und Geschichte der Weisheit*, Schmid
WL	*Wisdom Literature*, Murphy
WII	*Wisdom in Israel*, von Rad

Sigla and Technical Terms

A	Admonition (p. 2, n. 5; cf. p. 43, n. 11)
C	Comment (pp. 47-50; defined p. 50)
FA	Foolish Actant (p. 93)
FC	Figurative Comment (pp. 51-52; see Comment)
L	Level in the hierarchy of T-C structures of a S (pp. 50-52)
MC	Motive Clause (p. 44, n. 14)
MS	Motive Saying
NA	Negative Actant (p. 93)
P	Precept (p. 44)
Paradigmatic	(p. 40)
R	Result clause, a form of MC (p. 45)
RA	Relating Actant (p. 93, cf. pp. 122-123)
RT	Relational Topic (p. 89, n. 3)
S	Saying (p. 2, n. 5)
Syntagmatic	(p. 40)
T	Topic (pp. 47-50, defined p. 50)
/	Indicator of colon break or juxtaposition
>	"more than" in S's of "better . . . than" type (p. 46)
→	"so that, in order that" (p. 47)
↛	"lest, so that . . . not" (p. 47)
+	Broadly, the positive dimension of wisdom. Narrowly, a positive evaluation given to the *realia* depicted in a proverb colon or segment (pp. 45-47)
-	Broadly, the negative dimension of wisdom. See + (pp. 45-47)
∅	null: a colon which receives neither a + nor - valuation

Introduction

Perhaps the most crucial problem in the interpretation of literary texts is the determination and use of context in establishing meaning. This general problem touches virtually every aspect of the exegete's task, ranging from the broad horizons of the culture and language in which a text is written to the detailed questions of syntax, semantics, and orthography of a single line or word. In dealing with specific biblical texts, the problem often concerns the limits of a text: what, strictly speaking, defines this pericope? Here form criticism is of the greatest importance. But having delimited the smallest literary unit, further questions must be asked. Since a pericope exists in a larger work of some kind, how is a pericope to be related to its broader literary context? What constitutes legitimate, and what cavalier, use of context, whether proximate or distant? These questions, easy of formulation, are hard to answer. They involve all the issues and methods currently used in Old Testament studies, and they reveal the assumptions of the exegete who tries to answer them. Here, as Eissfeldt has said, form criticism "cannot deal with the larger units and is quite unable to deal with the books as we now have them."[1]

The problem of literary context also requires awareness of non-literary contexts. The enterprise of form criticism was founded upon the assumption that smaller oral or literary units had a *Sitz im Leben* out of which they arose and whose life concerns they served.[2] Moreover, the question of the relationship of a text to the realia of a world, whether actual or imaginary, cannot be avoided. For, as contemporary linguistics has made plain, though the words of a language form an interdependent system of meaning and though sense and reference are not coterminous, the meaning of words is generally tied to non-linguistic phenomena.[3] Much of the enterprise of Old Testament scholarship is obviously based upon the referential dimension of its texts.

The limitations of form criticism with its search for a *Sitz im Leben* and of the historical-critical search for concrete referents are particularly acute in certain Biblical texts. In the Psalms, in the wisdom writings, in many legal texts,

---

[1] O. Eissfeldt, *The Old Testament: An Introduction* (New York: Harper and Row, 1965), 4.

[2] M. J. Buss, "The Idea of *Sitz im Leben*—History and Critique," ZAW 90 (1978) 157-170.

[3] J. Lyons, *Introduction to Theoretical Linguistics* (Cambridge: Cambridge University, 1969) 54-55, 424-434.

and even in many prophetic passages, the givens for reconstructing the life situation or historical referent of a text are few or lacking. In these cases, apart from a broad cultural or historical context, one possesses only the literary context, the *Sitz im Buch*.[4] But even then, in many prophetic and legal texts, a considerable disparity of forms and contents often appears from pericope to pericope.

This problem appears in its most acute form in the book of Proverbs 10-22:16; 25-29. In these chapters, we find discrete, entirely self-sufficient literary units (Sayings or Admonitions) which are extremely terse in formulation and brief in compass, and virtually without historical "hooks." One is acutely aware that the briefer the literary unit the more difficult the interpretation. The problem is further complicated because the juxtaposed proverbs,[5] to a modern, western mind at least, often appear to have very little to do with one another either formally or materially.

The seeming isolation of the proverbs within the book raises an even deeper question which G. von Rad has formulated with his usual acumen:

> The sentence has to speak for itself. Here, however, we come for the first time to the most difficult problem, namely the question of the general religious and ideological sphere, of the context from which any given sentence comes and on the basis of which it is to be understood. . . . In the case of a modern sentence, we notice at once where a reliable interpretation or application stops and where an unreliable one begins. How much more easily, in the case of a sentence from antiquity, can one reach the point where the meaning of a sentence is falsified for the simple reason that one has lost sight of ideological and religious factors which were constitutive for the sentence.[6]

All interpretation involves a conscious or unconscious use of a complex of contexts both literary and non-literary, even when an isolated saying is being analyzed. The duty of the critic is not to ignore the contexts or "horizons" of meaning which affect interpretation but to become aware of their function and meaning, and of his own methods in dealing with them.

---

[4] For the distinction of the two types of *Sitz*, see G. Fohrer, "Remarks on the Modern Interpretation of the Prophets," *JBL* 80 (1961) 309-319. J. A. Gladson ("Retributive Paradoxes in Proverbs 10-29," Unpublished Ph.D. Dissertation; Vanderbilt [1978] 5) refers to "*Sitz in der Literatur.*"

[5] I will often use the word "proverb" in a non-technical sense to refer to the short Sayings and Admonitions which make up our texts. I use "Saying" as a t. t. equivalent to the German *Aussage* and "Admonition" (whether positive or negative) for *Mahnwort* or *Mahnung*. For this basic form critical distinction, see W. Zimmerli, "Concerning the Structure of Old Testament Wisdom," *SAIW* (1976, German original 1933) 175-207.

[6] *WII*, 32-33. Gladson ("Retributive," 146, cf. 156) speaks of "the contextless void" which bewilders the interpreter. The problem of context is also sharply put by R. N. Whybray ("Yahweh-sayings and Their Contexts in Proverbs, 10,1-22,16," [*SAT*, 1979] 153-165, especially 153-54).

If the broad problem behind our study is that of the context(s) which enable readers to understand ancient Biblical proverbs, the actual problem of our essay is narrower: to focus on their *literary* context, their *Sitz im Buch*.[7] It will be immediately obvious to the reader that two types of literary context are involved here. First is immediate context, which arises from the juxtaposition of letters, words, sentences, and pericopes, more or less in contiguity. The second is distant context, which arises when meaningful literary similarities or contrasts are created and discerned in texts that are not contiguous. Unconsciously or consciously, with methodological self-awareness or slumber, all readers of texts use both types of literary context in the process of understanding texts, not to speak of the non-literary baggage they bring to a text.[8]

Our study will focus on the question of contiguous context in the interpretation of Proverbs 25-27. If it appears that a proverb or group of proverbs have been consciously placed in a meaning-rich context, we must appropriate this fact and use it in our exegesis of the parts and the composite whole. In doing this, care must be taken that the exegete does not impose arbitrary connections but respects the text by asserting only such connections as he can explain.

This then is the problem of our essay. Are the proverbs and one brief poem found in Proverbs 25-27 arranged into a larger literary composition or compositions? And, if so, how? As formulated, this is a synchronic question. While synchronic and diachronic concerns can never be divorced, the necessity of the methodological priority of the synchronic question will be argued below.

---

[7] Our focus is in contrast to, but quite compatible with, the sociological focus of B. W. Kovacs' work, "Sociological-Structural Constraints Upon Wisdom: The Spatial and Temporal Matrix of Proverbs 15:28-22:16" (Unpublished Ph.D. Dissertation; Vanderbilt University, 1978). The contrast is one of focus; awareness of history and life setting must be a tacit dimension even of a literary study, and vice versa. See R. Wellek and A. Warren (*Theory of Literature*[3]; New York: Harcourt, Brace, and World, 1962) on the "extrinsic" and "intrinsic" approaches to literature. M. H. Abrams (*The Mirror and the Lamp: Romantic Theory and the Critical Tradition* [Oxford: Oxford University, 1953] 3-29) provides a useful analysis of four main types of criticism, based upon their primary focus on (1) the work itself, (2) its author (including *Sitz im Leben*), (3) its effect (on its audience), (4) its reference to a "universe" and its contents.

[8] "The education, the personality of every reader, the general cultural climate of a time, the religious or philosophical or purely technical preconceptions of every reader will add something instantaneous to every reading of the poem." Wellek and Warren, *Theory of Literature*, 146.

1
The Problem Pursued: Twentieth Century Research*

The student of Old Testament Wisdom is blessed with several recent and comprehensive surveys of the field, as are students of Ancient Near Eastern "wisdom." J. L. Crenshaw[1] and R. E. Murphy[2] have provided summaries of OT wisdom research with lucid statements of the basic issues and results. The collection edited by M. Gilbert[3] also includes a short survey of wisdom research. A recent volume of *JAOS* was entirely devoted to *Oriental Wisdom*,[4] including articles on Egypt and Mesopotamia. Ancient Egyptian wisdom research was also surveyed by M. V. Fox.[5] *The Aramaic Proverbs of Ahiqar* received a new edition with introduction and commentary by J. M. Lindenberger.[6]

*Commentaries are cited simply by author and page both in footnotes and in the text. See Bibliography for full details.

[1] Prolegomenon," *SAIW* (1976) 1-60; "Wisdom," *Old Testament Form Criticism* (ed. J. H. Hayes; San Antonio: Trinity University, 1974) 225-264.

[2] "Hebrew Wisdom," *JAOS* 101 (1981) 21-34; *Wisdom Literature* (FOTL 13; Grand Rapids: Eerdmans, 1981). See also J. A. Emerton, "Wisdom," *Tradition and Interpretation* (ed. G. W. Anderson; Oxford: Oxford University, 1979) 214-237. Due to a long publication delay, the last item was not as current as its date would suggest.

[3] *La Sagesse de l'Ancien Testament* (Gembloux: J. Duculot and Leuven: Leuven University, 1979) 7-13. Note also J. G. Gammie et al., *Israelite Wisdom: Theological and Literary Essays in Honor of Samuel Terrien* (Missoula/Chico: Scholars, 1978). Treating both Israel and the Ancient Near East is Leo G. Perdue, *Wisdom and Cult* (SBLDS 30; Missoula/Chico: Scholars, 1977).

[4] R. J. Williams, "The Sages of Ancient Egypt in the Light of Recent Scholarship," *JAOS* 101 (1981) 1-19; G. Buccellati, "Wisdom and Not: The Case of Mesopotamia," pp. 35-47.

[5] Two Decades of Research in Egyptian Wisdom Literature," *ZÄS* 107 (1980) 120-135. The Egyptian texts are now conveniently available in up-to-date translations by M. Lichtheim (*Ancient Egyptian Literature* Vols. I, II, III [Berkeley: University of California, 1973, 1976, 1980]) and in W. K. Simpson (*The Literature of Ancient Egypt* [New Haven: Yale University, 1973]). See also E. Hornung and O. Keel eds., *Studien zu altägyptische Lebenslehren* (OBO 28; Freiburg: Universitätsverlag and Göttingen: Vandenhoeck and Ruprecht, 1979).

[6] Baltimore: Johns Hopkins University, 1983. See the review by P. E. Dion in *SR* 12 (1983) 342-343.

5

For the purposes of this study, discussion may thus be limited to the tracing of those positions and problems which are of direct relevance to the thesis. First among these is the question of the demarcation of our text, Proverbs 25-27. Second is the problem which is our main focus, the question concerning the literary arrangement and unity of larger groups of proverbs in 25-27 (or elsewhere in the book). As presented in our Introduction, this is the problem of the immediate literary, interpretative context of the various proverbs. In the third place is a series of issues which, while not properly the business of the thesis, may be mentioned inasmuch as their solution cannot really be attained without more clarity concerning the basic literary problems of our document. If the text presents us with larger, unified blocks of proverbial material, the exegete possesses a much surer basis for interpretation than if only a random accretion of isolated proverbs exists.

Udo Skladny's work[7] set the stage for most subsequent discussion of the collections of proverbs which comprise the first and second "Solomonic" Collections (Prov 10:1-22:16; 25-29). Skladny, using analyses of form, content, and style, and employing statistics to quantify his findings, delineated four sub-collections: A (= 10-15), B (= 16-22:16), C (= 25-27), and D (= 28-29). Skladny's main contribution was to establish the individual character of the four collections, also with regard to content. It should be noted that Skladny's demarcations essentially follow the rubrics of the book itself (cf. 10:1; 22:17, 20; 25:1; 30:1), with an additional division in the middle of each Solomonic Collection.[8] Skladny dated the collections in the monarchical period.

There is no scholarly quarrel with Skladny's demarcation of the four Collections extant, and we will employ his designations (A, B, C, and D) to refer to them.[9] Nor is there now much debate concerning the *general* dating of these collections in the monarchical period. In particular, the date ascribed to Collection C by its attribution in 25:1 to the "men of Hezekiah" (even if the rubric is a later editorial insertion) is widely accepted, since there is no discernible *Tendenz*, other than historical interest, behind the attribution![10] The debate

---

[7] *Die ältesten Spruchsammlungen in Israel* (Göttingen: Vandenhoeck and Ruprecht, 1962).

[8] Skladny's basic divisions of the collections are fairly obvious and have long been commonplace. Even his separation of the sub-collections was not new. See, for example, J. Fichtner, *Die altorientlische Weisheit in ihrer israelitisch-jüdischen Ausprägung* (BZAW 62; Giessen: Töpelmann, 1933) 7, nn. 4, 5. Kovacs' suggestion ("Sociological") that Collection B should start at Prov 15:28 does not seem convincing.

[9] A sole exception is the highly idiosyncratic construct (as he himself admits, p. 27) of P. W. Skehan ("Wisdom's House," *CBQ* 29 1967 162-180). I cite the revised version in *Studies in Israelite Poetry and Wisdom* (CBQMS 1; Washington: Catholic Biblical Association of America, 1971) 27-45. Note also the slight dissent of Kovacs, cited in the note preceding.

[10] Skehan ("A Single Editor for the Whole Book of Proverbs," revised version in *Studies* 15-26) who does not mention Skladny, once again provides a dissenting voice. He asserts

which does exist concerns the *nature* of these "Collections" and the *manner* and *history* of their compilation. Two broad lines of argument may be traced: those which argue against unity in the collections and those which argue for.

Skladny's thematic treatment of the *Sammlungen* presupposed that these collections were not merely the result of a random accretion of sayings over the course of time, but that they arose in a relatively unified time-space frame and were each the product of the deliberate care and industry of a collector or collectors.

In sharp opposition to Skladny's view is that of W. McKane, who is perhaps the most prominent recent exponent of a long tradition in Proverbs studies[11] which takes the actual arrangement of proverbs in the collections as quite haphazard and thus virtually irrelevant for their interpretation. It is useful to take McKane as a representative figure, for he articulates in pointed fashion the unspoken assumptions underlying the practice of most exegetes:

> There is, for the most part no context in the sentence literature . . . for each sentence is an entity in itself and the collection amounts to no more than the gathering together . . . of independent sentences.

(17, 23; cf. "Wisdom's House," 44) that the mention of Hezekiah has an editorial function related to the number of lines in Collections C and D, and that, like Solomon, Hezekiah is mentioned as a fountainhead of wisdom tradition. However, the possible numerical usage of Hezekiah's name is not incompatible with an absolute dating of Collection C to his reign. See below.

For the generally accepted view on the date of C in Hezekiah's reign, see Skladny, *Spruchsammlungen*, 80-82 (with literature); R. B. Y. Scott (1965) xxxiv-xxxv, 21; W. McKane (1970) 577; H. J. Hermisson, *SIS* (1968) 16-18; von Rad, *WII* (1972) 15-17, (German original, 1970) 28-31; Crenshaw, *Old Testament Wisdom: An Introduction* (Atlanta: John Knox, 1981) 45. Cf. Murphy, "Hebrew Wisdom" (1981) 21.

[11] Actually one must speak of more and less here. Most commentators, from Ewald, Delitzsch and Toy onwards, have occasionally noted groupings (based on theme or poetic devices such as paronomasia) in the proverb literature of chapters 10-29. But for the most part these groupings, even when noted, are ignored in actual exegesis. R. N. Whybray ("Yahweh-sayings and their Contexts in Proverbs, 10, 1-22,16," *SAT* (1979) 153-165, 154) cites the commentaries of Gemser, Barucq, Scott, and Ringgren with McKane as representative of "the kind of approach which assumes that the material in these sections of Proverbs has been put together in an entirely haphazard way: that the authors or redactors were either indifferent to its arrangement or incapable of imposing any sustained logical structure on their ideas." Whybray here overstates the matter, though his assessment is correct in a global way. He could have added Gispen and van der Ploeg, among others. Cf. von Rad (*WII*, 113): "ordered arrangement of Proverbs occurs too sporadically to be of significance." B. S. Childs (*Introduction to the Old Testament as Scripture* [Philadelphia: Fortress, 1978] 557) notes the mixed character of the proverbs but argues from this for their "dialogic" character.

McKane does acknowledge, in deference to Gemser, that

> the atomistic character of sentence literature may be modified to some extent by a secondary grouping of sentences, whether this is based on purely mechanical considerations (word jingles, stitch-words) and is devised as a mnemonic technique to facilitate learning, or devices from editorial groupings based on common content in several sentences.

Nonetheless, McKane believes that these

> secondary groupings do not significantly alter the atomistic character of sentence literature. Further, these are not necessarily the principles of grouping which are best fitted . . . for the effective study of the wisdom tradition. . . . Consequently, I do not propose to concern myself with the principles which are employed to group sentences . . . but rather with a system of classification which is orientated towards an investigation of the history of the wisdom tradition in Israel, in so far as this can be reconstructed from the sentences.[12]

Thus, like every interpreter of the sayings, McKane needs some framework, an interpretive context to give meaning to the individual sayings he exegetes. To this end, McKane's 1970 commentary builds upon his theory of the history of Israelite wisdom adumbrated in his earlier *Prophets and Wisemen*.[13] Here wisdom is seen to develop from the secular to the sacred. The broad schema of this theory of wisdom's evolution can be found, for instance, already in J. Fichtner's 1933 work.[14] McKane, with reference to the sayings, formulates three classes which reflect this evolution:

---

[12] The foregoing quotations are from McKane (1970) 10, 413–414.

[13] (SBT 44; Naperville, IL: Alec R. Allenson, 1965). It should be noted that McKane's claim above to reconstruct the history of wisdom in Israel "from the sentences" is, strictly speaking, misleading inasmuch as its logic is circular. In fact, McKane employs a historical schema derived *extrinsecus* into which he fits the various proverbs. Cf. R. B. Y. Scott ("Wise and Foolish, Righteous and Wicked," *VTSup* 23 [1972] 146-165, 148): "It would appear that VON RAD and MCKANE differ so radically in their interpretation of the "Solomonic" sayings in Proverbs because they have reached their conclusions about the nature of old wisdom in Israel on other grounds, and then have read the sayings in the light of these conclusions."

[14] McKane (11) asserts his "general agreement" with Fichtner (*altorientalische Weisheit*, 24-25), Sellin, and Scott (commentary, 17). Various forms of this view (that wisdom evolves from universal, secular to sacred, Israelite concerns) are widespread in wisdom studies. Cf. G. E. Bryce (*A Legacy of Wisdom: The Egyptian Contribution to the Wisdom of Israel* [Lewisburg: Bucknell University and London: Associated University Presses, 1979] 220, n. 3) who asserts that this view was originally suggested in Rudolph Kittel's *Geschichte des Volkes Israel* (referring to the 1929 edition). Bryce himself treats the appropriation of certain Egyptian items in terms of three stages: the adaptive, the assimilative, and the integrative. But he considers the distinction of secular and religious inappropriate to Proverbs 25 (p. 154). Similarly, M. V. Fox ("Aspects of the Religion of the Book of Proverbs," *HUCA* 39 [1968] 55-69) finds in Proverbs an " 'Egyptian' stage" (which is already "religious") a " 'Yahwistic' stage" and a " 'Theological' stage." See also

Class A: These sentences are set in the framework of old wisdom and are concerned with the education of the individual for a successful and harmonious life.

Class B: Here the centre of concern is the community rather than the individual, and the sentences in this class have, for the most part, a negative character, in that they describe the harmful effects on the life of the community of various manifestations of anti-social behaviour.

Class C: These are identified by the presence of God-language or by other items of vocabulary expressive of a moralism which derives from Yahwistic piety.[5]

McKane's essential argument is that "the class C material represents a reinterpretation of the class A material and a later stage in the history of the Old Testament wisdom tradition."[16]

Similar to McKane's position of explicit rejection of the significance of grouping in Proverbs is that of C. Westermann[17] and R. B. Y. Scott. The latter scholar is less sanguine than McKane in expressing his aesthetic offence at the disorder he finds in the saying literature of Proverbs:

> The brevity of the proverbs in x 1-xxii 16, their miscellaneous subject matter and the discontinuity of their arrangement militate against the pleasure of reading them consecutively in their traditional order. . . . The parallelism of Semitic verse, which in prophetic oracles and longer poems can be a device of great beauty and effectiveness, produces in these lists of proverbs a tone of monotonous iteration. This second collection (xxv 1-xxix 27), like the first . . . is largely miscellaneous in subject matter and discontinuous in arrangement.[18]

Criticizing Skladny, Scott correctly points out that

> These bodies of material [Skladny's "collections"] are not homogeneous, and there is overlapping between them in subject matter, phraseology and literary forms. The

---

H. H. Schmid (*Wesen und Geschichte der Weisheit* [BZAW 101; Berlin: Töpelmann, 1966] 144-173) who finds three stages in Proverbs, but takes it as "heute unbestritten" that Israel's wisdom, like that of Egypt and Mesopotamia, was religious from the very start (p. 144).

[15] Commentary, 415. McKane concedes, "It is sometimes difficult to fit a sentence into this system of classification and, in particular, to decide whether it belongs to one class rather than another. . . ."

[16] Ibid., 11.

[17] "Weisheit im Sprichwort," *Schalom: Studien zu Glaube und Geschichte Israels* (A. Jepsen Festschrift; Arbeiten zur Theologie I/46; K. H. Bernhardt ed.; Stuttgart: Calwer, 1971) 73-85. Westermann based his arguments upon comparison with anthropological and missionary collections of proverbs from contemporary "traditional" societies. Westermann is correct in arguing that such sayings need a life-context to be meaningful. The question remains, however, whether the analogy made by Westermann to modern proverb collections is apt. The Sayings in Proverbs themselves bear a literary rather than oral character. Whether their compilation and arrangement are also deliberate and meaningful is precisely the question which Westermann begs.

[18] Commentary, 130, 24, 175.

differences among them are mainly differences in proportion of the several elements of their contents.[19]

A more subtle and complex analysis of the material than provided by Skladny's seminal work is called for. Scott, like McKane, sees a certain development over time of a more explicitly Yahwistic position in the book. Yet Scott seems more aware than McKane of the need to give account of the process of redaction or book-formation which led to our present document. Scott's basic model is that of a centuries-long process of accretion.

In contrast to the foregoing line of interpretation, which argues against the unity of proverb collections and against the significance of such smaller groupings as are discernible, is the line of research which argues for both unity and significance.

In 1968, H. J. Hermisson,[20] building upon earlier insights of Boström and Gemser (who himself used Boström) carried the analysis of Skladny a step further by trying to discern thematic and poetic unities in Collection A. G. Boström's important work, written in Swedish, has for obvious linguistic reasons not had the impact it merited, particularly in the Anglo-American world.[21] Boström's main focus was on the role of paronomasia of all sorts in creating the poetic unity of individual proverbs, especially in view of the bipartite form employed by most of them. Gemser (8-9) summed up Boström's contribution as follows:

> Wie ... vor allem G. Boström, Paron., gezeigt hat, wird fast in jedem Vers des Spruchbuches die eine oder andere Form von Paronomasie angewendet. Dabei ist die Paronomasie nicht nur ein Wort- und Klangspiel, sondern hat nach antiker Auffassung auch gedankenbildende, erklärende und überzeugende Kraft (Paron., S. 1-21).... Die Beachtung der Paronomasien ist zugleich ein wirksames Korrektiv gegen die Neigung zu Textänderung nach moderner, westeuropäischer Logik. Weder die Antithese noch die Synthese der parallelen Glieder darf forciert werden; das Unerwartete, Ueberraschende gehört vielmehr zum Maschalstil (Paron., S. 20. 122.135. 141 und sonst).[22]

Boström based his study of proverbial paronomasia on the view that for ancient Israel sound and meaning go together. Thus sound connections served to

---

[19] "Wise and Foolish," 149. Cf. Kovacs' account of Scott ("Sociological," 297-298).
[20] *SIS* 171-183.
[21] *Paronomasi i den äldre Hebreiska Maschallitteraturen* (Lunds Universitets Årsskrift. N. F. Avd. 1 Bd. 23; Lund: Gleerup and Leipzig: Harrassowitz, 1928). I am indebted to my colleague, Henry Vander Goot, for help with Boström's Swedish.
[22] N. H. Ridderbos (*Die Psalmen; Stilistische Verfahren und Aufbau* [BZAW 117; Berlin: de Gruyter, 1972] 75, 106-109) has pointed out that the sudden, unexpected transition from one sub-unit to another is also characteristic of the poetry of the Psalms. In this connection, it is interesting that Ridderbos, like Gemser, speaks of "Masjal-Stil": "Der Masjal-Stil hat tiefe Wurzeln in der gesamten israelitischen Literatur" (p. 108.).

strengthen the *sense* connection existing between the two halves of a proverb.[23] But Boström restricted the validity of this principle to the individual proverbs. And though he demonstrated the sound connections existing *among* distinct proverbs in meticulous detail (especially for Proverbs 25-27),[24] he viewed this as merely a matter of mnemonic convenience, having no significance for the interpretation of the proverbs so united.[25]

Hermisson objected to Bostrom's seemingly arbitrary restriction of the significance of paronomasia to the individual proverb:

> Verwunderlich is freilich, dass Boström den richtig erkannten Grund für die Anwendung von Paronomasien nur im Einzelspruch gelten lässt, während er Stichwortanordnung und Lautanklänge zwischen den Sprüchen nur als pädagogische Hilfsmittel zur Erleichterung des Auswendiglernens ansieht.[26]

This restriction, argued Hermisson, no doubt arose from the fact that the sound-plays existing among proverbs often connected proverbs which appeared to have widely varying *content*. Indeed, one may expect much stronger unity within a proverb than among them. Nonetheless, catch-words and sound-plays cannot be explained as mere mnemonic devices. For the sound-plays (*Lautanklänge*) at least cannot function as aids to memory, nor can the repetition of such common words as $sdyq$ and $rš'$. And, more importantly, the mnemo-technical view fails to take seriously the entire basis of this mode of thought: the connection between sound and meaning.[27]

Hermisson concluded that, though the proverb collections were comprised of traditional material — though not of folk-proverbs, in contrast to Eissfeldt — they revealed the hand of a unified artistic consciousness, so that Hermisson felt justified in referring to a *Verfasser* of this or that collection. Such a *Verfasser* employed both the paronomasia noted by Boström as well as themes which extended over several proverbs to create thematic-aesthetic sub-groups in chapters 10-15. And, in marked contrast to Scott's views, Hermisson insisted that the proverb groupings required thoughtful, aesthetically sensitive reading to be fully appreciated.

In explicit dependence upon Hermisson, O. Plöger[28] attempted to demonstrate the implications of Hermisson's position with detailed reference to

---

[23] Boström devoted careful attention to the individual proverbs in 25-27 (*Paronomasi*, 42-48, 73-86).
[24] *Paronomasi*, 87-102.
[25] In fact, Boström's argument (96) ran in the contrary direction: if sounds can unite where there are completely different meanings, how much more should this be the case in the individual proverb where meaning connection does exist.
[26] *SIS* (172) referring to *Paronomasi* (90).
[27] *SIS* 172; cf. 179-183.
[28] "Zur Auslegung der Sentenzensammlungen des Proverbiabuches," *Probleme biblischer Theologie. Gerhard von Rad zum 70. Geburtstag* (ed. H. W. Wolff; Munich: C. Kaiser, 1971) 402-416.

Proverbs 11, though his focus was mainly thematic. His conclusions were similar to Hermisson's: short groups of Sayings present a theme from a variety of angles. More recently, B. W. Kovacs[29] has produced a massive theoretical and interpretive study of collection B, which he begins a few verses before Skladny (15:28). In a number of respects, Kovacs' work is ground-breaking. He brings to bear the discipline of sociology as well as insights drawn from the phenomenological tradition. What Skladny had first ventured—the statement of a *Sitz im Leben* for proverb collections as opposed to individual sayings—Kovacs carries out in a more comprehensive way. Fundamental to Kovacs' enterprise is the insight that literature, including collections of sayings, is only preserved by a social group which has a more or less homogeneous worldview. Thus baldly stated, of course, the premise is too simplistic. Kovacs, however, may be said to employ this proposition, properly qualified, as a heuristic device leading to the delineation of a socially-perceived world which is the meaning-matrix of Collection B.

In contrast to the views of McKane and Scott that "no view unites any collection," Kovacs offers no less than eight reasons for the legitimacy of considering Collection B as the embodiment of a "consistent world-view." We quote Kovacs at some length since his work is not yet readily available:

> First, a long tradition of scholarship, from Casanowitz to Boström has shown the importance of paronomasia, assonance and catch-words to the structure of Hebrew poetry and particularly to the Book of Proverbs. Not only are word-plays and puns, repetitions of sounds, uses of different forms from the same root, spurious (for poetic effect) roots, and multiplication of synonyms employed to form individual sayings, but the same poetic devices appear to tie together successive sayings into a whole.... Paronomasia clearly establishes editorial intent when used as systematically as in Proverbs. The pattern cannot be either random or fortuitous; to attribute it to abstract verbal association or the mnemonic associative process of oral literature begs the question.... One may take issue with the term "collection" for describing the process whereby these blocks and other materials became a written document, but that such units existed seems as certain as anything in literary history can be.[30]

In the second place, Kovacs argues that Scott and McKane take insufficient account of

> the known rhetorical devices of the wise which would provide an alternate and less drastic explanation of some of their evidence. The wise, for example, clearly prefer in the context of brief sayings to state matters in general terms, without regard to exceptions and cases ... sayings which conflict may be resolved by appealing to relevant differences in situation—the wise man does not respond to life through the rote application of formulae to experience.... Further, repetition of sayings, the use of stock phrases, and repetition of sayings with small but all-important variations,

---

[29] "Sociological," (1978).
[30] "Sociological," 299-301.

all are known poetic devices in Israel as elsewhere. That the wise should use them in poetry scarcely requires resort to the atomization of wisdom writing and composition. The replacement of some phrase by a theological statement may represent theologization; it may also reflect *qol-wahomer* [sic] reasoning. If due piety be the sine qua non of wisdom, the irony of such substitutions would be obvious to the hearer. While one of the sayings may be original nevertheless, a long historical separation or some nationalization is not essential.[31]

Third, Kovacs argues that

> the nationalization of late wisdom [as in Ben Sirah] cannot be disputed, but a similar shorter process is hard to prove.... We should be careful not to historicize our philosophical precommitments ... or to make 'wisdom' so rigid and inflexible, so dogmatic in its assertions of retributionism, that it becomes a caricature.[32]

In the fourth place, Kovacs makes an important methodological point about the "relationship between language and context." The fact that certain language appears in the Yahweh sayings and not elsewhere does not necessarily entail two ideological spheres:

> To the extent that, for the wise, Yahweh limited or conditioned experience, one would expect these qualifications to appear only within the relevant generic statements, those about Yahweh himself, and typically not within sayings about the events conditioned.... To conclude that the theological language represents a later redaction on grounds of content, one must show that they present a world-view fundamentally at variance with that of the sayings-context in which they appear.[33]

Fifth, Kovacs points out that

> the aphoristic literature is terse.... The sayings are quintessentially poetry, to be related and understood in poetic terms.

Thus poetic connections are to be taken seriously and the demands of "non-poetic logic" are not to be imposed upon it:

> The poetic structure of the sayings also means that redactoral efforts should be fairly apparent through inconsistencies and problems in the text. The problems of "seamlessly" redacting a poetic text are nothing short of notorious. The traditional division of proverbs into "collections" is founded on precisely such problems. Alternative hypotheses of the composition of the book should present us with

---

[31] "Sociological," 301-303. Any proverbial system of thought encompasses "contradictory" sayings to accommodate different situations: "Look before you leap," but "He who hesitates is lost"; "Birds of a feather flock together," but "Opposites attract," and so on. See Prov 26:4-5; 17:17-18 (in Hebrew), 27-28, and Charles E. Carlston, "Proverbs, Maxims, and the Historical Jesus," *JBL* 99 (1980) 87-105.

[32] "Sociological," 303-304.

[33] "Sociological," 305-306. Cf. von Rad, *WII*, 53-73.

similar kinds of evidence to be convincing. In sum, the aphoristic literature amounts to poetic, not just "rational," modes of thought given poetic forms of expression.[34]

In the sixth place, Kovacs argues that

> however we understand the proverbs, we should offer an intelligible redaction history of the book. For example, the catch-word and paronomastic patterns which connect various proverbs simply cannot be adventitious nor accidental. They are intrinsic to the literature and require explanation. Groupings of sayings must be accounted for, along with disruptions and incursions into the text.

For Kovacs, this means that

> the sequence of events whereby the document came into being should be historically plausible, consonant with our understanding of the period, and should present a likely and understandable state of affairs and set of social processes to account for developments.[35]

But the prerequisite of such a redaction history is an analysis of the present texts. Kovacs appeals to von Rad who

> points out the need to deal, as first order of business, with the (traditional and historical) form of the materials in front of us. Blocks of distinctly-formed materials are recognizable in Proverbs and should first be understood as such. The classification approach of [McKane], therefore we submit, jumps a step in the analytic process.[36]

In particular, Kovacs argues, as his seventh point, that the widespread view that a process of theologizing or "yahwizing" of the sayings in Proverbs is improbable on the grounds of social history:

> If the early court circle included the priests, must any postulated theologizing, if it exists at all, be late? Contrariwise, given the increasing sedimentation of ideologies with time, is the increasing theological inclusiveness of wisdom under the monarchy consistent with increasing theological exclusivism? We submit that certain hypotheses about wisdom postulate sociological inconsistencies.[37]

Finally, in dependence upon Preuss, Kovacs argues that the theology of Hebrew wisdom is perhaps not so different from other Ancient Near Eastern wisdom. If this is the case, then even after taking the concept of the $yr't\ yhwh$ into consideration, there is no necessity of postulating a Yahweh redaction. The idea and theology of the "fear of the Lord" is

> entirely consistent with early wisdom, whether Hebrew or ancient oriental. Preuss' evidence certainly cannot be lightly dismissed. He suggests the reasons

---

[34] "Sociological," 306–307.
[35] "Sociological," 308.
[36] "Sociological," 310, with reference to G. von Rad, *Weisheit in Israel* (Neukirchen-Vluyn: Neukirchener, 1970) 24.
[37] "Sociological," 313.

educed for postulating either the random accretion of sayings or their redaction from changing theological needs are essentially phantom.[38]

Thus Kovacs would justify his enterprise of attempting to study Collection B as a unity. Finally, in direct continuation with the line of research extending from Boström through Hermisson and Plöger, is an important study by R. N. Whybray.[39] In this essay, independently of Kovacs, Whybray argued that the procedure of rearranging and reclassifying the material as employed by McKane and Scott involved

> a large element of subjectivity, both with regard to the point or intention of each saying, which is often ambiguous, and with regard to its religious or moral worth—questions to which the answer given is inevitably dependent on the interpreter's own set of values, imposed on the material from outside. Secondly, such classification, which really amounts almost to a complete rearrangement of the book, is manifestly not what the author or redactor intended. . . . If modern study of the problem has failed so far to discover the principles on which the material was arranged, this is more likely to be due to the interpreters' inability to find the key than to incompetence on the part of author or redactor.[40]

Whybray also launched a program of study which, while a good deal more modest than Kovacs', nonetheless attempted to take seriously the present form of the text as the necessary *starting* place for future progress in the field.[41] In brief, Whybray carefully showed that the placement of Yahweh-sayings was virtually always a deliberate editorial choice in chapters 10:1-22:16 and that the cluster of Yahweh-sayings at the center of the passage (15:33-16:9) served as its "theological kernel" which also helped clarify the use of Yahweh-sayings elsewhere.[42] It should be noted that Whybray combines his treatment of the *present* order of the sayings in the book with a view somewhat similar to McKane's concerning Wisdom's history. For Whybray, the deliberate, careful placement of Yahweh-sayings is evidence of meaningful "reinterpretation" of originally secular sayings by theological qualifiers. Nonetheless, his analysis seeks to make sense of the present form of the text and begins with it.

---

[38] "Sociological," 315-316. Kovacs is referring to H. D. Preuss, "Das Gottesbild der älteren Weisheit Israels," *VTSup* 23 (1973) 117-45, especially 136-45.
[39] "Yahweh-sayings and their Contexts in Proverbs, 10,1-22,16," *SAT* (1979) 153-165.
[40] "Yahweh-sayings," 153-54.
[41] Whybray speaks modestly of his essay: "To speak of 'conclusions' in connection with a branch of study which is clearly still in its infancy would be premature" (p. 165). His findings and method are more helpful than his modesty allows him to suggest. Earlier, J. L. Crenshaw had already pointed out the need for study of the phenomenon of the ordering of proverbs ("Wisdom," 229; "Prolegomenon," 14, 35).
[42] "Yahweh-sayings," 160.

The two streams here briefly sketched disclose several fundamental and interrelated issues.

First, are the sayings to be studied synchronically or diachronically? Put thus baldly, the question is of course a false either-or. Ideally, full understanding of a cultural product (language, graphic art, text, etc.) requires both diachronic and synchronic analysis. Nonetheless, I will argue below that synchronic literary analysis is a necessary prelude to diachronic analysis, just as synchronic linguistic study is a prerequisite to diachronic study. As far as the scholars surveyed above are concerned, the opposition between the two approaches is not of course, absolute. Skladny, for example, posits a sequence for his four collections, and none of the writers mentioned would wish to argue that the sayings exclude old and new elements. But, by and large, Skladny, *cum suis,* at least within the collections, may be said to take a synchronic approach to the exegesis of the sayings; contrast and contradictions are not immediately analyzed in terms of historical development but belong to the nature of situation-related, multivalent wisdom.[43] The second stream (McKane, *cum suis*) takes a more diachronic approach which is applied to the *individual* sayings, an approach which necessitates wresting the sayings from their present literary context. In addition, the two streams of interpretation treat complete or partial duplicates among the sayings differently: sayings like 13:14 and 14:27 (cf. 9:10) can be seen to reflect a process of Yahwistic influence on originally secular sayings (Whybray), or they can be seen as complementary statements within a single, complex worldview (Kovacs).

Second, both streams are opposed with regard to the *literary* character of the collections as a context for the individual sayings. Skladny found relatively unified collections. As Kovacs has emphasized, one must at least account for the fact that these sayings (and not others) have been preserved, brought together, and arranged in this and not some other way. But Scott and others see the juxtaposition of sayings as simply haphazard, the use of catchwords and wordplays not at all assisting the task of interpretation.

Third, the two streams, as well as other studies not strictly within these streams, diverge with respect to the religio-ideological context for interpreting the sayings. While this problem (and others mentioned below) are not strictly speaking a concern of this thesis, yet the thesis may aid in their resolution. For if literary studies establish larger units of meaning, the exegete has a much broader base upon which to found his interpretation of ideological and cultural issues.

Scott and McKane, in keeping with their diachronic view of wisdom, see within the sayings of Proverbs an earlier, empirical, virtually secular wisdom which tried to plot a course through life and statecraft by means of hard-headed analysis of the facts. This "old wisdom" is seen as overlaid with a veneer of Yahwistic reinterpretation which is not really true to the original character of old

---

[43] Cf. Kovacs, "Sociological," 301-303, and Carlston cited above.

wisdom. H. D. Preuss offers a variant on this perspective with an emphasis on the extra-Israelite affinities of wisdom to argue that wisdom, as found in the sayings, is for the most part incompatible with the authentic Yahwistic faith of Israel. That faith found its typical and normative expression in the features of salvation history and covenant, features utterly lacking in the wisdom sayings.[44] C. Westermann evinces similar convictions. These positions are characterized by the contrast, separation, or conflict of nature and grace, of reason and faith, and ultimately of creation and (redemptive-) history. Crucial to this problem is the decision with respect to the antiquity or modernity of such distinctions.

In opposition to the positions just mentioned, another stream of interpreters (somewhat overlapping with the Skladny tradition and including figures like R. E. Murphy, P. Skehan, and G. von Rad) argues that even the most "worldly" concerns in the sayings are to be seen within the context of Yahwistic faith.[45] This position in effect denies a split between faith and reason.

Finally, the question of the "structure" of wisdom thinking in the sayings must be raised. In his seminal article (1933), W. Zimmerli[46] argued against a rigid concept of order in wisdom and emphasized the role of the contingent and the subjective in wisdom thought and practice. Zimmerli's position has run into opposition from a variety of writers, mainly because a concept of (world-) order such as *maat* in Egypt seemed an essential ingredient also in Israelite wisdom with its *sdqh* (cf. *Dikē* in Hesiod). In a later article (1963/64) Zimmerli[47] modified his original rejection of the notion of world order in the face of hard evidence and strong consensus and spoke of wisdom thought in terms of "theology of creation." Yet the aspects of wisdom which Zimmerli pointed to in 1933 must be accounted for, even while the crucial role of order in wisdom thinking is acknowledged. The insights of Zimmerli (1933) and B. Gemser (1968)[48] need to be synthesized: What sort of world order makes possible the role of the subjective and contingent to which Zimmerli pointed?

Once again, the foregoing matters are beyond the scope of the thesis, but their resolution can only be furthered by better understanding of the actual literary units of interpretation — if such there be. The same may be said of other issues such as that concerning "retribution," the "deed-consequence" schema and its relation of world-order and Yahweh.

---

[44] H. D. Preuss, "Erwägungen zum theologischen Ort Alttestamentlicher Weisheitsliteratur," *EvT* 30 (1970) 393-417; "Das Gottbild der älteren Weisheit Israels," *VTSup* 23 (1972) 117-46.
[45] Murphy, "Wisdom—Theses and Hypotheses," *IW*, 40-41; Skehan, *Studies in Israelite Poetry and Wisdom* &CBQMS 1; Washington: Catholic Biblical Association, 1971) 23; von Rad, *WII*, passim.
[46] Translated and reprinted as "Concerning the Structure of Old Testament Wisdom,: *SAIW*, 175-207.
[47] "The Place and Limit of the Wisdom in the Framework of the Old Testament Theology," *SAIW*, 314-326.
[48] "The Spiritual Structure of Biblical Aphoristic Wisdom," *SAIW*, 208-219.

The connection in the thesis of the problem of interpretive context and the exegesis of proverbs 25-27 is not an arbitrary one for several reasons. First, this collection (= Skladny's *Sammlung C*) is generally acknowledged to have a rather tight literary organization by means of devices like catch-words (key-word is perhaps a better term in some cases), paronomasia, etc. Yet the possible implications that such literary organization may have for exegesis have hardly been explored. Second, there is within the collection itself a passage (26:1-12) which, in its own way raises the question of the use and meaning of sayings (*mšlym*) with a particular concern for the problem of *fittingness*. Here again we confront the basic hermeneutical problem of interpretive context (i.e., where and how does a proverb *fit*?) which makes meaning possible. Moreover, the passage in question implies that the 'world' or situation of the reader or user of a saying is essential in activating the meaning of a saying—rightly or wrongly (cf. 26:4,5,7,9).

Proverbs 26:1-12 is of crucial importance for the hermeneutical and methodological aspects of the thesis because it supplies a touchstone within the text itself for such reflection. The passage is further important for our thesis because it implicitly provides an ancient account of the nature and purpose of *mšlym* which can act as a much-needed corrective to some of the misunderstandings which have been imposed upon sayings in proverbs, often reducing them to an inadequate empiricism, easily destroyed in the crucible of human experience.

Finally, some comparative light can be shed upon our problem by reference to other Ancient Near Eastern literatures. The studies of B. Alster have shown the existence and importance of proverb arrangement in certain Sumerian collections[49] and W. G. Lambert has suggested arrangement in some Assyrian collections.[50] In the *Aramaic Proverbs of Ahiqar*, "The individual sayings are heterogeneous in form and content. But their arrangement is not random."[51] The importance of the order of sayings in Egyptian wisdom seems evident from an ironic passage in a letter from Hori to Amen-em-opet (whom the former actually considers an incompetent scribe):

> Thou art come provided with great mysteries, and thou tellest me a saying of Hordedef, (although) thou knowest not whether it is good or bad. *What chapter is before it, what after it?* Now thou art a scribe of experience at the head of his colleagues. The teaching of every book is engraved upon thy heart.[52]

A recent essay by M. Lichtheim in which she discusses the literary character and arrangement of sayings in Demotic wisdom (Ankhsheshonq, Papyrus démotique

---

[49] *The Instructions of Suruppak: A Sumerian Proverb Collection* (Mesopotamia 2; Copenhagen: Akademisk, 1974); *Studies in Sumerian Proverbs* (Mesopotamia 3; Copenhagen: Akademisk, 1975) especially 13-14.
[50] *BWL*, 213, 225.
[51] Lindenberger (*APA*, 21) provides examples.
[52] *ANET*, 476b. The text is late 19th dynasty.

Louvre 2414, and Papyrus Insinger) is especially suggestive, in my estimation, as a parallel to the composition of the saying collections in Proverbs.[53] Nonetheless, as Whybray has pointed out, the presence or absence of order and unity in sections of the book of Proverbs can only be established by investigation of that book itself.[54] This is the task of our thesis with respect to Proverbs 25-27.

[53] "Observations on Papyrus Insinger," *Studien zu altägyptischen Lebenslehren* (ed. E. Hornung and O. Keel; OBO 28; Freiburg: Universitätsverlag, 1979) 283-305, especially 284-290. According to M. V. Fox ("Two Decades," 130-31), I. Grumach (*Untersuchungen zur Lebenslehre des Amenope* [MAS 23; Munich/Berlin, 1972] not seen by me) has shown "that Amenope is a carefully structured work clearly composed by one author."

[54] "Yahweh-sayings," 154.

2
The Problem in Proverbs 25: The Work of Glendon E. Bryce

To Glendon E. Bryce belongs the credit of having first argued that Prov 25:2-27 constitutes a literary unit. He broached the matter in a 1972 article,[1] arguing on the basis of Egyptian parallels and internal stylistic and thematic factors that this passage was an intentional, artistic unity. He placed its social setting in aristocratic, courtly circles. In his recent book, *A Legacy of Wisdom*,[2] Bryce essentially replicated his earlier article. Finally, in "The Structural Analysis of Didactic Texts,"[3] which appears to be his most recent treatment of the passage, Bryce presents an account of the text using certain methods of French structuralism, especially as represented by A. J. Greimas, who himself stands in the line of the Russian formalist pioneer of folktale analysis, V. Propp.

In what follows, I shall first concentrate upon Bryce's 1972 essay in "rhetorical criticism" and the genuine contributions it made to our understanding of this passage. Secondly, I shall set forth the method and results of Bryce's structuralist essay (1978) in a critical way. My own use of certain "structuralist" techniques (sans commitment to a structuralist ideology) to elucidate particular aspects of our texts gains in methodological clarity when contrasted to the structuralist attempt of Bryce.

In discussing the 1972 article, my concern is not so much with the Egyptian parallels adduced by Bryce, though these are not without value, but with his account of the Proverbs text itself. Crucial to Bryce's delineation of a new "wisdom-'book' " in Prov 25:2-27 was his argument that Prov 25:27b formed an inclusio with v 2b, which opened the pericope. This reading of v 27b as an inclusio required only a repointing of vowels in one word (*kbdym*) of a colon which is otherwise obscure. While Bryce did not acknowledge his predecessors in this minor emendation, to my knowledge his discovery of the inclusio was

---

[1] "Another Wisdom-'Book' in Proverbs," *JBL* 91 (1972) 145-57.
[2] *A Legacy of Wisdom: The Egyptian Contribution to the Wisdom of Israel* (Lewisburg: Bucknell University, 1979). The preface is dated 1976.
[3] In *Biblical and Near Eastern Texts* (La Sor Festschrift; ed. G. A. Tuttle; Grand Rapids: Eerdmans, 1978) 107-121. The title is somewhat misleading, for only Proverbs 25 is analyzed.

original and strengthened the case for the correctness of the MT consonantal text of v 27b.[4]

Bryce further noted the correspondence of v 27a with v 16 so that these verses formed the "rubrics" or framework of his "wisdom-'book,' " on the analogy of the Egyptian wisdom of Sehetepibre. These rubrics formed a chiastic arrangement in certain of their key words: Glory (v 2) : Honey (v 16) :: Honey (v 27a) : Glory (v 27b).

Bryce also found a second chiastic feature in these verses. Each of the linked hemistichs (vv 2b and 27b; 16 and 27a) contains a word pair in common which is reversed in the second occurrence of the word pair:

| v 2 | kbd⟶hqr | v 16 | dbš⟶kl |
| v 27b | hqr⟶kbd | v 27a | 'kl⟶dbš[5] |

In Bryce's view, these rubrics marked the beginning, middle (i.e., the start of the book's second part) and close of the literary work, and also indicated its main themes and organization. Of course, the delimitation of Prov 25:2-27(28) can be, and had long since been, established on other grounds as well: the sub-title in 25:1, and the beginning in 26:1 of a clearly different group of sayings linked by the key-word *ksyl*. Yet Bryce's article contained an innovation whose significance and value are not to be minimized. For the first time someone was arguing for the careful literary interpretation of an extended group of proverbs upon the basis of an exposition of the aesthetic-thematic structure of the whole.[6]

Bryce employed conceptual as well as aesthetic criteria to establish the existence and shape of his "wisdom-'book' ":

> The first involves the ideological structure of the book and is concerned with content. The second treats . . . the formal structure and includes whatever poetic and literary devices may have been used to demarcate the outline of the book. Initially, we may raise the following two questions concerning the conceptual structure of the composition. Does Prov 25:2-27 form a clear conceptual unity with a sub-structure of thought which is integrally related? Moreover, apart from the formal structure, does it have a single theme to which each of the parts relates?[7]

It should be noted concerning this initial (1972) article that, though Bryce speaks of "structure," he is not employing a "structuralist" method or perspective, as is

---

[4] "Wisdom-'book'," 148-50, reading *kĕbēdīm* for MT *kĕbōdām* ("To eat honey . . . is not good, But to search out difficult things is glorious."). See the discussion in Delitzsch, 171 ("To surfeit oneself in eating honey is not good, But as an enquirer to enter on what is difficult is honour."). I discuss Prov 25:27 in my treatment of its chapter below.

[5] "Wisdom-'book'," 153-54.

[6] "Wisdom-'book'," 147, n. 8. For the more restricted scope of previous attempts, see Chapter 2 above. Of these, only Boström dealt with chapter 25.

[7] "Wisdom-'book'," 150-51.

the case with the essay discussed below (1978). In particular, his analysis of *form* and *content* remains on the level of "surface" structures and does not attempt to lay bare the "deep" structures which contribute to the "meaning effect" of the passage. Nonetheless, Bryce does here use these categories to refer to aspects of the literary work which must be accounted for. By "formal structure" Bryce means the "poetic and literary devices" such as are studied by "rhetorical criticism." Unfortunately, his analysis of this aspect of the pericope does not extend much beyond pointing to the above-mentioned "rubrics." The work of Boström, Gemser, and Hermisson seems not to have influenced Bryce.

Bryce's analysis of the conceptual or "ideological structure" of the passage concerns theme, and can be briefly summarized: Verses 2-5 constitute an introduction dealing with the book's two main subjects, the king (vv 2-3) and the wicked (vv 4-5). These subunits within the introduction present the two main subjects which are developed further: the ruler in vv 6-15 and the wicked in vv 16-26.[8]

Actually, Bryce vacillates on whether the second main section of the book includes the rubric (v 16 with or without its companion v 17) or not. In the latter event, the section would begin with v 17 or 18. This uncertainty is indicative of a failure in Bryce's analysis: he does not penetrate deeply enough into the details of his text to be totally convincing. Hence his argument that 'yš 'nh (v 18) and rš' (v 26) may form a sort of thematic "inclusio" (Bryce does not use the word here) for the second section must be deemed unsuccessful, both because Bryce is uncertain if v 18 actually begins the section and because of the absence of other examples where loose thematic links without any verbal resonance are clear delimiters of sections in composite literary works.[9]

Bryce further elaborates the ideological structure of the poem as follows. Verses 6-15, which comprise the first section after the introduction (vv 2-5) deal "with the relation of the courtier to his superiors," while the second major section deals with various wicked individuals. Within his sections, Bryce groups the subunits on the basis of themes and stylistic devices as follows:

| *Introduction:* | vv 2-3 | king |
| | vv 4-5 | wicked |

Section I king (ruler)	*Section II wicked characters*	
verses	verses	
6-7	16-17	hateful friend
8-9a	18	false witness
9b-10	19-20	faithless man/tormentor
11-12	21-24	enemy
13-14	23-24	backbiter/bad wife
15	25-26	the wicked

[8] "Wisdom-'book'," 151.

[9] "Wisdom-'book'," 151. In his later treatment ("Structural," 117), Bryce begins the new section with v 17. But this does violence to the obvious coherence of vv 16-17.

Inclusio: v 27[10]

In my judgement, Bryce has correctly discerned the main contours of Prov 25:2-27. His discovery of "rubrics" (by whatever name) and of the generally negative focus of Section II is important. Yet his treatment is too cursory to be wholly compelling. The purported unity among the proverbs in the pericope remains unexplained in the face of their striking diversity. Bryce has proposed a theory for the poem as a whole; his theory might have been more compelling had it more adequately accounted for the details on which the theory must rest.

Hence, various aspects of Bryce's exposition seem incorrect or misleading. For instance, his sub-groupings of the Admonitions within vv 6-10 will not survive a close study of the form critical pattern of these verses.[11] Nor does it appear with sufficient clarity how the Admonitions and Sayings in 25:6-15 can all be simply subsumed under the rubric of the "king."

Similarly, section II is not just a rogue's gallery of "wicked characters." The "hateful friend" in 25:17 is not wicked *per se*, but is in danger of coming into a relationship of conflict with the addressee of the Admonition. The point here, in connection with v 16, has more to do with excess and conflict than with the wickedness of the neighbor. It is the addressee who is in danger of doing the initial wrong and precipitating conflict. Again, v 25 is an entirely positive Saying, having nothing to do with the wicked. Either Bryce must exclude it from his Section II or offer an alternate explanation for its presence. Finally, Bryce's treatment fails to deal with the presence in this passage of two wisdom forms, the Admonition and the Saying, and the role these forms might have in shaping the passage as a whole.

Bryce's 1978 structuralist essay presupposes the rhetorical and thematic analysis of his earlier article. Hence, the later article might be anticipated to corroborate the results of the earlier study on a different level, by means of a different method.

Unfortunately, this is not the case. Bryce's structuralist study, in my view, suffers from some fundamental flaws on both the theoretical and practical (i.e., exegetical) level.

Like most structuralists today, Bryce employs insights and conceptual categories drawn from modern linguistics to understand the functioning of larger "linguistic" structures such as narratives. To quote D. Patte,

> According to this methodology the analyst first conceives, on the basis of a linguistic model, theoretical models of the structures he wishes to study, then transforms them (more or less radically) and revises them when applying them to texts. *This approach involves the danger that the analyst might project upon the text structures which are not at work in it.*[12]

---

[10] "Wisdom-'book'," 151.
[11] See the preceding diagram in the text and my account of these verses in the treatment of chapter 25 below.
[12] *What Is Structural Exegesis?* (Philadelphia: Fortress, 1976) 84; my emphasis.

Utilizing the linguistic distinction of form and substance, rather than form and content,[13] Bryce argues that

> form is not a specific configuration of content determined by a variety of variable historical and cultural factors, i.e., the *Sitz im Leben* as Gunkel defined it. Rather, it is the ensemble of structures found within the content, the system that organizes and shapes the substance.[14]

While Bryce's "either-or" (*Sitz im Leben* versus an a-cultural, intrinsic "system") seems unwarranted, his concept of form is quite legitimate, also in its application to literary texts. Its use can lead to genuine new insights, as I hope to show later. However, the sentence which follows the preceding quotation occasions serious theoretical and exegetical difficulties for Bryce: "The form, which is articulated in the act of communication, is the system that exists before it and that makes signification possible." This last statement is, of course, relatively true of the linguistic substrata of human communication: "Form is the structuring system, the organizing principles that produce meaning, what is, with respect to the lexical entries, the grammar of language."[15] One might add that these statements apply on other linguistic levels as well, the phonological and morphological, for example. Bryce's assertion that the form exists prior to the act of communication also has a certain validity when it is applied to large literary units such as a narrative or poem. It is true that a literary form, whether deep or surface, can structure a poem and "exist" prior to the poem, just as the system of norms which hold for a declarative sentence in English exists prior to any particular declarative utterance, and makes such an utterance possible. So also a certain pattern of rhyme, meter, and other conventions defines a sonnet.[16]

This "priority" is, however, a *normative* one, and not always a temporal one. The formal structure of the sonnet did not exist prior to the creation of the first sonnet sometime after 1200 A.D. Since then this structure has become a normative convention which exists prior to the creation of any new sonnet. If the new poem does not abide by the structural "rules," it is not a sonnet, but something else, or perhaps a poor sonnet.

The scholar can abstract such a traditional, normative structure from those works of art which conform to it. Thus Propp was able to lay bare the structure of the Russian folktale, including the conventional substitutions and variants permissible in it. But this abstractive activity must be based upon the empirical investigation of a number of works which consistently reveal the structural pattern. A work that does not abide by the conventions is thus not a "Russian folktale" but something else, and the structure which it embodies must similarly be abstracted. It is a fundamental error to assume that a normative structure discovered in one genre of literature is an *a priori* structure which holds for all

---

[13] Cf. John Lyons, *Theoretical*, 54–70; D. Patte, *What Is*, 28–30.
[14] "Structural," 109.
[15] "Structural," 108.
[16] For our purposes, the various subtypes of sonnet may be ignored.

genres of literature![17] One could with equal validity assume, as did Bishop Lowth, that the English language was something the rules of Latin syntax applied to.

Bryce's structuralist treatment of Prov 25:2-27 is an example of the error just described. He takes the analysis of narrative as it has been developed by Propp and Greimas[18] and attempts to apply it to the proverbs in our text. Bryce seems to assume that the structure of a literary text must necessarily be a *narrative* structure, and that it must necessarily reveal the narrative *sequence* described by his structuralist mentors.

Thus Bryce believes that "a narrative consists of a series of interlocking levels. . . ." This series has three components:

> These three narrative components on the syntagmatic plane, the qualifying test, the principal test and the glorifying text, form a narrative isotopy, the common axis of meaning being the struggle of the Subject![19]

Consequently, Bryce sees Prov 25:2-27 as the narrative of a quest containing several stages and encompassing several sub-quests. Both the hero (the addressee of the Admonitions) and the king are involved in a quest for wisdom or knowledge (vv 2-17b). The narrative begins with a situation of lack which determines the major narrative programs of the text as a whole:

> If the situation of lack is that the king is surrounded by the wicked, the task enjoined by "The Book of the Men of Hezekiah" is to remove the wicked from the presence of the king so that he can be united with the righteous in a long and just rule.[20]

This overarching task comprises the quest of the hero (Subject proper) who is seeking a position among the great who stand before the king (25:6-7). Enroute to this goal the Subject encounters the three "tests" dictated by Bryce's *a priori* model: "The first test of the courtier occurs when he has an altercation with a colleague, a serious incident that provokes him to consider legal action (vv 7-8)." By resisting this temptation, and by gaining the proper volition and the ability to speak wisely, moderately (not too much), and thus persuasively, the

---

[17] Compare T. Hawkes' remarks on the novel and short story: "Because the novel concerns itself centrally with sequence, with the continuous passage of time, it offers no other pre-existing concrete material. . . . Moreover, there are no laws governing the novel as a form separable from its narrative content. Each novel is different, and each invention of content 're-invents' the form of the novel. The same is not true of the short story, which can be reduced to laws. We can that is to say, identify the non-story, but not the non-novel." *Structuralism and Semiotics* (Berkeley and Los Angeles: University of California, 1977) 65.

[18] Lucid accounts of Propp and Greimas are available in Patte (*What Is*, 36-52) and Hawkes (*Structuralism*, 67-69, 87-95). For critique of Greimas, see J. Culler, *Structuralist Poetics: Structuralism, Linguistics, and the Study of Literature* (Ithaca: Cornell University, 1975) 75-95, 213-14.

[19] "Structural," 111.

[20] "Structural," 114.

courtier is able to "change his potential Opponent into an actual Helper."[21] Consequently, for Bryce, vv 7-15 present the "qualifying test," and the virtues and proper volition which must be obtained if the test is to be passed. The proper volition is represented by the honey (vv 16, 27), of which one ought not to desire too much, i.e., too grand a place at court.[22]

The second, the "principal test" occurs in vv 17-26. "Having acquired a Helper [i.e., a persuaded opponent, cf. vv 7-10 and 15] in the first part, the Subject is now equipped to confront the Opponent." The sayings of this section (especially vv 18-20) give advice concerning the conflict which the Subject is entering:

> Before entering the arena of conflict, the contestant is given the tactical advice enabling him to identify his opponent and assess his strength. . . . Whereas the task enjoined in the first part of the instruction is one of persuasion, the role of the courtier has now changed. His task is one of interpretation, to scout the enemies' positions, to identify potential sources of conflict, and to be prepared to confront the enemy in strength.[23]

The climax of the "principal test" occurs in vv 21-22 where the courtier shows his enemy mercy:

> Having confronted the Anti-Subject in the principal test, and not only having defeated him but also having shown mercy to him, the courtier will be rewarded by Yahweh (v 22). What is this reward? Apart from the context of the instruction it is unspecified, but within this specific wisdom-'book' it cannot be other than the reward envisaged by the quest itself, a position in the presence of the king and a place with the great.[24]

Finally, in vv 26, 27, Bryce finds evidence for Propp's "glorifying text." For in v 26, the courtier is addressed, says Bryce, "as the righteous man." By his righteousness, the courtier has gone from a potential to an actual "great man" in the court. Thus he searches out glorious things as a companion to the king (vv 2, 27b).

This attempt to find all three of Propp's tests in Prov 25:2-27 is symptomatic of the lack of concern for detail which plagues Bryce's attempts to provide an account of the pericope as a literary whole. His theories lead him to eisegesis. For instance, the "glorifying test" appeals to v 26 since there the "hero" is supposedly addressed as one who has now attained the title and status of "righteous." But this verse describes the evil of the righteous giving way ($m\underline{t}$) before the wicked. If the verse is taken seriously, we have a tragedy rather than the folktale happy ending envisioned by Bryce.

---

[21] "Structural," 115. One wonders if Bryce's "plot" here is not borrowed from *Ptahhotep*, chapters 2-4 and 13-14 (Lichtheim, *AEL* I, 63-64, 67). Much of Proverbs 25 is similar to *Ptahhotep*.
[22] "Structural," 117.
[23] "Structural," 117.
[24] "Structural," 117-18.

Thus, for a number of reasons, Bryce's narrative structuration of 25:2-27 must be judged unsuccessful (though various of his insights must be acknowledged). Most basic is that his "narrative" is like the "emperor's new clothes"; it does not exist. A collection of Admonitions and Sayings, no matter how tightly interrelated and organized, does not constitute a narrative. The *sine qua non* of narrative is that a temporal sequence of events is presented in a meaningful way. This does not happen in Proverbs 25. Hence, Bryce violates his own structuralist principle: "The first task of a structural analysis is to determine the precise limits of the discursive unit under scrutiny."[25] In Proverbs 25 the primary units are the Sayings and Admonitions, not the whole. If this passage has a meaningful structure—as I shall argue—this structure must be of another sort than narrative.

What sort of "structure" might a collection of small units embody? One might say that since the Admonitions and Sayings are the primary units, no structure is to be found in the whole. Such a tack is taken by scholars such as Scott, McKane, and Westermann, even though they have not put the question in "structuralist terms." Yet on the assumption that human artifacts generally exhibit some structure, one is entitled to ask, "How are these small proverbs, relatively complete in themselves, related to one another? How are they ordered?" The answers to these questions may not be *a priori*. The possibilities range, theoretically at least, all the way from "no relation, no order" to "highly significant relation, careful order."

Before we attempt to answer such questions in terms of our text sample (Prov 25-27), we shall present a fuller account of our operating assumptions concerning literary works (including Proverbs 25-27) and our methods of analysis: structural, poetic, and semantic.

[25] "Structural," 113.

3
Heuristic Assumptions*

In an oft-quoted dictum, the paroemiologist W. Mieder has said that "the proverb in a collection is dead." Mieder's remark is exemplary of the contextualist or functionalist school of folklore studies and is, in a certain sense, correct.[1] Many twentieth-century collections of proverbs made by missionaries, folklorists, and anthropologists were of little value since they gave no account of the role or function of the sayings in their live cultural context; indeed they were often taken from a culture which itself was largely misunderstood.

But one may not assume that the ancient creators of the wisdom literatures of the Ancient Near East were engaged in the same sort of haphazard collection of verbal curios from a culture strange to themselves. They collected and compiled and created documents according to their own literary canons of taste and meaning and to serve themselves or their contemporaries.[2]

One should be aware here of the contrast between the oral use of proverbs and their literary development and use in a collection. While it is true that the ancients did not read silently (recall St. Augustine's surprise at Ambrose's silent reading), this fact should not obscure the difference between written and merely oral works. One obvious difference is that a writer is more able to juxtapose radically contrasting forms and sentiments and to hold them together in a

---

*Parts of this chapter are adapted from my unpublished M.A. Thesis, "The Day of Yahweh: Theme and Form in Amos 4 and 5" (St. Michael's College/Toronto School of Theology, 1975).

[1] Cited by C. R. Fontaine (*Traditional Sayings in the Old Testament* [Sheffield, Almond, 1982] 54) from W. Mieder, "The Essence of Literary Proverb Study," *Proverbium* 23 (1974) 888-94, p. 892; also in *New York Folklore Quarterly* 30 (1974) 66-76. On the "contextual" approach see L. Rohrich and W. Mieder (*Sprichwort* [Stuttgart: Metzler, 1972] 78-82) and J. H. Brunvand (*The Study of American Folklore* [second ed.; New York: Norton, 1978] 19, 23) with bibliographies.

[2] On this see especially Hermisson (*SIS*, 171-183) and B. Kovacs ("Structural"). The work of J. M. Thompson (*The Form and Function of Proverbs in Ancient Israel* [The Hague/Paris: 1974] 68-83) suggests the primary function of biblical proverbs is "philosophical" (i.e., concerned with worldview and meaning) and lists "Entertainment," "Legal Usage," and "Instruction" (of youth) as "Sub-Functions." Thompson's analysis is a bit cursory and outstripped by the ambition of his title.

complex whole than is a speaker. The reader is forced by their static proximity on the page to assimilate in one experience even harshly contrary elements. John W. Rogerson has noted that

> Writing enables knowledge to be extracted from the social contexts with which it is inextricably bound up in 'oral' societies and situations. Because of it, traditions can be compared side by side, enabling critical faculties to be developed.[3]

Rogerson's observation is based on the anthropological work of Jack Goody:

> The influence of writing manifests itself even upon such thoroughly 'folk' material as proverbs, those encapsulations of popular wisdom. One of the favourite subjects for scholars wishing to write down a language for the first time is folk literature, proverbs especially. The effects, particularly upon utterance-embedded forms, is interesting. For by taking the proverb out of the context of speech, by listing it along with a lot of other similar pithy sentences, one changes the character of the oral form. For example, it then becomes possible to set one proverb against another in order to see if the meaning of one contradicts the meaning of another; they are now tested for a universal truth value, whereas their applicability had been essentially contextual (though phrased in a universal manner).[4]

Rogerson notes that Goody's account "entirely contradicts" the position of von Rad with respect to the juxtaposed contraries in Prov 26:4-5. For von Rad, says Rogerson,

> The apparent contradictions . . . do not invite us to see a mutually enriching combination of insights based upon the juxtaposition of the sayings. According to von Rad, it is simply that the thought passes from one area of interest to another without any concern for co-ordination. . . . Careful study of Goody's thesis may well result in a re-appraisal of the implications of the so-called Wisdom Literature. . . .[5]

While we will argue, in connection with Prov 26:1-12 (especially vv 4-5, 7, 9), that the juxtaposition of contradictions is not intended to test "for a universal truth value" (as Goody has it), his and Rogerson's observations on the (con)textuality of Biblical proverbs are important for our project. In fact, Prov 26:1-12 suggests that the compiler was himself aware of the functional, contextual nature of *mšlym,* and that they could be well or ill used depending upon their fittingness in a given extra-textual context.

Hence, a fundamental heuristic assumption of this thesis is that the writers of our text sample (Prov 25-27) attempted to create literary contexts for individual sayings which would compensate for their loss of life-context and

---

[3] J. W. Rogerson, *Anthropology and the Old Testament* (Atlanta: John Knox, 1979) 117. One implication of this is that the critic can no longer be content with the quest for a life-setting for the individual units (a sometimes impossible quest in any case), but must ask after the *Sitz* of the literary composition, as Kovacs ("Structural") has done.

[4] Jack Goody, *The Domestication of the Savage Mind* (Cambridge: Cambridge University, 1977) 125-6. Cf. Fontaine, *Traditional,* 139-146.

[5] *Anthropology,* 118.

which would be sufficiently elaborate to provide hermeneutic parameters within which they could be understood. This heuristic assumption is furthered by the realization that these writings are not simply products of the *Volksmund,* but are, as individual sayings, themselves the products of sophisticated literary art. Our heuresis leads us to ask, if the micro-structures are aesthetically well-crafted, why not the macro-structures? The issue of *Sitz im Leben* when raised is thus more properly and profitably pursued with respect to the creation of the larger units.

A corollary assumption would be that the poetic and other techniques employed to create larger, unified blocks of meaning would have to be the same devices known to us elsewhere in the poetry of ancient Israel and Northwest Semitic, and in the poetry of the Sayings and Admonitions themselves.[6]

Assuming the presence of meaningful units which comprehend several proverbs, how then are we to discern such a meaning-rich context which constitutes a unified whole? It is here that the *methodological* priority of synchronic analysis over diachronic analysis must be made clear. It is incorrect to say that students of Proverbs are presented with the hopeless task of synthesizing the broken fragments created by form critical analysis. For the literary work of Proverbs with its clearly marked major sections is given to us as a whole, prior to all abstraction of glosses, textual errors, and textual accretions, and prior to any other historical mode of analysis. This actual Hebrew text with its subsections is the primary datum, the most ancient information we have. Study of a text may indeed very quickly compel us to diachronic explanations, especially when account is taken of the versions. But the attempt to understand the text which lies before us as a unit or complex of units is the precondition of all subsequent analysis. The text (or its marked subsections) exists as a synchronic, static entity, hence a unit of some sort. Only upon the basis of a prior perception of unity of style, theme, language, usage of forms, and so on, is it possible for the critic to declare that a word, line or section is secondary or editorial. For without a clear notion of what *belongs* to a text one cannot judge what is foreign to it. Without a prior intuition of the *Gestalt* of a musical piece in its cultural context—a *Gestalt* in which melody, harmony, rhythm, style, and instrumentation all find their place—one cannot say what is a "wrong note" or why a given instrumentation is inappropriate, say, for a piece of the Rococo period. Comprehension of a text as it "stands" may indeed require the interaction of a diachronic and synchronic modes of analysis, but there must always exist a minimal perception which says, *this* and not *that* is the text.[7]

---

[6] This point is implicit in the comments made by Kovacs ("Sociological," 299–301) quoted on pp. 12ff. above.

[7] I mean to suggest that diachronic and synchronic modes of analysis can on occasion be virtually simultaneous or interacting in the mind of the reader, while maintaining nonetheless that diachronic analysis always and necessarily presupposes the *pou sto* of some synchronic entity or unity.

In a different context, the matter has been well put by the classicist, K. von Fritz:

> Dass A und O [omega] der klassischen Philologie und jeder Philologie ist die Interpretation und das dadurch zu erzielende Verständnis der Texte. Dazu können freilich unter gewissen Umständen auch Interpolationskritik, Echtheitskritik, Schichtanalyse and Entwicklungstheorien sehr wesentlich beitragen. Aber es sollte sich von selbst verstehen, dass diese überhaupt erst anfangen können, wenn die einfache Wort- und Sachinterpretation, und zwar nicht nur einzelner Stellen, sondern der Stellen im Zusammenhang der ganzen Werke, zu denen sie gehören, so weit getrieben ist, dass es möglich wird einigermassen gesicherte weiterreichende Schlusse zu ziehen.[8]

For example, one may find in the book of Amos several instances of composite literary unities in which the meaning of the whole is more than the sum of its form critical parts. It is generally acknowledged, even by those who see some of the oracles as not by Amos, that the "Oracles against the Nations" in chapters 1-2 are to be read not merely as discrete units, but as one complex unit culminating in the Oracle against Israel.[9] Again, in chapter 5, literary complexes are created which transcend form critical distinctions.[10]

Hence, our task is not to effect a synthesis which is alien to the text. Rather, we need first to arrive at a judgment or standard of unity, against which such things as fragmentation and disorder can be measured. Second, after this global perception or comprehension of the text has been achieved, this original perception can be elaborated, deepened, changed, or corrected by analysis and reflection, and by comparison with other relevant writings or knowledge, e.g., of grammar, genres, archeology, history, theology and the like. Perhaps this secondary reflection will lead one to conclude that there is more than one whole to be dealt with. That is, study of the text as given drives one to perceive it diachronically. The classic example of this is Eichhorn's separation of the two Isaiah's in his *Einleitung* of 1783, an analysis which has since become a critical commonplace.[11] One might even conclude that there is no literary "work" in the

---

[8] "Ziele, Aufgaben und Methoden der klassischen Philologie und Altertumswissenschaft," *Vierteljahrsschrift für Literaturwissenschaft und Geistesgeschichte* 33 (1959) 528. Cited from M. Weiss, "Die Methode der 'Total-Interpretation'," *VTSup* 22 (1972) 88-112, 95.

[9] S. M. Paul, "Amos 1:3-2:3: A Concatenous Literary Pattern," *JBL* 90 (1971) 397-403. K. N. Schoville, "A Note on the Oracles of Amos Against Gaza, Tyre, and Edom," *VTSup* 26 (1974) 55-63. S. M. Paul, "A Literary Reinvestigation of the Oracles against the Nations of Amos," *De la Tôrah au Messie. Mélanges Henri Cazelles* (ed. J. Doré, P. Grelot, and M. Carrez; Paris: Desclée, 1981) 189-204.

[10] J. De Waard, "The Chiastic Structure of Amos v 1-17," *VT* 27 (1977) 170-177. N. J. Tromp, "Amos V 1-17, Towards a Stylistic and Rhetorical Analysis," *OTS* 23 (1984) 56-84. Cf. Van Leeuwen, "The Day of Yahweh."

[11] It is significant that contemporary scholarship, while recognizing the growth of the Isaiah book in time, is nonetheless returning to the question of the book's unity. R. E. Clements, "The Unity of the Book of Isaiah," *Int* 36 (1982) 117-129.

strict sense. But if this should be the case with a collection of proverbs, one will at least have to acknowledge a certain sociological unity to the collection, as obviously follows from B. Kovacs' trenchant question: "Do groups with any significant frequency involve themselves in preserving works that lack some salience or affinity for them?"[12]

Third, from this secondary, perhaps diachronic, activity, one can return enriched, and with greater clarity, to the problem of the whole and its meaning. At this stage the exegete is ready to present his results and conclusions![13]

This threefold process, by which a whole and its parts are known, is here presented in schematic fashion. In the actual process of understanding, the various steps may mutually interact or overlap. Nevertheless, it remains true that an original intuition of unity is the basis for all consequent analysis, even if this intuition contains only the perception of so broad a unity as that of a common language.

The extent to which such an intuition of unity is correct depends both upon the reader and the written document. While intuition and analysis are subjective processes, they have, however, an "objective correlative" to which they respond and are responsible. Thus an account of a literary unit rests both on the text itself and upon the literary ability, sensitivity, and training of the reader![14]

---

[12] Cited in J. Gladson, "Retributive Paradoxes in Proverbs 10-29," (Unpublished Ph.D. Thesis; Vanderbilt University, 1978) 62.

[13] The threefold process of analysis here presented differs, for example, from the procedure presented in W. Richter's *Exegese als Literaturwissenschaft: Entwurf einer alttestamentlichen Literaturtheorie und Methodologie* (Göttingen: Vandenhoeck and Ruprecht, 1972) mainly with respect to our first and third stages. Richter lists what he considers to be the sum and proper *order* of literary analysis: "*Text- und Literarkritik, Form-, Gattungs-, Traditions-, und Redaktionsgeschichte*" (19-21). His list of methods omits poetic or stylistic analysis, especially in connection with redaction studies and thus remains largely limited to our second stage. Many critics, including Richter, appear unaware that the first stage, the intuition of some whole, has already taken place—often through the spectacles of the secondary literature—before their secondary analysis begins. Cf. Kovacs' criticism that McKane's classification system "jumps a step in the analytic process" (quoted on p. 17 above). See also K. Koch, *The Growth of the Biblical Tradition* (New York: Scribners, 1969) 77-78: "In the exegesis of a passage it is usually best for practical reasons to start with the present final form, and to work back, on the basis of the literary-critical method, to the first literary form. Only then is it possible to tackle the other aspects of form criticism."

[14] See p. 4, n. 8 above. The term "objective correlative" was apparently coined by W. Allston in 1850 and made famous in this century by T. S. Eliot in his essay "Hamlet and his Problems." For the concept and its history, see A. Austin, *T. S. Eliot, The Literary and Social Criticism* (Bloomington, IN: Indiana University, 1971) 99. Compare Wellek and Warren (*Theory of Literature*, 150) who argue that "the real poem [literary work] must be conceived as a structure of norms, realized only partially in the actual experience of its many readers. Every single experience ... is only an attempt—more or less successful and complete—to grasp this set of norms or standards." They compare the poem and its many

Consequently, for an exegete to present an adequate account of a literary work's unity requires that the text indeed hold its diverse parts together, that the exegete be able to experience the work's unity, and that he explain the means by which the diversity is unified. That is, he must be able to explain the nature of the unity in its various aspects of structure, form, language, style, and theme.

Since Proverbs as a whole and chapters 25-27 within it obviously consist of parts such as words and sentences and diverse forms, we must first consider how *any* such diversity can be experienced as a more or less harmonious unit. This general question can be applied to every written work or poem. T. Munro has given a useful description of the subjective process by which the objective unity of the artwork is experienced. This description corresponds to our idea of an original intuition of unity which must precede analysis. From the description given by Munro, it appears that this primary manner of experiencing a work is different in character from the analytical knowing which can follow and enrich or correct intuition. While Munro's account refers to Western poetry, it applies equally well, *mutatis mutandis,* to Hebrew poems, including—as we shall argue—the subsections of Proverbs 25-27. In literary works or poems, says Munro,

> . . . a special kind of reading and perhaps of thinking and feeling is appropriate. . . . Words are to be grasped, not quickly for their obvious, literal meanings only, but slowly and with some relaxation of strict logical and practical attitudes, to let their diversified suggestive power awaken deep reverberations in the mind.
>
> One does not stop at every word. The rapid reader quickly fuses a group of separate symbols into a composite block of meanings, then moves on to the next. Even the leisurely reader, who stops to imagine along the way, will grasp the text in blocks of words, in phrases and sentences. Each of these in sequence will start a train of associations within his mind. . . . Each group of words, in starting a new train of thought, tends partly to arrest previously started trains. But not entirely, for their memory remains and accumulates to build up a composite meaning. This in turn acts as context and background to each new succeeding train of thought, directing it and assimilating it into an even larger form.
>
> Images and ideas may be conveyed from the start in such a way that each is clear by itself, so that each can be clearly apperceived as read and succeeding ones fitted immediately into the cumulative group of meanings. But important key words are often postponed until well along in the passage. . . . There the reader tends to apperceive the earlier ones only partially, to hold them in suspense within his memory, vague or ambiguous as they may be, until he comes upon the clue which directs him how to narrow them down to relevant meanings and fit them together into a coherent whole. In some literature which aims to trick and surprise, he may be led to interpret and combine the earlier words in a certain way, yet find later on that all must be reinterpreted in the light of a different clue just provided.[15]

---

readings to de Saussure's distinction "between *langue* and *parole,* the system of language and the individual speech-act . . ." respectively (p. 152).

[15] *Form and Style in the Arts: An Introduction to Aesthetic Morphology* (Cleveland:

We may say, then, that the intuition of a literary unity, especially of poetry, takes place through a process of intuition or *apperception* of elements which somehow belong together, albeit complexly. But this subjective process must have its "objective correlative" in the poem itself. As Munro suggests, this objective structure can develop its concepts, moods, and images in a rather straightforward manner, where one thought naturally leads to another. Or it can develop by way of surprises, using a process of partial revelation and ambiguity, and then suddenly forcing the reader to reconsider the poem's meaning by providing a new clue. In either case, we must say that a poem bears its total meaning by way of *accretion* of its large and small parts. Thus, accretion is the "objective correlative" of subjective apperception.

It should be noted that this situation obtains also in the other arts. For instance, a melody is a string of notes which accrue to one another in time, yet a melody is an aesthetic and emotional unit both objectively and subjectively—at least if it is a good melody. Of course a melody, like a narrative, is a form of art in which the meaning of the individual units or "notes" is powerfully determined by syntagmatic sequence. Obviously, a proverb collection must be arranged on somewhat different, non-syntagmatic principles, as the failure of Bryce's structural attempt made plain. But there is a widespread European iconographic tradition of popular broadsheets, often associated with contemporary proverbs, which provides a closer parallel to the sort of paradigmatic[16] arrangement of units which we may expect to find in a proverb collection where each unit, unlike a musical note, has a relative autonomy with respect to the whole. A note cannot exist apart from the composition; a proverb can. The pictorial tradition in question is that which represents the topos of "The World Upside Down."[17] In this broadsheet tradition, we find a series of pictures, each complete in itself and often existing in other contexts, all of which are considered to depict the World Upside Down. The same pictures are found repeatedly in the different nations and are often visual counterparts to contemporary proverbs. In a typical example, a Dutch woodcut of the late sixteenth century (reproduced at the end of this chapter) we find the following images juxtaposed as described by Kunzle:

Case Western Reserve University, 1970) 71. E. M. Good ("The Unfilled Sea: Style and Meaning in Ecclesiastes 1:2-11," *JW* [1978] 59-73) provides a reading of his text which illustrates the accretion of meaning described by Munro.

[16] The terms paradigmatic and syntagmatic are discussed in the chapter next.

[17] The literature on the subject is large and the topos is itself virtually universal in distribution, appearing in the Ancient Near East and surviving in all the modern European traditions. For an initial orientation, see David Kunzle, "The World Upside Down: The Iconography of a European Broadsheet Type," *The Reversible World: Symbolic Inversion in Art and Society* (Barbara A. Babcock, ed.; Ithaca: Cornell University, 1978) 39-94, with bibliography. Also, Hedwig Kenner, *Das Phänomen der verkehrten Welt in der griechisch-römischen Antike* (Klagenfurt: Geschichtsverein für Kärnten, 1970).

Top row: peasant rides while king walks, child teaches professors, wife goes to war and husband spins, tower inside bell. *Second row:* servant arrests master, cripple carries healthy man, blind man guides seeing one, poor man gives to rich. *Third row:* birds eat man, ass drives master, child punishes father, child rocks father. *Fourth row:* sheep eat wolf, peasants [sic] drive men at plough, young ladies draw carriage bearing horses, sheep shears shepherd. *Fifth row:* cart pulls oxen, ox flays butcher, pig guts butcher, chickens eat fox. *Sixth row:* hen sits on cock, fish nest in trees, women storm building, parrot teaches caged man to talk. *Seventh row:* mice catch cat, child feeds mother, little birds eat big one, fish catch birds. *Bottom row:* wild animals chase hunter, world upside down, sick man inspects doctor's urine, ships travel overland![18]

What concerns our project with Proverbs 25-27 is that the widely diverse images and topics depicted in numerous broadsheets are seen to belong to *one* visual artwork whose theme, "The World Upside Down," is manifest in the discrete pictures which can also exist independently of the larger artwork. Our argument concerning structure will be that similar, "paradigmatic" principles of arrangement are among those at work in the ancient saying collections of Proverbs 25-27. Similarly some of the techniques of juxtaposition found in the pictures (father beside father, eating beneath eating, ox beside ox, cocks beside cock, butcher beside butcher and so on) will also be seen to function among the Biblical sayings as binders of contiguity which strengthen the general unity of the whole work.

It goes without saying, of course, that the process of accretion of meaning has validity only within the bounds of a genuine unit. The accretion of meaning and its apperception by the reader can take place only within a true literary unit or poem. Thus, in regard to Proverbs (and certain prophets, for that matter), the question arises, "How do we define the poem or larger unit, within which the process of meaning-accretion takes place?" As mentioned above, form criticism tends to restrict the "poem" to the smallest oral forms or literary *Gattungen*. From this viewpoint, Proverbs 25-27 can only be an *artificial,* inauthentic unit of a number of proverbs arbitrarily gathered together.

One cannot impose an *a priori* method on a text, but one can certainly approach the text with questions. Yet, if the questions ignore the nature of the text, they will lead either to no conclusion or, worse yet, to false conclusions. Hence we must seek grounds for the appropriateness of our methodological questioning in the text itself.

Proverbs 25-27, simply stated, is a collection of ancient Hebrew wisdom forms. It is not one proverb, but a number of proverbs concluded by a short poem brought together to form a new whole. This whole includes several subsidiary wholes (25:2-27; 26:1-12, 13-16, 17-28; 27:1-22, 23-27). Since the very nature of proverbs is to function as short, discrete utterances, and since there is a diversity of forms in the various subsections, we cannot think simply of these

---

[18] "World Upside Down," 45. The reproduction at the end of our chapter is found on pp. 46-47.

passages as original unities. Yet these texts have been brought together and arranged by one or more individuals who were consciously engaged in literary, redactional activity *as they understood it*. Indeed, there is some evidence that individual units were either adapted or created *ad hoc* to fill a role in the larger proverbial composition.[19] It is this fact that constitutes our problem. In order to understand the mutual significance the various proverbs in chapters 25-27 have for one another, we need to recreate[20] the principles, structural, poetic, and semantic, of selection, composition, and editing according to which the compiler(s) of these passages went to work.

These principles must be manifest in the object created, subject to the limitations of its linguistic and literary raw materials and to the limitations of the compiler's talent. That the poet-compiler, for so he will be understood in this work, did select is suggested by the text itself (cf. 25:1)[21] and seems obvious from the existence of doublets and variants of the same saying. That the proverbs were edited with a view to forming a literary whole is further evident from the fact that some of them only possess an intelligible meaning by virtue of their *Sitz im Text* and from the artful character of the juxtaposition of the individual units.[22] In the combination and arrangement of these forms we may find that the meaning of the whole is more than the sum of its parts.

---

[19] For this process in Egypt, see M. Lichtheim, "Observations on Papyrus Insinger," 286-290. Regarding the Sumerian collections edited by Gordon, J. Goody (*Domestication,* 125) notes that "there is even a question as to how many of these proverbs had a popular as distinct from a 'literary' origin. For there is a special group of proverbs dealing with scribes, while others display an abundance of rhetorical figures and numerous complex forms of parallelism, which suggest their composition by the literati. . . . In any case it was the scribes who selected and arranged the proverbs in the more or less standard order in which they are found in collections." Goody bases his Sumerian references on the early work of E. I. Gordon (*Sumerian Proverbs: Glimpses of Everyday Life in Ancient Mesopotamia* [Philadelphia, 1959]), but his observations are borne out by the later work of B. Alster (*Studies in Sumerian Proverbs*).

[20] R. G. Collingwood (*The Idea of History* [Oxford: Clarendon, 1946]) argued that the task of the historian was to recreate the mental processes which shaped events and artifacts. Our interest, however, is not so much in the mental processes as in the actual artifact, the poem which is a product of much more than just individual genius.

[21] Unfortunately the exact sense of h'tyqw is uncertain.

[22] N. H. Ridderbos (*Die Psalmen: Stilistische Verfahren und Aufbau* [BZAW 117; Berlin: de Gruyter, 1972] 74-78, 106-109). "Allgemein kann gesagt werden, dass die Uebergänge zwischen den einzelnen Teilen in der Regel eher abrupt als fliessend sind. Das Aphoristische ist kennzeichnend für viele Psalmen. Der Psalmendichter stellt die eine Aussage mehr oder weniger unvermittelt neben die andere. Das bedeutet keineswegs, dass die verschiedenen Aussagen untereinander nicht zusammenhängen, jedoch bleibt es oft dem Einfühlungsvermögen des Lesers überlassen, herauszufinden, welcher Art diese Zusammenhänge sind" (p. 75). Recent work in Hebrew poetics and parallelism demonstrates that one is not entirely cast upon the subjectivity of his Einfühlungsvermögen (see Chapter 4 on Method below).

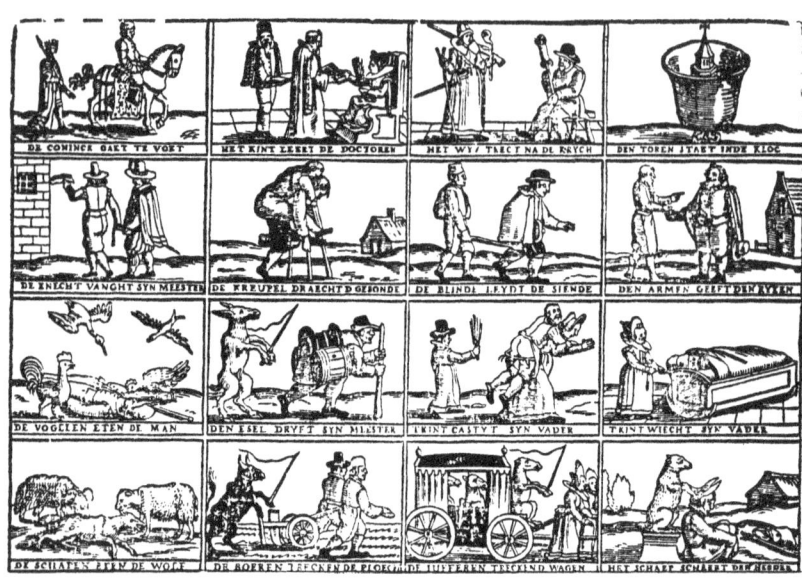

4
Methods: Structural, Poetic, Semantic

In a previous chapter, I discussed the contributions made by G. E. Bryce to the analysis of Prov 25:2-27 as a literary unit. As noted, in spite of genuine advances, Bryce's work did not pursue its analysis in sufficient detail and, particularly in its structuralist aspects, showed itself to be methodologically unsatisfactory. The following chapters of the thesis undertake a positive analysis and exposition of the subsections of Proverbs 25-27. To anticipate the results of this study, Prov 25:2-27; 26:1-12, 13-16, 17-28; 27:1-22, 23-27 are units which use various literary devices, and present varying degrees of coherence, ranging from a complex, tightly organized "proverb poem"[1] like 26:1-12 to the proverb miscellany found in 27:1-22. Each "poem" needs to be analysed on its own terms and with respect to several aspects. It is ultimately the cumulative force of all these aspects working together which reveals whether a passage is a literary whole or not.

To create a poem out of Sayings and Admonitions,[2] which can and usually do function independently, is not easy. The authors of 25-27 use a variety of means: whatever will work. They have at hand a vast store of tradition — linguistic, poetic, formulaic, metaphoric, and thematic. By his craft the poet welds these raw materials into a coherent structure of meaning, a verbal work of art, embued with a certain spirit and style, and expressive of an overarching view of reality in contact with the details of life.

As poets, the authors of Proverbs 25-27 are very much like the *bricoleur* of Claude Levi-Strauss[3] who creates something new out of materials old and new, whatever is at hand for his purposes (cf. Matt 13:52). Our task is to perceive what is in the text — even if the text operates and exists differently than we might expect at first glance.

---

[1] The expression derives from B. Alster, *Studies in Sumerian Proverbs* (Mesopotamia 3; Copenhagen: Akademisk Forlag, 1975) 14.
[2] For these terms, see p. 5, n. 3 supra and n. 11 below.
[3] *The Savage Mind* (London: Weidenfeld and Nicolson, 1972) 16-36. Cf. the description of compositional technique in M. Lichtheim, "Observations on Papyrus Insinger," in *Studien zu altägyptischen Lebenslehren* (E. Hornung and O. Keel eds.; OBO 28; Göttingen: Vandenhoeck und Ruprecht, 1979) 286-290.

To this end we will employ three primary methods: structural, poetic, and semantic. Our first step is to lay bare the basic structures which give pattern and coherence to the poem's macrostructure.

STRUCTURES

Any structuralist analysis (i.e., one ultimately based on modern linguistics) of a literary text entails the question of *syntagmatic* and *paradigmatic* relations. For our purposes, John Lyons' description of these terms will suffice:

> By virtue of its potentiality of occurrence in a certain context a linguistic unit enters into relations of two different kinds. It enters into *paradigmatic* relations with all the units which can also occur in the same context ... and it enters into *syntagmatic* relations with the other units of the same level with which it occurs and which constitute its context.[4]

Thus, the pronouns *I, you, he, she, it* are in paradigmatic relations with one another, while they are in syntagmatic relations with verbs like *fell, fall, will fall* (which are in paradigmatic relations among themselves). The paradigmatic options are in tacit contrast with one another and the implicit meaning-context of each option is the set of unused options. The *explicit* meaning-context of any unit is the units in syntagmatic relation with it. It is crucial to note the interrelation and interdependence of syntagmatic and paradigmatic relations in structuring and conveying meaning:

> the same information may be conveyed in language either syntagmatically or paradigmatically. ... One can say either *I'm flying to New York* or *I'm going to New York by air*, either *I'm driving to New York* or *I'm going to New York by car*. In one case the distinction is made by the paradigmatic choice of the verbs *fly* and *drive*, in the other by the syntagmatic modification of the more general verb *go*.[5]

Bryce's treatment of Proverbs 25, as laid out above, is primarily syntagmatic and assumes that the "narrative syntax" put forth by Greimas provides a *temporal* sequence which determines the structure of the chapter. However, syntagmatic relations need not be sequential (*Caesarem necavit Brutus = Brutus Caesarem necavit*).[6] Furthermore, they need not be presented in a temporal sequence when they are of narrative character (Brutus killed Caesar. Three days before they had been out drinking together.).

For our purposes, it is crucial to see that there can be syntagmatic relations which are not temporal or narrative in character. Moreover, these relations must be studied in connection with the paradigmatic options[7] available to the writer

---

[4] *Theoretical*, 73. See also Patte, *What Is*, 25-27.

[5] Lyons, *Theoretical*, 542.

[6] On sequence and syntagmatic and paradigmatic relations, see Lyons, *Theoretical*, 70-81.

[7] Only with reference to Prov 25:4, 5 does Bryce bring up the interaction of paradigmatic and syntagmatic analysis ("Structural," 114). He is aware that these two

of a text. In short, at this stage of research into the problem of order in the book of Proverbs, care must be taken to begin with analysis of the text itself to determine the possible options and structures employed in the text. Inasmuch as our task is a "structural" one, our approach must not be *a priori* but empirical:

> Another structural methodological approach is used by many analysts. Each text is analyzed on its own merits so as to discover the constraints, or structures, which contribute to the production of its meaning effect. No model is consciously presupposed by the analyst. In such a case the analyst is led to emphasize the constraints closest to the surface of the text, i.e., the structures of the enunciation and the cultural structures. Without this type of analysis models for the various structures could never be established. They should indeed be multiplied in order to identify the cultural codes and the structures of the enunciation which characterize each biblical text.[8]

In the sort of literature at hand, it is necessary to address the question of structure by beginning with the Sayings and Admonitions themselves, and by admitting their relative self-sufficiency. These units will thus have their own internal paradigmatic and syntagmatic options and patterns. But with respect to the macro-structure of a literary work which incorporates such small wisdom units into a larger whole, the Sayings and Admonitions present themselves as the paradigmatic "building blocks" of the whole.

For example, where the paradigmatic units consist of a two-item string of options (AB), various syntagmatic macro-structures of junction or disjunction can be created by sequences of juxtaposition.

1. High degree of homogeneity or coherence:
   AB
   AB
   AB
   etc.

---

verses exist in a paradigmatic relation, but seems to think that one can read the verses syntagmatically without reading them paradigmatically—which is not the case. Other than this instance, Bryce does not explore the paradigmatic relations which exist among the sayings. On page 109, Bryce contrasts the Proppian model he employs as a "syntagmatic" one in contrast to the primarily "semantic" one which C. Levi-Strauss uses. But "semantic" is not a meaningful opposition to "syntagmatic" in this context. I assume Bryce means "paradigmatic," which would fairly characterize Levi-Strauss' somewhat one-sided but suggestive method of arranging "mythemes" paradigmatically without much concern for the sequence in which they occur in a story. Cf. C. Levi-Strauss, "The Story of Asdiwal" (*"La Geste d'Asdiwal"*), *The Structural Study of Myth and Totemism* (ed. E. Leach; London: Tavistock, 1967) 1-47; and Hawkes, *Structuralism*, 39-49.

[8] Patte, *What Is*, 84-85.

2. Junction with disjunction:
   AB/AB/AB
   BA/BA/BA

3. Chiasmus of paradigmatic options:
   ABBA
   ABBA
   etc.

As the number of elements and hence the complexity of the basic paradigmatic units (our A's and S's) increases, so does the complexity and number of macro-syntagmatic possibilities. But if a poet wishes to create a larger unity out of discrete paradigmatic units, he will naturally select a relatively simple pattern of juxtapositions to avoid the chaotic centrifugal force of unordered proverbs.

A warning is in order, however. It is by no means necessary that the compiler of wisdom units choose to arrange his material in terms of the contrast between Admonition and Saying, or even in terms of variations among Sayings or Admonitions. He may choose other principles of organization. A parallel on the level of grammatical syntax would be a language that minimized the role of word order in syntagmatic relations (*Caesarem necavit Brutus* = *Brutus Caesarem necavit*). But when such syntagmatic patterns do appear in a collection of short wisdom utterances, they constitute a major piece of evidence in the cumulative argument that a collection of Sayings and Admonitions is not random but meaningful in arrangement and coherence.

Assuming for the moment that we will find meaningful macro-structures in our texts, the analysis of their syntagmatic structure, at the least, must elaborate the arrangement of and the relations among the Sayings and Admonitions incorporated into it. That is to say, in contrast to Bryce, our analysis must have a paradigmatic emphasis. As Viktor Shklovsky, the Russian formalist, had already pointed out, some genres operate primarily in an "associative" or "vertical" (i.e., paradigmatic) mode, while others mainly employ the syntagmatic mode:

> Where the lyric is in a sense "static" in respect of its object, instantaneous in its import and graspable as a single unity, the novel's commitment to narrative, to movement in and through time, makes it an essentially dynamic and active entity. . . . If the lyric operates . . . on static objects and institutions in what, to use Saussure's term, could be called an *associative*, "vertical" mode, the overriding necessity of narrative in the novel forces on it a mode appropriate to its investment in temporality: the *syntagmatic*, horizontal mode.[9]

While the above formulation may require qualification, it makes a point important for our study of Proverbs: some genres highlight paradigmatic arrangement,

---

[9] So T. Hawkes, *Structuralism*, 65.

while others emphasize sequential syntagmatic arrangement. Obviously this is not a matter of either-or, but one of *emphasis*. The great linguist R. Jakobson has put this insight in terms of "metaphor" and "metonymy" which for him have paradigmatic and syntagmatic connotations respectively:

> Jakobson offers the ... proposal that the metaphoric mode tends to be foregrounded in poetry, whereas the metonymic mode tends to be foregrounded in prose.... "The principle of similarity underlies poetry; the metrical parallelism of lines, or the phonic equivalence of rhyming words prompts the question of semantic similarity and contrast.... Prose, on the contrary, is forwarded essentially by contiguity. Thus, for poetry, metaphor, and for prose, metonymy is the line of least resistance...." By the use of complex interrelationships, by emphasizing resemblances and by promoting through repetition "equivalences" or "parallelisms" of sound, stress, image, rhyme, poetry patterns and "thickens" language, "foregrounding" its formal qualities, and consequently "backgrounding" its capacity for sequential, discursive and referential meaning. Words similar in sound are "drawn together in meaning"; ambiguity is consequently favoured, and equivalence is promoted to the status of a "constitutive device" of the art![10]

Hence our analysis must focus upon the basic paradigmatic units (Sayings and Admonitions) to determine if syntagmatic patterns emerge from their juxtaposition. We will employ two types of structural analysis of the basic wisdom units. The first proceeds from the well-established form-critical distinction of *Admonition* (= A) and *Saying* (= S);[11] the second is based upon paradigmatic variation among the Sayings only. These small forms, S and A, the basic aesthetic units of wisdom, have a relative completeness in themselves, though they are by no means atomistic utterances without broader linguistic and non-linguistic contexts. Our focus in the following chapters will be upon their immediate literary context.

---

[10] Hawkes, *Structuralism*, 80, 81. See also R. Jakobson, "Grammatical Parallelism and its Russian Facet," *Language* 42 (1966) 399-429. Hebrew *parallelismus membrorum* may be considered in terms of paradigmatic variation or substitution.

[11] For a brief account with literature, see J. L. Crenshaw, "Wisdom," in *Old Testament Form Criticism* (J. H. Hayes, ed.; San Antonio: Trinity University Press, 1974) 235-236. W. Zimmerli, "Concerning the Structure of Old Testament Wisdom" (1933) in *SAIW*, 180-183. R. E. Murphy, *Wisdom Literature*, 48-82, the first volume to appear in a series entitled "The Forms of the Old Testament Literature," contains much of value. Nonetheless, Murphy's distinctions are not entirely clear, nor are they consistently applied to the texts. On pp. 4-6, "The Saying" and "Commands and Prohibitions" are presented as the two "Basic Wisdom Genres." Yet page 6 tells us that "commands and prohibitions abound in the genre of INSTRUCTION," and that they can also appear in isolated form. In the passages treated in this thesis, Murphy assigns 25:16-17 to the genre of INSTRUCTION, while the other Admonitions with motivations in chapter 25 (vv 6-7, 8, 9-10, 21-22) are properly identified. Prov 26:4-5 is described as "a striking form of antinomies," while no mention is made of the form-critical status of these verses as *Admonitions*. Similarly, the A's in 26:25; 27:1, 2, 11, 13 (?) go unmentioned.

Structural Analysis of S and A, + and -[12]

Biblical scholars have long been using form-critical distinctions to determine coherences and disjunctions in more extended passages. Less frequently have they enquired whether there might be a pattern in the arrangement of form-critical units. This step is crucial in the study of larger sections of Proverbs, precisely because the formal units are so small.

Proverbs 25:2-27:22 (excluding the title in 25:1 and the poem in 27:23-27) is entirely composed of S and A units which extend over one or two poetic lines.[13] The A is a two-part form comprised of imperative or vetitive *Precept* (= P) and a *Motive Clause*.[14] While there are a variety of types, depending upon the nature

---

[12] The + and - sigla are explained in the immediately following paragraphs of the text.

[13] I use "line" in the sense of a poetic unit, usually in parallelism, comprised of 2 or 3 cola. Thus my "line" corresponds to J. L. Kugel's "parallelistic line" (*The Idea of Biblical Poetry* [New Haven: Yale, 1982] 1-58) more closely than it does to M. O'Connor's "line" which equals my "colon" (*Hebrew Verse Structure* [Winona Lake: Eisenbraun's, 1980] 52).

[14] B. Gemser ("The Importance of the Motive Clause in Old Testament Law," *VTSup* 1 [1953] 50-66) was seminal. R. Sonsino (*Motive Clauses in Hebrew Law: Biblical Forms and Near Eastern Parallels* [SBL Dissertation Series 45; Chico: Scholars, 1980] 109-117) gives four categories of motive clauses which are theoretically possible for wisdom as well as legal forms: "(1) motive clauses which express God's authority, (2) motive clauses which allude to historical experiences of the people, (3) motive clauses which instill a fear of punishment, (4) motive clauses which promise well-being to the compliant" (p. 109). Sonsino's third and fourth categories are expressed in a moralistic way which seems uninformed by the discussion begun by K. Koch ("Gibt es ein Vergeltungsdogma im AT?" *ZThK*, 52 [1955] 1-44, and the collection edited by Koch, *Um das Prinzip der Vergeltung in Religion und Recht des Alten Testaments* [WdF 125; Darmstadt: Wissenschaftliche Buchgesellschaft, 1972]). See Carl-A. Keller, "Zum sogenannten Vergeltungsglauben im Proverbienbuch" in H. Donner et al., eds., *Beiträge zur alttestamentlichen Theologie* (W. Zimmerli Festschrift; Göttingen: Vandenhoeck and Ruprecht, 1977) 223-238. The relationship of Precept and Result (Consequence) is better expressed in terms of the now common idea of "The Act-Consequence Relationship" (G. von Rad, *WII*, 124-137)—however one may wish to account for that relationship theologically. It may be noted that, in terms of the system used in the present thesis, Sonsino's third and fourth categories are consequential; furthermore, number (3) corresponds to our "R-" (= Result-) and number (4) to our "R+" respectively. For "Result" see below in the text.

H. J. Postel ("The Form and Function of the Motive Clause in Proverbs 10-29" Ph.D. Dissertation; University of Iowa, 1976 58, 144-171) distinguishes motive clauses that appear in Admonitions (= A, with negative Precept denoted as A-) or Sentences (= S). "The type of motive is identified as : P = promissory; D = dissuasive. The content of the motive clause is identified as: C = consequential; E = explanatory; T = explicitly theological" (58). Postel's P. and D correspond roughly to our R+ and R- respectively. There is some confusion and overlap among Postel's "type" and "content" categorizations of motive clauses. A "P" motive must necessarily imply a positive consequence, while it is possible for a dissuasive motive ("D") to be of a non-consequential type (e.g., Prov 26:25b, "for there are seven abominations in his heart"). Similarly, 25:22, which Postel calls a T (p. 85), is with equal validity designated C. In Prov 25:2-27, Postel rightly classifies

of the Precept and especially of the Motive Clause, in Proverbs 25-26, only one type occurs, the *Consequential* (we will discuss chapter 27 later). That is, these Admonitions motivate their positive or negative Precepts by spelling out positive or negative consequences of the actions entailed.

With the foregoing observations, we have arrived at the essential requirements of a structural analysis of the Admonitions in Chapter 25 which will be helpful in laying out the macro-structure of the whole passage. The form-critical pattern of Precept and *Result* (= R) clause intersects with the positive (= +) and negative (= -) dimension of wisdom. By the positive and negative dimension, I mean the fundamental contrast of good and evil—in the broadest sense—which in its various aspects premeates all of wisdom thought![15] This

---

all the motive clauses as C (with the exception just noted); his grouping of D and P for this chapter corresponds in all but one case (25:7; p. 85) to our R- and R+ respectively.

With regard to form-critical considerations, P. J. Nel's recent work (*The Structure and Ethos of the Wisdom Admonitions in Proverbs* [BZAW 158; Berlin: de Gruyter, 1982]) is problematic. One example should suffice. Nel does not understand his own categories. In Hebrew it is often impossible, on a grammatical level, to distinguish final or purpose clauses from result clauses (cf. T. O. Lambdin, *Introduction to Biblical Hebrew* [New York: Scribner's, 1971] 119). Yet Nel's motivational types include "Final Clause" (pp. 18-26) and "Result Clause or Result Description" (pp. 28-36). Nel sometimes translates his final clauses as result clauses (e.g., Prov 22:10; 9:9; p. 20) and defines the same in terms more appropriate to a result clause: "They are . . . *factual statements* about the final consequence of the prescribed behaviour in the admonitions" (p. 20, my emphases). Conversely, Nel classifies Prov 27:11b as a result clause, but translates it as a final clause: "that I may answer my contemner." Nel's comment on this verse expresses his confusion of result and purpose succinctly: "The result clause is expressed in the form of a wish, with *we* and *Cohortative*" (p. 29).

[15] H. H. Schmid, *WGW*, 159 (cf. 155, 161): "Auch die Welt muss sich aufteilen lassen können in die Antithetik von Gutem und Bösem, Rechtem und Unrechtem." See especially the exposition of G. von Rad, *WII*, 77-82: The "reality of good and evil [is] . . . life-forming; . . . knowledge of them was the prime conviction on which all individual teachings rested and from which they proceeded. . . . The good man is the one who knows about the constructive quality of good and the destructive quality of evil and who submits to this pattern which can be discerned in the world. . . . Behind this concept of life there lies not the dispassionate utilitarian standpoint of the man who has taken life into his own hands, but the action, which has to be constantly repeated, of pious integration into a divine order which is imposed on man and in which alone he can find blessing" (pp. 78-80). Cf. H.-J. Hermisson, *SIS*, 154-156. Much confusion has resulted from the failure to realize that the Sayings which contrast good and evil (e.g., those with the opposed roots *SDQ* and *RŠ‛*) *are not merely existential statements but normative* statements which contrast two things with respect to some norm. J. Lyons' remarks, based upon a semantic analysis of antonymic word pairs, are germane: "Many pseudo-problems have arisen in logic and philosophy as a consequence of the failure to appreciate that such words as *big* and *small*, or *good* and *bad*, do not refer to independent, 'opposite' qualities, but are merely lexical devices for grading as 'more than' or 'less than' with respect to some implicit norm." Thus

contrast comes to explicit expression in opposed, fixed word-pairs like *righteous-wicked* and *wise-foolish,* and in the more or less explicit valuations which the Sayings often place upon certain states of affairs. This contrast, which is profoundly related to the writer's worldview, presupposes a normative world-order which provides the standards by which things, events, and people are judged.

Addison G. Wright has shown that the opposition of positive and negative can be used to organize the material of wisdom poems and that the discernment of such a pattern contributes significantly to our understanding of the poem's meaning.[16] Once again, to anticipate our analysis, similar patterns are operative in our text sample, most significantly in Prov 26:1-12.

In the Admonitions of Chapter 25, the good-evil contrast appears in positive and negative Precepts and Result clauses. Similarly, the Sayings, or their parts, may be broadly characterized as + or - inasmuch as they depict matters which are evaluated as good or evil respectively. Since the Sayings in Proverbs are usually of two parts, the following internal patterns are possible: 1. +/+, 2. +/-, 3. -/+, 4. -/-. (Patterns 2. and 3. are of course very common in antithetical parallelism. Cf. Proverbs 10-15 *passim.*) In these patterns, the slash (/) indicates juxtaposition with varying degrees of semantic relatedness between the two parts. The "Better-than" Sayings are similar except that a "greater than" sign (>) is used to separate the more valued from the less valued Saying-half (cf. 25:24).

---

the sentence, "*A small elephant is a large animal*" is not contradictory because "the implicit 'size-norm' for elephants is not necessarily the same as the implicit 'size-norm' for animals taken as a whole class. . . . Explicitly ungraded antonyms are to be understood as implicitly graded with reference to some relevant norm . . ." (*Theoretical,* 465-466). Even those Sayings which are often pointed to as being morally neutral, as simply describing states of affairs without value judgment explicitly attached, are nonetheless generally value-laden. A Saying like 27:19 ("As in water face answers to face, so the mind of man reflects the mind of man" RSV.) seems quite value-free, but this is only because "is" and "ought," the "fact" and its norm, are congruent. Like the "law" of reflection this "law" of human nature is simply a given. In 13:23 ("The fallow ground of the poor yields much food, but it is swept away through injustice."), once again a "fact" is described, but the reader is expected to know that the whole complex described is a wicked one. Prov 18:17 ("He who states his case first seems right, until the other comes and examines him.") is somewhat ambiguous in its details (which can only be made clear through the application of the Saying to a situation); nonetheless, the Saying is clearly heavily value-laden in terms of what constitutes righteousness in the lawcourt.

[16] " 'For Everything There is a Season': The Structure and Meaning of the Fourteen Opposites (Ecclesiastes 3, 2-8)," *De la Tôrah au Messie . . . Mélanges Henri Cazelles* (ed. J. Doré, P. Grelot, M. Carrez; Paris: Desclée, 1981) 321-28. Following J. A. Loader, Wright analyzes the poem to disclose a pattern based on the categories "desirable" and "undesirable" ("D" and "U") which conform to our + and - respectively. Cf. C. R. Fontaine, *Traditional,* 66.

A further word of explanation concerning my use of + and - is necessary. Normally grammar and sense are congruent.[17] A vetitive (*'l* plus short imperfect) is used to forbid a bad action as in *"Do not go* when the light is red." However, the same negative sense can be provided by the use of a positive grammatical form as in *"Stop* when the light is red." The imperative lexeme "stop" is a sense-substitute for the more cumbersome "do not go." In Hebrew, the point is illustrated by Nebuzaradan's offer to Jeremiah of a choice to go to Babylon or not (*b'* versus *hdl;* Jer 40:4; cf. also Ps 119:60a). Similarly, the use of a negative particle or a negative phrase in a Saying or Admonition does not necessarily give it a negative sense. In the analysis which follows, when grammar or other surface phenomena "conflict" with sense, my account will be based upon the deeper form-critical criterion of sense. Form-criticism ought not to be reduced to grammar; its ultimate principles are semantic. Thus both "Do not go" and "Stop" are to be considered negative Precepts (P -).

The foregoing considerations permit us to diagram sections of Proverbs so that the structures of the Sayings and Admonitions are laid bare. In terms of deep structure, there are four possible patterns for the consequential Admonition: 1. P+ → R+, 2. P- → R+, 3. P- ↛ R-, 4. P+ ↛ R-. In this schema, P is a precept to do (+) or not to do (-) something good or bad respectively. R is a good (+) or bad (-) Result of Precept. The sign → indicates that the Result following upon the Precept is either intended or anticipated. The sign ↛ , which often corresponds to Hebrew *pen*[18] ["lest"], indicates that the Result following upon the forbidden action is to be feared and avoided. Thus in the patterns above, number 1. (P+ → R+) may be read, "Do x so that y may ensue." Number 3. (P- ↛ R-) may be read, "Don't do q lest p ensue."

The underlying "logic" of the Admonitions is thus quite simple: The world is so constructed that doing good leads to good; doing evil leads to evil![19] Consequently, Number 1. and Number 3. in the preceding paragraph are the simplest forms of Admonition. Numbers 2. and 4. are variations on this basic principle where doing good avoids or prevents some evil and not doing evil makes possible some good. Upon these basic structures various surface patterns can be elaborated.

Structural Analysis of Sayings: Topics and Comments[20]

While the analysis of S and A patterns in intersection with + and - values provides us with a valuable means of discerning macro-structures based on

---

[17] J. Lyons, *Theoretical*, 135. See also R. Murphy's critique of W. McKane (*WL*, 51).

[18] See note 14 above. Admonitions are able to use a variety of particles or asyndeton to connect the P with its Motive Clause. For the various possible connections, see Sonsino, *Motive Clause*, 70-76, and Heribert Rücker, *Die Begründungen der Weisungen Jahwes im Pentateuch* (Erfurter Theologische Studien 30; Leipzig: St. Benno-Verlag, 1973) 3-7.

[19] It should be noted that this presents a caricature of wisdom thinking, which is quite aware of exceptions to the tidy consequential scheme just described.

[20] These terms are explained in the immediately following paragraphs of the text. Topic

paradigmatic continuity or contrast, it does not in itself provide an adequate means of discriminating patterns among the *Sayings*. For instance, in Proverbs 26:1-3, 6-12 (vv 4-5 are A) all the Sayings have a -/- structure, a situation which may be significant (deliberate homogeneity) or meaningless (the method of analysis does not discriminate).

Consequently, we employ a second method of structural proverb analysis. Our argument here is similar to the preceding one concerning Admonitions and Sayings in that it takes the line or couplet as the basic paradigmatic unit and asks if these units are related in a syntagmatic way. This analysis, however, does not pertain to the contrast of A and S, but only to contrasts and coherences within the Sayings. My point of departure is the Topic-Comment analysis of Sayings (= S) developed by the paroemiologist A. Dundes and modified by others and myself.[21] Carole R. Fontaine has shown the fruitfulness of this method for biblical studies, and we will adopt and adapt it for our purposes, after making some necessary clarifications.[22]

The method developed by Dundes, like all structuralist methods, has its roots in modern linguistics. Dundes argued that all proverbs could be analyzed into "descriptive element(s)" consisting of *Topic(s)* (= T) and *Comment(s)* (= C). The simplest form of Proverb will have one descriptive element: "Money (T) talks (C)." More complex proverbs will have several descriptive elements which will form various patterns of identity and contrast.

Though Dundes did not spell it out, his use of T and C stems from developments in the Prague School of linguistics going back at least to the 1930's.[23] What Dundes calls Topic and Comment is by the Prague linguists

---

= T; Comment = C.

[21] A. Dundes and R. A. George, "Toward a Structural Definition of the Riddle," in A. Dundes, *Analytic Essays in Folklore* (Studies in Folklore 2; The Hague: Mouton, 1975) 95-102. A. Dundes, "On the Structure of the Proverb," *Analytic Essays*, 103-118. C. T. Scott, "On Defining the Riddle: The Problem of a Structural Unit," in D. Ben-Amos ed., *Folklore Genres* (Austin and London: University of Texas, 1975) 77-90.

[22] C. R. Fontaine, *Traditional Sayings in the Old Testament: A Contextual Study* (Sheffield: Almond, 1982) 34-38, 63-67. Fontaine applies Dundes' method to all the traditional sayings she treats; e.g., Jud 8:2 (pp. 81-82). Fontaine follows Dundes' in his important distinction of proverb "image," proverb "message" and proverb "architectural formula" (pp. 34-35). It is the "architectural formula" which receives the T-C analysis. Hermisson's analysis of Sayings (*SIS*, 141-171) is essentially a grammatical one which does not serve our purposes well.

[23] F. Daneš, ("Functional Sentence Perspective and the Organization of the Text," [*Janua Linguarum*, Series Minor 147, *Papers on Functional Sentence Perspective*; Prague: Academia/The Hague: Mouton, 1974] 106-128, 106) cites a 1939 paper by V. Mathesius. I am indebted to my colleague William Vande Kopple for discussion and bibliography concerning the Prague School.

usually called Theme and Rheme.[24] Unfortunately, these terms are regularly used equivocally to refer to a variety of linguistic functions, some of which overlap, most of which interact; we must be clear as to which is at stake in our analysis.[25] The two most common and important uses of T and C are 1) the opposition of Given and New[26] and 2) the opposition of what "is spoken about in the sentence" (the sentence "theme") and "what the speaker says about this theme."[27] It is this second opposition which, correctly, is used by Dundes in his structural analysis of proverbs and riddles:

> The *topic* is the apparent referent; that is, it is the object or item allegedly described [in the riddle]. The *comment* is an assertion about the topic, usually concerning the form, function or action of the topic.[28]

Thus Dundes' T will often correspond to a grammatical subject and his C to a grammatical predicate, but this is not necessary, and Dundes rightly insists that *proverbial* T-C structure and grammatical structure are not always coterminous.[29]

Yet, as Charles Scott has shown, Dundes did not adequately pursue the connection between linguistic analysis and T-C analysis of riddles and proverbs.[30] When subjected to linguistic rules of transformation, proverbial

---

[24] For a brief treatment of Topic and Comment as linguistic notions, see Lyons, *Theoretical*, 334–340. For convenience we will employ the terms T and C and ignore Theme and Rheme.

[25] Z. Palkova and B. Palek ("Functional Sentence Perspective and Textlinguistics," *Current Trends in Textlinguistics* [Research in Text Theory 2; ed. W. Dressler; Berlin: de Gruyter, 1977] 212–227, 213) note that "The terms employed . . . are not standardized; some of them are divergent and some correspond only partially." They point out five uses of, or factors in the use of, the terms Topic and Comment.

[26] For example, the following paragraph was found to be "rather incomprehensible" by subjects not possessing an antecedent topic: " 'The procedure is actually quite simple. First you arrange things into different groups depending upon their makeup. Of course, one pile may be sufficient depending on how much there is to do. If you have to go somewhere else due to lack of facilities that is the next step, otherwise you are pretty well set. It is important not to overdo any particular endeavor. That is, it is better to do too few things at once than too many. . . .' " Other subjects who were told that the topic of the paragraph was "washing clothes" had no difficulty construing its meaning. Susan E. Haviland and Herbert H. Clark, "What's New? Acquiring New Information as a Process in Comprehension," *Journal of Verbal Learning and Verbal Behavior* 13 (1974) 512–521, 520.

[27] Daneš, "Functional," 107.

[28] Dundes, "Riddle," 97. In "Proverb" (p. 108), Dundes assumes these definitions apply to the proverb as well as the riddle, with the difference that in the proverb the referent is known to both speaker and addressee.

[29] "Proverb," 104. See for example Dundes' analysis of the following proverb (110): Many (C) men (T) = many (C) minds (T), where each of the two descriptive elements has a C and T which are not Predicate-Subject but adjective-noun respectively.

[30] "On Defining the Riddle: The Problem of a Structural Unit," *Folklore Genres* (ed.

Topics and Comments can be restated as subjects and predicates. Moreover, Topics and Comments can often be further broken down into smaller T-C units which correspond to the basic linguistic deep structure of subject and predicate.[31]

However, Scott's attempt to reduce all T-C relations to a deep *grammatical* structure of subject and predicate seems not wholly satisfactory. For example, *on a certain level,* a direct object (or some other verbal adjunct) can be considered to *comment* upon or modify a verb. In this case, the verb thus relates as *Topic* to the direct object as *Comment.* That is to say, whenever a word is modified by a second word, they, in a certain sense, relate to one another as T and C respectively. Moreover, the notion of transitivity must be seen as equally primordial a deep structure as the "subject-predicate" relation and is not reducible to it, though both may be described in terms of Topic and Comment. When a direct object (John hit *the ball.*) is transformed into the passive subject (*The ball* was hit by John.), what had been C on a *secondary* level (i.e., hit [T]/ *the ball* [C]) has become the Topic as well as the grammatical subject on the primary level of the new sentence. Nonetheless, in this transformation, the passive structure is derivative of the active, transitive structure.

At this point our own definition of Topic and Comment may be introduced:

A *Topic* is a semantic unit, on any level, which is spoken about or qualified by another semantic unit.
A *Comment* is a semantic unit, on any level, which speaks about or qualifies another semantic unit.

For our purposes of proverb analysis, the smallest semantic unit may be taken to be a word. Moreover T may, but need not, correspond with what is "Given" and C may, but need not, correspond to what is "New."

The foregoing definition enables us to clarify and simplify the process of Topic-Comment analysis, and fosters a more precise application of these terms. The definition of T and C is given in terms of semantic *relations* on various *levels.* Hence, in the treatment of proverb structure, it is necessary to be aware of *a hierarchy of Topics and Comments,* so that one's presentation of structure manages to convey clearly which Topics and Comments belong to the same level.[32] In the proverbs which are composed of more than one "descriptive

---

Dan Ben-Amos; Austin: University of Texas, 1976) 77-90. Reprinted from *Genre* 2/2 (1969) 129-142.

[31] "On Defining." To take the proverb of note 29 above, "many men" = "men are many" while "many minds" = "minds are many."

[32] On the concept of *level,* see J. Lyons, *Theoretical,* 144, 218. C. R. Fontaine's exemplary work (*Traditional*) would be more lucid, I think, had she made clear that her analyses of "Type" of traditional saying was simply a deeper level of T-C analysis, in which one multidescriptive element (A) is related as Topic to another multidescriptive element (B) as Comment by way of identification (=), opposition (≠) or comparison (>). Thus, for her,

element" (each containing a T-C relation) one thus discovers that, on a deeper level, the one descriptive element functions as C to the other's T (Many men [T], many minds [C]). Moreover, the smaller the T-C (sub)units, the closer one is to surface structure.

Some further comments are necessary before presenting a T-C analysis of our texts. Congruence of T-C structure among Sayings may not be apparent at first glance. The proverb maker is able to employ the same deep structure while varying the surface structure. Here too the necessity of analyzing Sayings on at least two levels is apparent. Almost every Saying in our passage, as in most of Proverbs, comprises two cola. Each of the cola may be a complete descriptive element composed of a T and C, while on a deeper level the entire first colon may be a figurative C upon the second colon which is the true Topic of the Saying as a whole. For instance, Prov 11:22, "A gold ring in the snout of a pig (C),/ a beautiful woman without sense" (T). The reverse pattern is also possible. Alternately, one colon may provide a contrast or antithesis to the other: "A soft answer (T) turns away wrath (C), ≠ but a harsh word (T_2) stirs up anger (C_2)" (Prov 15:1).

These points are crucial in the analysis of Proverbs 25-27 because those passages frequently employ a *Figurative* (= F) descriptive element in the first colon, the whole of which acts as a Comment upon the non-figurative descriptive element forming the second colon. Thus both cola contain their own T-C units (either expressed or implicit), while on a deeper level the first colon relates to the second as Figurative Comment to literal Topic. These structures are most easily grasped when presented in the form of "phrase-marker"[33] diagrams employed by linguists to indicate the structure of Sentences with their phrases and "immediate constituents." One should note that the lower levels of such a diagram bring one closer and closer to the actual surface structure or phenomena of the Saying. An example of the Saying type just described in this paragraph is Prov 27:17:

Topics and Comments are sometimes congruent with the "A" and "B" of her Types (p. 76; cf. p. 82 on Jud 8:2; p. 116 on 1 Sam 24:14), but sometimes (p. 103 on 1 Sam 16:17) the Topics and Comments are incongruent with A and B (they are constituent elements of A and B). Clarity can be achieved by distinguishing the various levels of T-C in a saying. Fontaine's insight that in proverb performance a traditional saying functions as a *Comment* on a life situation as *Topic* is very helpful (p. 237 on 1 Sam 16:7), but her regular use of Seitel's "social metaphor" model of proverb performance does not employ this insight.

[33] A succinct account of "phrase marker" analysis is given by J. Lyons ("Linguistics," *Encyclopaedia Britannica, Macropaedia* Vol. 10 [1978, fifteenth edition] 998-1003).

Diagram 1

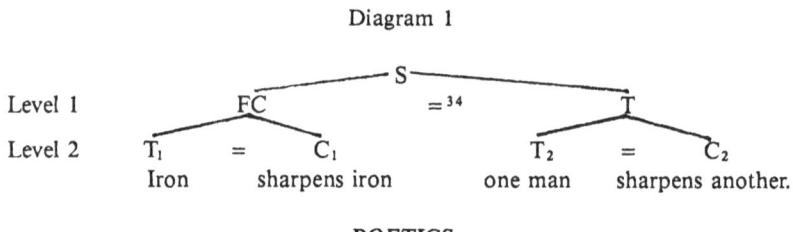

POETICS

As a complement to the structural methods just presented, our study of Proverbs 25-27 will employ an analysis of the sort commonly called "rhetorical criticism" in contemporary OT studies.[35] Such an undertaking at this time

---

[34] It should be noted that the "=" sign here does not function to indicate identity, or even strict predication of Comment to Topic. Its usage varies from strict predication to mere juxtaposition, the significance of which the proverb user must discern. Where I use "≠", it is to indicate that the elements so related are in contrast or antithesis to one another. The sign ">" is only used to indicate a Saying of the "Better . . . than" type. There is a host of gradations from the *seeming* identity of "Business is business" (T = C!) to *absolute* antithesis which cannot occur. In any case, on any level, the main concern is designated T, while that which illuminates, modifies, or provokes thought about T is designated C.

[35] "Rhetorical criticism" is more a conventional rubric than a precise descriptive term in current OT studies: J. H. Jackson and N. Kessler eds., *Rhetorical Criticism, Essays in Honor of James Muilenburg* (Pittsburgh: Pickwick, 1974). In practice, OT critics often use the phrase as a name for what is more properly stylistic or poetic criticism. That is, the actual focus is on the literary work itself as art object, rather than on its reader-relatedness, as "rhetorical criticism" in the strict sense implies. See M. H. Abrams, *The Mirror and the Lamp: Romantic Theory and the Critical Tradition* (Oxford: Oxford University, 1953) chapter 1. Abrams provides a classic typology of various criticism as oriented primarily towards 1) the work, 2) the referents of the work, 3) its writer and his life-world, and 4) the reader. The aspect of the critical task which here concerns us is 1) the artwork in its stylistic or poetic aspect. For general theory and method, R. Wellek and Austin Warren (*Theory of Literature*[3] [New York: Harcourt, Brace, and World, 1962]) is still basic. For Bibliography from the ancients to the present: L. T. Milic, *Style and Stylistics: an Analytic Bibliography* (New York: The Free Press, 1967). In OT studies the following are noteworthy. L. Alonso-Schökel, *Das Alte Testament als literarisches Kunstwerk* (Köln: Bachem, 1971) a translation of the second, methodological part (i.e., pp. 71-355) of his *Estudios de poética hebrea* (1963). A. Schökel (sic), "Poésie Hébraïque," *DBSup* 8 (1972) 47-90. M. Dahood, "Hebrew Poetry," *IDBSup* (1976) 669-672. N. H. Ridderbos, *Die Psalmen: Stilistische Verfahren und Aufbau, mit besonderer Berücksichtigung von Ps 1-41* (BZAW 117; Berlin: de Gruyter, 1972). W. Bühlmann and K. Scherer, *Stilfiguren der Bibel* (Fribourg: Schweizerisches Katholisches Bibelwerk, 1973). James L. Kugel, *The Idea of Biblical Poetry: Parallelism and its History* (New Haven and London: Yale University, 1981). M. O'Connor, *Hebrew Verse Structure* (Winona Lake: Eisenbrauns, 1980). J. P. M. van der Ploeg, "Zur Literatur- und Stilforschung im Alten Testament," *ThLZ* 100 (1975) 801-814. John H. Stek, "The Stylistics of Hebrew Poetry," *CTJ* 9 (1974) 15-30. Further

requires no justification. What is somewhat new (though anticipated by Hermisson and others) is the assumption that the devices of Biblical Hebrew poetry have significance for large units of proverbial material, and the systematic exploitation of that assumption. Our focus here will not fall upon the individual Sayings per se, but upon those rhetorical or stylistic devices which relate the various Sayings and Admonitions to one another. Since the Sayings and Admonitions can exist on their own, our treatment naturally concentrates upon those devices which resist the inherent centrifugal force of the small units to bind them together into one literary whole.

Though stylistic features of a poem are inseparable from its meaning, they can be abstracted to highlight their role in the poem's meaning. They can bind units of meaning (words or groups of words) together; they can heighten contrasts, emphasize key meanings through repetition of sound and sense and so on. To present this aspect of the larger poetic units in Proverbs 25-27 exhaustively is beyond the scope of this thesis. For our purposes it suffices to present enough detail so that the poetic meaning and unity of the whole poem becomes clearer.

The rhetorical devices in Proverbs with which we are concerned may be separated into two sorts on the basis of function: 1) those which bring together and foster mutual "commentary" among *separated* units in the poem and 2) those which bring together contiguous units in the poem. The former devices create or foster non-contiguous context, while the latter create contiguous context. The former function (of bringing together separated units) is especially important for the structure and unity of the poem as a whole; the second gives coherence or contrast to the smaller sections within the poem. In fact, one can pursue this function from smaller contiguous units to larger ones. For example, $qsyr$ and syr bind together the two cola of 25:13; hgw unites vv 4-5, as does $\acute{s}b^c$ vv 16-17.[36]

The presence of contiguous rhetorical binding in chapters 25-27 through catchwords, puns, and phonetic relations has been carefully studied in G. Boström's much cited but little used Swedish work of 1928.[37] Boström has firmly established that the same rhetorical devices which bind together parts within individual Sayings also unite disparate Sayings and Admonitions. Though one may question individual connections made by Boström—some of the phonetic links may be happenstance—his major connections are firm. His analysis of chapter 25 shows that in it not a single verse is without rhetorical binding to contiguous verses. Our treatment will not repeat Boström's work. We will

---

bibliography in D. J. A. Clines, "Story and Poem: The Old Testament as Literature," *Interp* 34 (1980) 115-127.
[36] G. Boström, *Paronomasi i den äldre hebreiska maschallitteraturen* (Lunds Universitets Arsskrift, N. F., Avd. 1, Bd. 23, no. 8; Lund: Gleerup, 1928) 76, 94, 95.
[37] *Paronomasi.* Cf. Chapter 1 above, pp. 10-11.

mention only such contiguous rhetorical devices as have a salient role in shaping the meaning of greater or lesser units in the poem.

What is more important for our work are techniques of literary binding which operate over a distance. On this D. Pardee has made some important observations. Pardee is concerned with "expanding our analytical tools so as to be able to discern all the means whereby poetic units were bound together, on the level of micro-parallelism as well as of macro-parallelism. . . ." His questions concerning the poetic devices of parallelism are similar to the structural questions we have asked in the preceding section of this chapter: "How are these types of parallelism distributed over the entire work? or, in slightly different terms, How do these micro-structural devices contribute to macro-structure?"[38] Pardee's observations on half-line and near parallelism lead him to suggest that their major function "was to bind together units not otherwise characterized by semantically strong parallelism. . . ." More important for us is his observation that "Distant parallelism, by its very nature as distant, seems to function primarily as a binder of larger structures."[39]

In discussing the relative strength of poetic binders, Pardee classifies the binding power of different types of parallelism with respect to large and small units as follows:

[1] Repetitive parallelism is the strongest binder, though it is usually linked with semantic parallelism. . . . [2] Semantic parallelism is the next strongest binder, used in half-line, regular, near, and distant distributions, *though my impression is that the greater the distance of distribution, the more likely it will be that semantic parallelism will be linked with repetitive parallelism.* [3] Grammatical parallelism is not nearly so strong a binder as the previous two types. . . . [and requires contiguity (near distribution) to function] [4] The same appears true of phonetic parallelism: the high occurrence of a given sound almost certainly serves to bind a half-line and a bicolon together but a sound element alone is not distinctive enough to bind larger sections unless it be linked with semantic or repetitive parallelism. . . . Thus repetitive parallelism, because it englobes all the other types is the strongest; semantic parallelism is next in strength because of its broad lexical and ideational basis; grammatical and phonetic parallelism are largely limited to micro-structures, unless linked with one of the stronger types. . . .[40]

These observations will prove useful in gauging the significance of the various poetic devices found among the proverbs in our texts.

---

[38] "Types and Distribution of Parallelism in Ugaritic and Hebrew Poetry" (unpublished Communication prepared for the Annual Meeting of the Society of Biblical Literature, New York, December 21, 1982) 6. I am indebted to Professor Pardee for a copy of his paper.
[39] "Parallelism," 7, 8.
[40] "Parallelism," 9, my emphases.

SEMANTICS

I use the word "semantics" broadly to refer to the task of explicating the "sense" of a passage in its parts and as a whole. Two things ought to occur if we are dealing with an actual proverb poem. First, the structures and poetic devices described will be shown to work together with other aspects of a text to produce a pattern of meaning that is more than the sum of its parts. Secondly, such a whole, in a way appropriate to its genre, must then be explicated as a literary whole, just as the Broadsheet of the World Upside Down (p. 38 above) must be viewed as one multiplex pattern of meaning even though its pictures exist discretely.

Our sections labelled "Sense" are not so much a matter of "method," though they could not exist without the panoply of methods, but of the patient listening which is the beginning and ending of reading. M. Greenberg has put the matter well:

> There is only one way that gives any hope of eliciting the innate conventions and literary formations of a piece of ancient literature, and that is by listening to it patiently and humbly. The critic must curb all temptations to impose his antecedent judgments on the text; he must immerse himself in it again and again, with all his sensors alert to catch every possible stimulus—mental-ideational, aural, aesthetic, linguistic, visual—until its features begin to stand out and their native shape and patterning emerge.[41]

---

[41] *Ezekiel 1-20* (AB 22; Garden City: Doubleday, 1983) 21.

5
Proverbs 25:2-27

Translation

v 2	God's glory is to conceal a matter and kings' glory is to search a matter.
v 3	Heavens for height and earth for depth and kings' hearts are unsearchable.
v 4	Remove dross from silver and a vessel comes forth[1] for the silversmith.
v 5	Remove the wicked from before the king, and his throne will be established with righteousness.
v 6	Do not aggrandize yourself before the king, nor stand in the place of the great,
v 7	for it is better one say to you, "come up here," than that you be put down before nobility.
vv 7c/8	What your eyes have seen, do not hastily bring to trial, lest . . . what will you do at its conclusion, when your peer exposes you (as in the wrong)?[2]
v 9	Argue your own case with your peer (*scilicet*, if you must) but do not divulge the confidences of another,

---

[1] Some commentators are puzzled by the use of *yṣ'* in 25:4. See R. C. Van Leeuwen, "A Technical-Metallurgical Usage of [*yṣ'*]," *ZAW* 98 (1986) 112-113.

[2] Verse 8: *'šr*, cf. Ps 69:5; Jonah 2:10. *tṣ'*, read as hiph. *pn mh*, anacolouthon. *bhklym:* M. Klopfenstein (*Scham und Schande nach dem Alten Testament* [ATANT 62; Zürich: Theologischer Verlag, 1972] 110-116) has established the visual component ("*blossstellen*") of *klm* in connection with Akkadian *kullumu*. Unlike the Akkadian, in Hebrew the root always has pejorative connotations, and in the earliest usages already appears as a technical legal term for accusation or counter-accusation in the court. The disputant, as it were, "exposes" his opponent's person and case as in the wrong. In Prov 25:8 and 18:13, the root has this technical legal sense (129-131, 138).

v 10 lest the arbiter pronounce you guilty
       and the accusation against you sticks.³

v 11 Apples of gold in a design of silver,
       a decision made according to its circumstances.
v 12 A ring of gold, an ornament of fine gold,
       a wise arbiter to a hearing ear

v 13 Like cool snow on a harvest day
       is a faithful messenger for his sender;
       he restores the spirits of his lord.
v 14 Clouds and wind and no rain
       is a man promising a fraudulent gift.

---

³ Verses 9–10 are admittedly difficult, but some of the difficulties disappear when close attention is paid to text and context. Verses 7c–8 have presented legal action mainly in optical imagery (*r'w 'ynyk, hklym;* see preceding note). Verses 9–10 do the same in aural imagery (*swd, šm', dbtk*). In each case one wrongly enters a *ryb;* first with what he has seen, secondly with what he has heard (*swd*). In the first case the *lex talionis* leads to a visual retribution (*hklym*), in the second case to an aural retribution (*dbtk*): an accusation against one which does not return to the accuser. For *l' tšwb* (lit. "does not return" [to its source]) as "sticks," cf. McKane and contrast *l' tb'* in 26:2.

For the concessive character of v 9a, see "Sense" below. *yhsdk* is a hapax. (Sir 14:2 probably provides another instance, emending *hsrtw* to *hsdtw* after LXX.) Bühlmann (*RR*, 248) wishes to take this as a privative piel ("jem. die Gunst entziehen") assuming that hearers in general will remove their *hsd* from the addressee. This is improbable. For it fails to perceive the technical legal usage of *šm'* here. Cf. 2 Sam 15:3, (*wšm' 'yn lk m't hmlk*) and K. W. Whitelam's discussion thereof (*The Just King: Monarchical Judicial Authority in Ancient Israel* [JSOTSup 12; Sheffield: JSOT Press, 1979] 140–142). Further examples provided by Whitelam include Deut 1:16, 17; Judg 11:10; 2 Sam 14:16–17; 1 Kgs 3:9, 11; Job 31:35; Prov 21:28. Note also the first word (*yšm'*) *in the judicial plea of the Mesad Hashavyahu (Yavneh Yam) ostracon* (D. Pardee, *Handbook of Ancient Hebrew Letters* [SBL Sources for Biblical Study 15; Chico: Scholars Press, 1982] 20). It seems therefore more natural to take *yhsdk* here as an example of "Deklarativ-ästimatives Pi'el" (E. Jenni, *Das hebräische Pi'el* [Zürich: EVZ Verlag, 1968] 40–43) along with certain piel uses of verbs like *sdq, nqh* which have judicial significance. Thus the verb would be a denominative based upon *hsd*. In my judgment the noun is best understood to mean something like "guilt" or "condemnation" (vs. *BDB* "shame, reproach"). These meanings fit both occurrences well (Lev 20:17; Prov 14:34). Translate the latter text, "Righteousness exalts a nation, sin is the condemnation of peoples." This interpretation also does justice to the LXX reading of Sir 14:2 (*katagignōskein*). The LXX of Prov 25:10 is badly jumbled.

Finally, *dbh* in 25:10 is not just "a bad report" or "reputation." In all occurrences except Ezek 36:3 (which is uncertain) and Ps 31:14 (which is ambiguous), *dbh* clearly means an "accusation" which people bring out (*ys', hiph.; once bw', hiph.) against something (Num 13:32; 14:36, 37) or someone (Gen 37:2; Prov 10:18). This sense also fits Ps 31:14. Note the Akkadian cognate *dabābum* with its legal sense of accusation (Fabry, *TDOT*, III, 72–73).

| v 15 | The prince is persuaded by a slow temper, |
| | a soft tongue breaks bones.[4] |

v 16	Of the honey you've found, eat what's right for you,
	lest you be (over) filled and vomit it.
v 17	Keep your foot from your neighbor's house,
	lest he have his fill of you and hate you.[5]

v 18	A scatterer with sword and sharpened arrow
	is a man bearing false witness against his neighbor.[6]
v 19	A crumbling tooth, a shaky foot
	is false security on a day of trouble.[7]
v 20	Taking off a cloak on a cold day,
	vinegar on a wound
	is singing songs to a sad heart.[8]

---

[4] Verse 11. *dbr dbr* = "decision," see the treatment in "Sense" based on M. Weinfeld. *'l 'pnyw* remains uncertain (though note that in 20:26 *'wpn* appears in a royal judicial context). McKane (584) translates v 11b, "a phrase which is well-turned." Bühlmann (*RR*, 45) is similar. Ringgren (99), Van der Ploeg (87) and others, on the analogy of *b'tw* (15:23b), translate "at the right moment." In his note (91) but not in his translation (90), Gemser follows Delitzsch (155–157), "according to its circumstances," that is, as time "turns" with respect to circumstances. The use of *tšwbh* in *tšwbt hšnh* "the turning of the year" (2 Sam 11:1 etc.) may be a similar semantic development.

Verse 12. On *mwkyḥ* as a technical judicial term see below. One should note the fine play of images between the cola of this Saying: it is really the jewelry of the first colon which adorns the ear!

Verse 13. *lšlhyw* and *'dnyw*, construe as sg. So B. Lang, "Vorläufer von Speiseeis in Bibel und Orient. Eine Untersuchung von Spr 25,13," *Mélanges bibliques et orientaux en l'honneur de M. Henri Cazelles* (A. Caquot and M. Delcor eds.; AOAT 212; Neukirchen-Vluyn: Neukirchener Verlag, 1981) 219, n. 1, and *GKC* §124k.

Verse 15. *ypth* = "persuaded" in a non-sexual, neutral sense. D. J. A. Clines and D. M. Gunn, "'You tried to persuade me' and 'Violence! Outrage!' in Jeremiah xx 7–8," *VT* 28 (1978) 20–27.

[5] On v 16 cf. Sir 37:29–30. *hqr rgl:* a variety of similar idioms with *rgl* are found in Prov 1:15; 3:23; 7:11; Jer 2:25; 14:10; Ps 119:101.

[6] *Mpys* "scatterer" is usually emended to *mps* "mace" with LXX. But note Ps 18:15, *wyšlḥ ḥṣyw wypysm* "he shot his arrows and scattered them," and Ps 144:6. It is not the "arrows" which the warrior scatters but his enemies (Ps 68:2) by means of his weapons. Thus in Nahum 2:2 MT *mpys* can also stand: "The scatterer has come up against you" (against RSV, "The shatterer"). Cf. Prov 26:18 (which echoes the theme and imagery of 25:18). For wicked speech as a "sharpened arrow" see Ps 120:3–4.

[7] *r'h* = *r"h*, "crumbling"; so Delitzsch (164), McKane (586). *mw'dt* = pual part. without preformative *m* or repoint as qal part. (*GKC* §52s), so Gemser (92).

[8] *ntr* = *nāter*, "wound," (Arabic *natratu*), McKane (588) after Driver. *'l lb r'*, cf. Isa 40:2, against McKane (251), "with a sad heart."

v 21	If your enemy hungers, feed him, if he thirsts, give him water to drink,
v 22	then you will be snatching coals (from) upon his head and Yahweh will recompense you.[9]
v 23	A north [hidden] wind produces a downpour, and a "hidden" tongue (produces) angry faces.
v 24	It is better to live on the corner of the roof than in a shared house with a quarrelsome wife![10]
v 25	Cool waters on a failing throat is good news from a far land.
v 26	A trampled spring and a ruined fountain is the righteous slipping before the wicked.
v 27	To eat too much honey is not good, and to seek difficult things is (no) glory![11]

Using the method developed in the previous chapter, we are now ready to present an outline of the structure of Prov 25:2-27 based upon the two form-

---

[9] Verses 21-22 are straight-forward—except for the puzzling imagery of v 22a. S. Morenz, "Feurige Kohlen auf dem Haupt," *ThLZ* 78 (1953) cols. 187-92. L. Ramaroson, " 'Charbons ardents': 'sur la tete' ou 'pour le feu'?" *Bib* 51 (1970) 230-34. I follow M. J. Dahood ("Two Pauline Quotations from the Old Testament," *CBQ* 17 [1955] 19-24) and A. R. Ceresko (private communication). Ceresko suggests the imagery is that of dehydration and heat prostration with fever ("fiery coals") cured by giving water to drink. He compares the "refreshment" motif in vv 13 and 25. For *'l* = "from" Ceresko cites Ps 81:6; cf. LXX and Jerome.

[10] For the meteorological difficulties of a "north wind" producing rain in Palestine, see McKane (582-583). With van der Ploeg (89; following Boström, *Paronomasi,* 42), however, I am inclined to take seriously the word-play on *spwn* ("north wind/ hidden") and *str* ("hidden"). The thought seems to be that as the North wind is an unanticipated (hidden) source of rain contrary to the observer's expectation, so talk in secret suddenly produces outrage from an unexpected—perhaps trusted (cf. v 19b!)—corner.

Proverbs 25:24 = 21:9. For the difficulties of this verse and of *byt hbr,* McKane (553-55). Note that *'št mdwnym* provides a verbal echo (*dyn*) of the conflict theme.

[11] Verse 27b is notoriously difficult. Suggestions for interpreting or emending it are manifold—while some throw up their hands at "an obviously corrupt text" (Toy, 470). For recent suggestions, see Bühlmann (*RR* 179-83) and A. A. MacIntosh ("A Note on Proverbs xxv 27," *VT* 20 [1970] 112-114) who essentially follows the Vulgate. Many of the "modern" solutions already appear in Matthew Poole's *Synopsis Criticorum* (vol. 2; London [1671] cols 1735-1736). The solution offered here builds primarily upon the work of Delitzsch (170-72) and Bryce ("Wisdom-'Book,' " 148-50) but follows the Syriac and Targum in reading the *l'* of v 27a as double-duty. See further R. C. Van Leeuwen, "Proverbs xxv 27 Once Again," *VT* 36 (1986) 105-114.

critical categories (A and S) in intersection with the dimension of good and evil (+ and -). The outline is of course proleptic to the argument and exegesis to follow; it also contains some elements not mentioned in the discussion so far. These elements, such as the grouping into couplets, will be explained and justified later. The purpose of the outine at this stage is to provide a preliminary overview of the macro-structure of the passage, and a point of reference for our subsequent discussion (See diagram 1).

The data underlying the analysis implicit in Diagram 1 are, of course, not without ambiguity. In the process of exegesis, where the various aspects of analysis are brought together, this ambiguity is greatly reduced. On the other hand, one must not destroy for the sake of theory a poem's artful ambiguities The analysis developed here attempts to account for the form-critical data as well as data on other levels. Our goal is an integrated interpretation of the proverb poem as a whole.

Diagram 1

Form-Critical (A/S and +/-) Structure of Prov 25:2-27

Verse	Introduction	Form
2	kbd 'lhym hstr dbr/ wkbd mlkym ḥqr dbr	S:+/+
3	šmym lrwm w'rṣ l'mq/ wlb mlkym 'yn ḥqr	S:+/+
4	hgw sygym mksp/ wyṣ' lṣrp kly	S:Prot+ →R+
5	hgw rš' lpny mlk/ wykwn bṣdq ks'w	S:Prot+ →R+

	Section I	
6	'l tthdr lpny mlk/ wbmqwm gdlym 'l t'md	A:P-
7	ky ṭwb 'mr lk 'lh hnh/ mhšpylk lpny ndyb	⊬ R-
7c-8a	'šr r'w 'ynyk/ 'l tṣ' lrb mhr	A:P-
8b	pn mh t'śh b'hryth/ bhklym 'tk r'k	⊬ R-
9	rybk ryb 't r'k/ wswd 'hr 'l tgl	A:P-
10	pn yḥsdk šm'/ wdbtk l' tšwb	⊬ R-
11	tpwḥy zhb bmśkywt ksp/ dbr dbr 'l 'pnyw	S:+/+
12	nzm zhb wḥly ktm/ mwkyḥ ḥkm 'l 'zn šm't	S:+/+
13	kṣnt šlg bywm qṣyr/ ṣyr n'mn lšlḥyw/ wnpš 'dnyw yšyb	S:+/+/+
14	nśy'ym wrwḥ wgšm 'yn/ 'yš mthll bmtt šqr	S:-/-
15	b'rk 'pym ypth qṣyn/ wlšwn rkh tšbr grm	S:+/+

Section II A

16	dbš mṣ't 'kl dyk/ pn tśb'nw whq'tw	A:P-⇸ R-
17	hqr rglk mbyt r'k/ pn yśb'k wśn'k	A:P-→R-
18	mpys wḥrb wḥṣ šnwn/ 'yš 'nh br'hw 'd šqr	S:-/-
19	šn r'h wrgl mw'dt/ mbṭḥ bwgd bywm ṣrh	S:-/-
20	m'dh bgd bywm qrh/ ḥmṣ 'l ntr/ wšr bšrym 'l lb r'	S:-/-/-

Section II B

21	'm r'b śn'k h'kylhw lḥm/ w'm ṣm' hšqhw mym	A:P+
22	ky gḥlym 'th ḥth 'l r'šw/ wyhwh yšlm lk	→R+
23	rwḥ ṣpwn tḥwll gšm/ wpnym nz'mym lšwn str	S:-/-
24	ṭwb šbt 'l pnt gg/ m'št mdwnym wbyt ḥbr	S:-/-
25	mym qrym 'l npš 'yph/ wšmw'h ṭwbh m'rṣ mrḥq	S:+/+
26	m'yn nrpś wmqwr mšḥt/ ṣdyq mṭ lpny rš'	S:-/-
27	'kl dbš hrbwt l' ṭwb/ wḥqr kbdm kbwd	S:-/-

In Diagram 1, it should be noted that the FORM column represents the deep structure of the form in each instance. Normally this is congruent with the surface structure, but sometimes it is not, as can be seen with the Admonitions of Proverbs 25. My purpose in diagramming only the deep structure is to bring the form critical and thematic coherence of the Admonitions in vv 6-10 to light, and to highlight the contrast between the Admonitory pairs in vv 16-17 and 21-22. Nonetheless, it should be noted that this is achieved at the cost of minimizing fine stylistic and semantic nuances on the surface level. These nuances are created by artful and meaningful variations on basic formal conventions. The poet plays upon the deeper convention and gives it a new twist![12] For our present purpose of discerning the macrostructure of the poem, however, it is the deeper patterns that are most significant. Hence, for lucidity's sake, in the *Admonitions* I have reduced +/+ to +, and -/- to -.

The form-critical classification of vv 4-5 is at first glance uncertain. (In Diagram 1 the Prot refers to *Protasis*.) In terms of grammar, the *hgw* is an infinitive absolute which may function as an imperative. But this grammatical

---

[12] See R. Alter's comments (*The Art of Biblical Narrative* [New York: Basic Books, 1981] 47-62) on literary conventions and form criticism, "which is set on finding recurrent regularities of pattern rather than the manifold variations upon a pattern that any system of literary conventions elicits" (p. 47). Further, "The process of literary creation ... is an unceasing dialectic between the necessity to use established forms in order to be able to communicate coherently and the necessity to break and remake those forms because they are arbitrary restrictions and because what is merely repeated automatically no longer conveys a message" (p. 62).

ambiguity calls attention to the transitional character of the form in 25:4-5. It is not a true Admonition, giving advice that ought to be followed. Rather, this Saying pair comprises two conditional utterances with the following form: "If you do x ... then y results."[13] The English, "Take two from three and you get one," is similarly not a command or Precept, but a statement.

Prov 25:4-5 with vv 2-3 forms an "introductory" block of Sayings. Together, these two proverb pairs delineate the worldview parameters within which the other Sayings and Admonitions of the poem are to be understood. Verses 2-3 establish the God-King-subject social hierarchy which encompasses all that follows (as will be argued below). Verses 4-5 set forth, in a nutshell, the normative world order (all that is *sdq*, "righteous") in terms of the opposition of good and evil. These two verses also reveal the poem's primary locus of concern: the presence of the King (*lpny mlk, ks'*). Nonetheless, like certain Egyptian royal *Instructions* which freely move from the court to other spheres of life,[14] Prov 25:2-27 also addresses and engages life beyond the court. Wisdom presumes a world-order encompassing all of life and disdains hermetic compartmentalization.

At the same time, the formal ambiguity of vv 4-5 nicely reinforces its connection with the Admonitions which follow in vv 6-10. This connection is also strengthened by other means such as the catch-phrase *lpny-mlk* (see below).

The incongruencies between deep and surface structure in the Admonitions of Chapter 25 may be explained as follows. In v 6 there is a double Precept (P-/-) followed, in v 7ab, with a "Better ... than" Saying introduced with *ky*. This Saying serves as a Motive to the preceding Precepts. It not only warns of the likely negative consequence of failing to obey the negative Precepts (to be put down before the nobleman), but delightfully captures the social ambiguity of a young courtier's situation: He might, after all, be elevated! The surface form of v 7ab may be diagrammed thus: MS:+ >- (where MS indicates a *Motive Saying*).

In v 9 there appears to be a conflict between surface and deep form because v 9a is positive Precept (P+): "Fight your fight...." This precept in its context, however, is ironic or concessive. It might be paraphrased, "Fight your personal fight then, if you must (but don't divulge the secret concerns of another....."). This interpretation is supported by 25:8a and 20:3 ("It is a man's glory to refrain from a quarrel [*ryb*]...."). Verse 9a serves to contrast one's personal matters with one's responsibility to the other. That v 9a does not function on the deep level is evident from its total lack of contact with the Result clause in v 10. Verse 9a may be diagrammed thus: P [+]/- (where square brackets indicate an element which is non-functional for form critical purposes).

---

[13] So McKane, 578, and Murphy, *WL*, 77-78. Cf. Prov 27:22.

[14] So H. H. Schmid (*Wesen und Geschichte der Weisheit: eine Untersuchung zur altorientalischen und israelitischen Weisheitsliteratur* [BZAW 101; Berlin: Töpelmann, 1966] 43) on Egyptian royal *Instructions* and *maat*. One notes a similar juxtaposition of the royal and the domestic in the 16th-century broadsheet on p. 38 above.

Finally, the imperatives in 25:16, 17 are positive on the surface, but negative on the level of deep form, on the principle explained above in our treatment of method. The main point in v 16a is *"Don't* eat too much . . ." (cf. v 27a), and of v 17a, *"Don't* enter too often. . . ."

The majority of the form-critical evaluations outlined in Diagram 1 are, I believe, clear. A number of the +/- evaluations cannot be established until our actual exegesis of the verses in question (for instance, the notorious crux in v 27b). In a proleptic way the analysis implicit in Diagram 1 may be summed up as follows.

The "Introduction" consists of a solid block of positive Sayings. If, as I shall argue, it forms a sort of ideological prologue to the individual concerns addressed by the following Admonitions and Sayings, a well-organized and coherent form-critical and +/- pattern emerges. After the "Introduction" (vv 2-5), in what may be called the "Body" of the poem, we find a thrice repeated pattern of Admonitions followed by Sayings:

Diagram 2

Introduction   S:+ (vv 2-5)
Body   I.   A:- (vv 6-10)
                    S:+ (vv 11-15; except for v 14 which is S:-)
             IIA.   A:- (vv 16-17)
                    S:- (vv 18-20)
             IIB.   A:+ (vv 21-22)
                    S:- (vv 23-27; except for v 25 which is S:+)

Diagram 2, as a summary of certain elements in Diagram 1, makes clear that Prov 25:2-27 is carefully constructed with regard to form-critical and +/- options. The writer uses only a few of the forms available to him, though he varies these on the surface level. Moreover, he uses his forms to create coherences and contrasts![15] He does not in general mix his forms, nor does he mix the +/- contents of his forms, either in groups or within individual Sayings (i.e., in the +/- dimension, there are no antithetical Sayings). The two exceptions to this rule also fall into a pattern:

---

[15] That groupings of + or - Sayings are a matter of design and not happenstance becomes evident when one compares the groupings of Sayings in Proverbs 25 and 26 with those in chapter 27. The groupings in chapter 25 have been given above, in Diagram 1. In chapter 26, *all* the Sayings are negative (-) except for vv 20 and 26 which may be described as negative transitional. By contrast, a cursory look at chapter 27 shows that here homogeneous grouping of + and - plays no role in organizing the Sayings.

Diagram 3

v 13	S:+	v 25	S:+
v 14	S:-	v 26	S:-
v 15	S:+	v 27	S:-

The anomalous verses (14 and 25) both occur in the final three verses in the two major sections of the poem (vv 2-15 and 16-27). The last couplet (vv 13-14, 25-26) in each case reveals a +/- pattern while the final solitary verse reverts to the predominate + or - value of its section.

This pattern at the close of each major section of the poem is reinforced on other levels. Verses 13 and 25, which begin the sequence of three final Sayings in each section, are closely linked in message and imagery. The report from a far land needs a messenger to bring it, as does the cold snow. Both Sayings use the imagery of coldness (snow, cool water) upon the *npš* of the person affected positively by the message. Nowhere else in this chapter do these themes and images occur![16] The echo of v 13 in v 25 thus seems to reinforce, on a different level, the closing pattern suggested by the sequence of + and - mentioned above.

The grouping of lines into couplets in Diagram 1 must await our exegesis to be vindicated in every instance. However, some of these groupings are obvious even at this stage. Such are the Admonitions which encompass two lines (vv 6-7, 7c-8, 9-10, 21-22). The pattern of grouping which I will defend is this. There are fourteen units in the poem: eleven couplets (of varying cohesion), one triplet (18-20), and two single lines which close off sections (vv 15, 27). Thus after the single one-line Saying or Admonition, the predominant secondary compositional unit in the poem is the two-line couplet. The frequency of the "proverb pair" as a compositional unit is one of the features that seems to set off chapter 25 from other sections of Proverbs. The lines within the couplets are themselves able to function with varying degrees of autonomy. Some two-line Admonitions would be incomplete if one line were taken away, while some of the Sayings can function quite well on their own (e.g., vv 5, 11, 12, 13, 18), having been brought into the couplet relationship within the poem for the purpose of qualifying and enriching the meaning of the Saying, or of giving it a more particular focus.[17]

---

[16] On the actual practice of bringing compacted snow or ice from distant mountains, see now the delightful and learned essay of B. Lang, "Vorläufer," 218-232. Lang considers that Prov 25:13c is not a gloss. Even if it is, it correctly interprets the sense of v 13ab and highlights the connection between vv 13 and 25 by its use of *npš*. Lang's suggestion that 25:25, in contrast to 25:13, entails the method of cooling by evaporation in a porous vessel appears to me mistaken; it would make the comparison with a good report from a *far land* inconsequent (p. 221).

[17] Murphy (*WL*, 63-64) mildly objects to this line of interpretation as found in Hermisson and Plöger. McKane (*passim*) and others object more strenuously (cf. pp. 413-414, 577). See our treatment of the question in Chapter 1 above and R. N. Whybray ("Yahweh-sayings," 153-165).

Finally, the grouping of the poem into two major sections (the second containing two subsections) preceded by an Introduction will find its grounding in the rhetorical and thematic analysis to follow. But on the basis of the foregoing, one should note that the boundaries set agree with the form-critical groupings and that the second half of the poem has blocks of negative Sayings while the first half (including the Introduction) has positive Sayings, with the solitary exceptions noted above.

In sum, the foregoing analysis indicates that the writer of 25:2-27 did not randomly toss Admonitions and Sayings together. Rather, he builds his composition out of homogeneous blocks of similar (+ or -) Sayings and Admonitions. While the Admonitions display some variety of surface structure and rhetorical features, the poet has avoided using anything but the consequential type of Admonition. Similarly, the Sayings are homogeneous in terms of the +/- criterion. As with the Admonitions, the homogeneity of the S's in increased by the eschewal of other Saying forms (like the antithetical Saying) within the poem. That is, the poet has restricted his choice of possible forms at the outset and has carefully used his limited stock of forms to create block-like sections. Diagram 1 suggests that after an "Introduction," the poet consistently follows a repeated A/S scheme. The validation of this suggestion must await the exegetical argument and comparison with 26:1-12 below.

Leaving behind the pattern of Admonitions and Sayings for the moment, we now turn to our second structural analysis as developed in the preceding chapter (cf. Diagrams 4 and 5). This approach will be seen to corroborate my A and S analysis of the poem with respect to its coherence and structure. As it happens, all the Sayings in Prov 25:2-27 display the same Topic-Comment structure on Level 1, except for vv 2, 4-5, 15, and 24. Verse 24 retains the structure except for its comparative ($>$) relation between FC and T.[18] Verses 4 and 5, which form a proverb pair, each have cola linked in terms of dynamic result ($\rightarrow$), but within this proverb pair the first Saying provides a Figurative Comment (FC) to the second (v 5) which is the Topic (T). (Among the Admonitions, vv 16-17 stand in a similar relation: v 16 provides the figurative foil to the plain sense of v 17.) Thus among all the Sayings in this passage, only vv 2 and 15 fail to show the FC-T pattern. These two verses mark the beginning of the entire poem and the end of the first major section respectively. Verse 2 is unique and deserves closer analysis; v 15, while providing contrast to its companion Sayings on the deepest level, nonetheless is congruent with many of them at Level 2 ($T_1 = C_1 = T_2 = C_2$).

---

[18] It may be significant that this form occurs near the end of the poem. See G. E. Bryce, " 'Better'-Proverbs: An Historical and Structural Study," *Book of Seminar Papers* 2 (L. C. McGaughy, ed.; Missoula: SBL, 1972) 343-354, especially 346-348, 352; G. S. Ogden, "The 'Better'-Proverb (Tob-Spruch), Rhetorical Criticism, and Qoheleth," *JBL* 96 (1977) 491, 497. See the discussion of Prov 26:12, 16 in the next chapter.

In all the Sayings (with the exception of v 15), where the Figurative Comment is employed on Level 1, the FC makes up the first colon and the T the second. Consequently the Core of these Sayings always occurs in the second colon. On Level 2, however, these Sayings reveal artful variation: elements can disappear through ellipsis or through transferal from one colon to another, for example. Prov 25:3 may elucidate this point:[19]

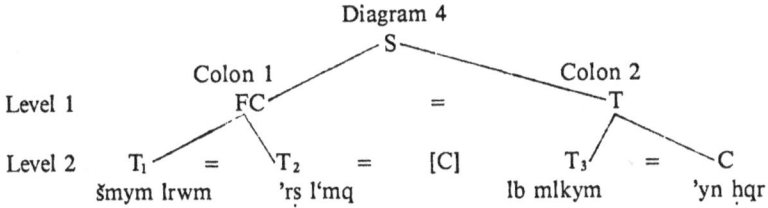

Diagram 4

Level 1 — Colon 1: FC = Colon 2: T

Level 2 — T_1 = T_2 = [C] T_3 = C
šmym lrwm   'rs l'mq   lb mlkym   'yn ḥqr

The following diagram presents a summary of the structures used by the poet in the Sayings of Prov 25:2-27:

Diagram 5

Verse	Level 1		Level 2	
	Colon 1	Colon 2	Colon 1	Colon 2
2	T_1 = C_1 ≠	T_2 = 1/C_1	T_1 = T_2 =	T_3 = C
3	FC	= T		
4 (FC	T	→ R		
5 = T)	T	→ R		
11	FC	= T	T_1 = C_1 =	T_2 = C_2
12	FC	= T	T_1 = T_2 =	T_3 = C
13	FC	= T = C (Colon 3)	T_1 = C_1 =	T_2 = C_2 = C_3
14	FC	= T	T_1 = C_1 =	T_2 = C_2
15	T	= FC	T_1 = C_1 =	T_2 = C_2
18	FC	= T	T_1 = T_2 = T_3 =	T_4
19	FC	= T	T_1 = T_2 =	T_3
20	FC	= T	T_1 = T_2 = T_3	

[19] Our multi-level analysis resolves McKane's quandary (578; cf. Toy, 459) whether this verse is a *Priamel* (Delitzsch, Boström, Gemser), that is, a Saying with three Topics and a concluding, common Comment, or—as McKane prefers—a Saying having two images in Colon 1 illustrative of the main concern in colon 2. The first option (*Priamel*) is correct on the Second Level, but fails to catch the more basic pattern on Level 1. The second option (McKane) makes plain the FC-T pattern that characterizes the Sayings of this chapter, but confuses the First and Second Levels.

23	FC = T	$T_1 = C_1 =$	$C_2 = T_2$
24	FC > T	$C = T_1 >$	T_2
25	FC = T	$T_1 = C_1 =$	$T_2 = C_2$
26	FC = T	$T_1 = T_2 =$	T_3
27	FC = T	$T_1 = C_1 =$	$T_2 = C_2$

The analysis embodied in the foregoing diagram permits several conclusions and requires several comments. Verse 2 is unique; its peculiar symbol ($1/C_1$) and subtleties will be discussed below. It is possible that colon 1 of v 24 ("to dwell on the corner of a roof") is not fully figurative, in that it might be taken literally (cf. Judith 8:5; 2 Kgs 4:10). Nonetheless, the change of image in the parallel Saying 21:19 ("to dwell in a desert land") suggests that the emphasis is not on a literal alternative to living with a shrew, but on a metaphoric evaluation of that sad wedded state.

Occasionally there may be some ambiguity, on Level 2, concerning the immediate constituents of a T-C analysis. For instance, in v 14b it is possible to give the following analyses: 1) *'yš* (T)/*mthll bmtt šqr* (C); or 2) *'yš mthll* (T)/*bmtt šqr* (C). For various reasons, the second analysis is preferable: the poetic balance of the line is more natural in context (cf. v 14a) and, most important, a boasting man is not per se bad (Jer 9:22-23); rather, it is the *object* of the boasting which qualifies or comments upon the boasting. (Note again, Topic and Comment do not always correspond to grammatical subject and predicate.) The case of v 13b similarly must be decided by extra-structural concerns: not *ṣyr* (T)/*n'mn lšlhyw* (C), but *ṣyr n'mn* (T)/*lšlhyw* (C). This division is suggested by the third colon in 25:13, by the parallelism with *ṣnt šlg* in v 13a (cf. v 25a), and by the implicit opposition of "reliable messenger" to a bad or foolish, and hence unreliable, messenger (cf. 13:17 and 26:6). These considerations, however, do not affect our main concerns as reflected in Levels 1 and 2.

Prov 25:18-20 are linked by a common T-C pattern on Level 2 which also appears in v 26. In these Sayings, on this level, there is no explicit Comment. Rather, the two or three figurative Topics in the first colon imply a strong but unstated Comment which applies to themselves and thus, more importantly, to the core Topic in the second colon. For v 18, such an implied Comment might be "does harm"; for vv 19 and 26 "is not good" (i.e., *l' ṭwb*); and for v 20 "is not fitting" (i.e., *l' n'wh*, cf. 26:1). The goodness or badness of an initial Figurative Comment (= Topic on Level 2) is so obvious that it does not need explicit expression. This tacit dimension is a necessary part of the art of the Saying: one cannot waste words! The tacit dimension must be made explicit in analysis so that the connection of these Sayings without a "Comment" to other Sayings with evaluative Comments may be made clear (cf. vv 24, 27).

Within Prov 25:2-27, v 2 occupies a special place. The first unit in the poem, it alone of all the Sayings is contrastive ($\neq$) rather than identifying (=) in T-C

Structure. Yet this Saying is a marvelous combination of identifying and contrastive elements:[20]

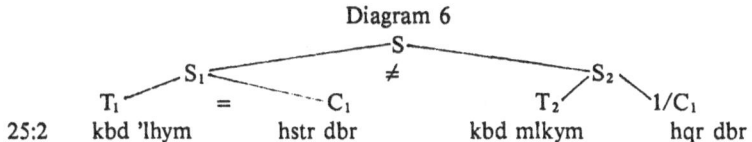

Diagram 6

| | | 25:2 | kbd 'lhym | hstr dbr | kbd mlkym | hqr dbr |

Though Prov 25:2 is a contrastive Saying, its verbal structure serves to relate what it contrasts. God has a certain *kbd* which is uniquely his own; the king also has his *kbd*. The two-fold repetition of *kbd* both distinguishes and associates the respective glory of God and king. The king's glory basks in and is qualified by God's ultimate majesty. The glory of God and king is further related by the repetition of *dbr*, and by the converse relation existing between *hstr (dbr)* and *hqr (dbr)* which is symbolized by C_1 and $1/C_1$. God's prerogative (*kbd*) is a transcendent hiding or revealing of matters (cf. Deut 29:29) while the king's prerogative is to sort out matters.

Thus God and king are intimately related in their glory and activity. Yet they are profoundly contrasted. If we eliminate the identifying features of the Saying (*kbd, dbr*), we arrive at a simpler contrastive Saying made up of two contrastive pairs: *'lhym ystr/ mlkym yhqrw** "God hides, kings search out." Thus underlying the actual Saying found in 25:2 is a contrastive Saying of the type "Man proposes, God disposes" (cf. Prov 16:1, 9; 19:21; 21:1, 30-31) which sets sharp limits upon the prerogatives or glory of men and kings in relation to Yahweh.

To return to the main point of Diagram 5, it provides another line of confirmation in our argument for the poetic coherence and organization of Prov 25:2-27. With the understandable exceptions of the poem's opening line (v 2) and the closing line of the first section (v 15), the poet consistently employs the FC/T pattern in his Saying material. Where this pattern does not appear in individual lines, it appears in the couplet which comprises the two lines in question (vv 4-5). On one occasion, a pattern similar to the FC/T relationship also links together a pair of one-line Admonitions (vv 16-17).

Thus the T/C analysis reveals a great deal of coherence among the Sayings of 25:2-27. The paradigmatic units (Sayings and Couplets) are combined into the simplest of all syntagmatic relations: congruence on the deepest level (Level 1) with greater or lesser degrees of variation on levels closer to the surface.[21] The

---

[20] Cf. A. Dundes, "Proverb," 114-115.
[21] On Level 2, the extent of variation is still quite limited:
1) $T_1 = T_2 = T_3 = C$ (vv 3, 12)
2) $T_1 = C_1 = T_1 = C_2$ (vv 11, 13, 14, 15, 25, 27)
3a) $T_1 = T_2 = T_3 = T_4$ (v 18)
3b) $T_1 = T_2 = T_3$ (vv 19, 20, 26)
4) $C = T_1 > T_2$ (v 24)

variations patent on Level 2 do not seem to have a significant role in organizing the Sayings, except for an occasional cluster effect. By way of contrast, Prov 26:1-12 will reveal such an organizing role for this level.

Finally, we note that while the beginning of the poem (v 2) and the end of the first major section (v 15) stand out because of their structural uniqueness, the end of the poem (v 27) displays no *structural* reasons for consideration as the final paradigmatic unit in the syntagmatic grouping. Indeed v 28 displays the FC = T pattern typical of the Sayings in vv 2-27. Thus another criterion must be brought to bear in establishing the end of the poem. This criterion appears in the area of poetic macro-structure.

POETICS

As noted in the previous chapter, Boström has carefully pointed out the means by which contiguous verses in Proverbs 25-27 are linked together, and that such linkage is ubiquitous in these chapters. We will occasionally point to devices which strongly accentuate sense connections, but for the most part we will not duplicate Boström's work. Hence, our main task in this subsection is to take up the incomplete analysis begun by Bryce in his 1972 article discussed above. Bryce himself termed his study a "rhetorical" analysis. In it, he gave minor attention to the role of contiguous stylistic features, and focused upon certain non-contiguous features. His attempt to clarify these features helps us to detect the contours and emphases of the poem as a whole, and aids in answering questions that our foregoing structural analysis could not settle.

As noted in our earlier treatment, Bryce thought that Prov 25:2-27 was bounded by "rubrics" linking v 2 with v 27b and v 16 with v 27a by means of chiastic patterns of word pairs. Bryce discerned three chiastic word-pair patterns: 1) kbd-$db\check{s}$ in vv 2, 16, 27; 2) kbd-hqr in vv 2, 27b; and 3) $db\check{s}$-kl in vv 16, 27a. As it turns out, Bryce missed two further instances of this phenomenon, each of which links key units in the poem: 4) $r\check{s}^\text{c}$-sdq in vv 5, 26; and 5) 'kl-$\acute{s}n$'k in vv 16-17, 21-22.[22] Furthermore, he failed to note, perhaps partly because of the difficulty of v 27b, that each instance of reversal of word order is accompanied by a switch in the plus or minus (+/-) value of the respective Sayings or Admonitions.

In sum, the stylistic device pointed out by Bryce is part of an elaborate system of interrelationships within the poem, binding together key elements in it. The use of this device occurs in three ways: 1) to create an inclusio for the entire poem, 2) to create a minor inclusio for the second section of the poem (II; vv 16-27), and 3) to link the otherwise separated Amonition forms in Section

---

5) $T_1 = C_1 = C_2 = T_2$ (v 23).

[22] As Pardee points out ("Types," see p. 54 above) repetition of words and roots is the strongest of all poetic binders and serves especially to bind large literary units together.

II (vv 16-17 and 21-22). To this third function, one may compare the clear contiguous links which exist among the three Amonitions in vv 6-10. The three patterns may be diagrammed as follows:

Diagram 7

1) v 2   kbd   hqr (+)   2) v 16   dbš⟍⟋'kl   (+/-)[23]
   v 5   rš' sdq   (+)   v 27a   'kl⟋⟍dbš   (-)
   v 26   sdq rš'   (-)   3) 16-17   'kl⟍⟋śn'k (-)
   v 27b hqr   kbd (-)   21-22   śn'k⟋⟍'kl (+)

Some comments are in order with respect to each part of the diagram: 1), 2) and 3). With regard to 1), when in v 27b the two-fold repetition of *kbd* appears, the poet is virtually waving a red flag in the reader's face: this colon must be construed with vv 2-3. The urgency of the inclusio is intensified by the further repetition of *ḥqr* in 27b. Both cola of v 27 are dependent upon previous key verses (cf. 27a and 16); the vocabulary of v 27b is entirely derived from v 2. Thus Bryce was quite correct in tying the interpretation of v 27 to that of v 2, but he failed to exploit the connection with v 16. While the Saying is somewhat obscure when taken in isolation, its difficulties become less awesome when the verse is read in terms of its two-fold inclusio function (see "Sense" below). The poem begins and ends with the themes of *glory* and *enquiry,* or social order (God-king-subjects) and the limits appropriate to king and subjects. With the stereotyped opposition of *ṣdq* and *rš'*, we discover that the poem has a double inclusio.[24] The first inclusio (*kbd-ḥqr*) links the first *couplet* (vv 2-3) with the last verse, while the second inclusio links the second *couplet* (vv 4-5) with the penultimate verse 26. Several factors suggest that this second inclusio is not just chance but design. First, while the opposition of *ṣdq* and *rš'* is a common one, found often in the Psalms and especially in Proverbs 10-15, in Collection C of Proverbs (25-27) it occurs *only* in 25:5, 26. By contrast, this opposition resumes its regular appearance in Collection D, occurring in 28:1, 12, 28; 29:2, 7, 16, 27. Secondly, as will be argued more fully in the exegesis below, the two introductory couplets (vv 2-3, 4-5) have a fundamental worldview function within the poem. They set the parameters of meaning within which all the Sayings and Admonitions are to be understood. Verses 2-3 establish the God-king-subject hierarchy, while vv 4-5 posit the fundamental conflict of good and evil that permeates reality. That the poem begins and ends with this structure serves as a structural

---

[23] Honey is a liminal symbol: it is good but too much is not good, and "what is enough for you" (*dyk*) is precisely at the limen. Hence on the surface v 16a is positive (+) while in terms of the deep structure of the Amonition, it is negative (-). This ambiguity must simply be acknowledged in its thought-provoking force. With regard to the present pattern, the positive side of the ambiguity is relevant.

[24] Murray H. Lichtenstein ("Chiasm and Symmetry in Proverbs 31," *CBQ* 44 [1982] 202-211, 207) has shown a similar double chiastic inclusio in Prov 31:1-29 (just before the "two-verse coda"): *ḥyl* (v 10), *b'lh* (v 11), *b'lh* v 28, *ḥyl* (v 29).

metaphor: the meaning of the included Sayings and Admonitions are to be seen in terms of these ultimate parameters. Thirdly, in v 5 the conflict of *rš‛* and *ṣdq* is dealt with in a normative or positive manner (+). But in v 26, corresponding to the inversion of word order, this normative situation is inverted (-) as good is overcome by evil.

With regard to 2), in vv 16-17, the eating of honey occupies the boundary between what is fitting and unfitting (the "too much" that leads to social conflict). In v 27a the +/- tension found in v 16a is unambiguously resolved; the "golden mean" is overreached and the possible bad has become actual (-).

With regard to 3), the word-pair relationship here (vv 16-17 and 21-22) is also a striking inversion of words and corresponding situations. The word pair (*'kl-śn'k*) first of all binds together Admonitions that might otherwise be unconnected in the reader's mind, just as the Admonitory couplets in Section I (vv 6-10) are more obviously joined by contiguity. Secondly, in vv 16-17 "eating" runs the risk of creating a "hater," while in vv 21-22 the problem of the "hater" is positively resolved by giving him something "to eat."

Another non-contiguous linkage, pointed out above in the subsection on structure, is the relationship of imagery and theme existing between vv 13 and 25. Finally, a minor long-range connection appears in the two-fold occurrence of *r‛* in vv 8, 9 and 17, 18.[25]

SENSE

In this subsection we will argue that for all the diversity of its individual topics and themes, Prov 25:2-27 is a composition united by two main concerns: 1) social hierarchy, rank, or position; and 2) social conflict and its resolution.[26]

---

[25] The sound pattern *r‛* occurs in every verse from 25:17-21 inclusive, a phenomenon first noted by Delitzsch (163), slightly inaccurately, and followed by Boström (*Paronomasi*, 95-96), more accurately and adding other factors. For the importance of this *r‛* pattern for the sense of the passage, see our treatment of these verses below.

[26] After arriving at this formulation, I discovered L. G. Perdue's suggestive essay, "Liminality as a Social Setting for Wisdom Instructions," *ZAW* 93 (1981) 114-126. His use of social anthropologist Victor Turner's concepts of "structure and anti-structure" corresponds to my "two main concerns." "V. Turner defines structure and anti-structure (*communitas*) as follows: 'It is as though there are here two major "models" for human interrelatedness, juxtaposed and alternating. The first is of society as a structured, differentiated, and often hierarchical system of politico-legal-economic positions with many types of evaluation, separating men in terms of "more" or "less." The second, which emerges recognizably in the liminal period, is of society as an unstructured or rudimentarily structured and relatively undifferentiated *comitatus,* community, or even communion of equal individuals who submit together to the general authority of the ritual elders' (The Ritual Process 96)." G. E. Bryce ("Structural Analysis") als perceived these two aspects of Prov 25, but, as we saw above, his treatment was marred by its attempt to create a narrative out of the chapter.

The primary address of this chapter is to the young men of the royal court.[27] As many have noted, 25:1-7 in particular requires a courtly setting.[28] Yet, by their very nature, these sayings have a wide applicability beyond the court.[29]

The poem begins with statements which organize social positions and set limits for humankind. Verses 2-3 are bound together by one of the poet's favorite literary devices: the two-fold repetition of a word, root, or sound within a unit.[30] As *kbd* and *dbr* twice repeat in the first Saying, so *mlk* and *ḥqr* link vv 2 and 3 together.

As noted earlier, vv 2-3 establish the proximity of God and king,[31] while making clear a hierarchy of prerogatives and glory: God above all, then king, and finally the king's subjects for whom the king's heart is inscrutable. These subjects, especially those of the court, come into play in the following verses. James G. Williams has rightly sensed the worldview potency of these two Sayings:

---

[27] Most extensively argued by G. E. Bryce (*LW*, 162) and followed by W. Lee Humphreys ("The Motif of the Wise Courtier in the Book of Proverbs," in *IW*, 185). Lindenberger (*APA*, 21, 32, n. 32) argues for a similar original setting for the Aramaic Ahiqar proverbs.

[28] S. R. Driver, *Introduction to the Literature of the Old Testament* (9th edition [1913]; reprinted, Gloucester, Mass.: Peter Smith, 1972) 400; Boström, *Paronomasi*, 94; H. Cazelles, "A Propos d'une Phrase de H. H. Rowley," *VTSup* 3 (1955) 25-30; Gemser, 93, 101; Barucq, 201; G. von Rad, *WII*, 17, n. 6; Postel, *Form and Function*, 61-62; R. E. Murphy, *WL*, 77. U. Skladny's (*ASI*, 55-57) idea that the Collection is directed at the lowest class of society, the farmer, is due to a literalistic misreading of the metaphorical imagery of several Sayings, for which see our treatment below. Postel ("Form and Function," 61-62) and McKane (10-11) provide critique of Skladny's general characterization of Collection C.

[29] See the reference to Skladny in the preceding note. H. H. Schmid (*WGW* 43 and n. 163) notes that in Egyptian Instructions designed for the training of young court officials, the teaching quickly broadens to include a wide variety of non-courtly topics. This movement from topic to topic presupposes the all-inclusive world-order of *maat* which encompasses even the smallest details of ordinary life.

[30] The frequency of this device was first discussed by Boström (*Paronomasi*, 44-52), though Boström's treatment does not seem to make the distinction between mere sound repetition and the more forceful device of repeating entire words or word-sounds in a small poetic unit. The sound patterns can also be inverted like a canon theme in contrary motion. Notable examples of entire word or word sound repetition include the following: 25:2 (*kbd/dbr*), 9 (*ryb*), 11 (*dbr*), 13 (*ṣyr*), 20 (*šr*), 27 (*kbd*). The same device can be used to tie poetic lines to one another, e.g. vv 4-5 (*hgw*), 16-17 (*śb'*). The connections among 25:18-20 will be discussed in the text. Cf. 26:4-5 (*'wlt*), 1-12 (*ksyl*), 13-16 (*'ṣl*), 17 (*'br*); 27:1-2 (*hll*), 3 (*kbd*), 10 (*r'*), 16 (*spn* ?), 17 (*yhd, brzl*), 19 (*pnym, 'dm*), 20 (*śb'*), 22 (*ktš, 'wl*), 23 (*yd'*), 24 (*dwr*), 27 (*lḥm* ?).

[31] Cf. Prov 16:1-15; 24:21-22 and R. N. Whybray, "Yahweh-Sayings," 159-160, 164-165. Cf. G. von Rad (*OTT* II, 218-219) on Jer 23:5-6; 30:21; Ps 110:1.

There are occasionally sayings that are enigmatic in their compactness. A whole mythology may be compressed within 25:2-3. One senses that if one were to 'crack these nuts' it would be like splitting an atom. An entire world ready to explode from a proverb.[32]

To use a less violent image, the world hidden in these verses is revealed when we carefully trace out its tendrils of language and thought. These, with vv 4-5, lead us to Judean royal ideology[33] and to the creation theology[34] of the wisdom tradition.

God's glory is of course manifold, having many aspects. That he conceal a matter, however, focuses upon his transcendent wisdom as creator and Lord of history. The use of the common ANE merism, "heavens and earth," in v 3 could not but remind the ancient reader of Yahweh's sovereignty:

... the Lord, who made heaven and earth
The heavens are the Lord's heavens,
but the earth he gave to the sons of men (Ps 115:15-16).

In Prov 25:2-3, God does not hide himself (so McKane) or his face,[35] rather, he hides a *dbr*, something in the earth, the created realm where men and preeminently the king have the task of searching out matters. That the heavens and earth are inscrutable is a function of the wisdom hidden in them. The king and mankind are engaged in a search for wisdom (world order)[36] especially —

[32] "The Power of Form: a Study of Biblical Proverbs," *Semeia* 17 (1980) 43.
[33] This ideology appears explicitly in v 5 with which vv 2-4 must be construed. See notes 34, 51, 52 below.
[34] That wisdom theology is creation theology has become a commonplace since Zimmerli's statement to this effect in 1964. W. Zimmerli, "The Place and Limit of the Wisdom in the Framework of the Old Testament Theology," *SAIW* (original 1964) 316; G. von Rad, *WII* 77-78, 92, 115-137, 144-176. J. Crenshaw, "Prolegomenon," *SAIW*, 22-55; H. J. Hermisson, "Observations on the Creation Theology in Wisdom," *IW*, 43-57; R. E. Murphy, "Wisdom—Theses and Hypotheses," *IW* 36-37, among many others. Perhaps it is better to speak of world-order theology since the *act* of creation is not a primary concern in much of the literature, as Hermisson's article shows by its paucity of texts.

In my judgment, Judean royal ideology and creation theology are two sides of one ideological complex: God-king-world-order and justice go together. So J. Vermeylen, "Le Proto-Isaïe et la Sagesse d'Israel," *SAT*, 45-48. Contrast W. McKane (*Prophets and Wise Men* [London: SCM, 1965]) who in effect separates courtly wisdom from Yahwism.
[35] These are expressions of anger or abandonment. S. E. Balentine, "A Description of the Semantic Field of Hebrew Words for 'Hide,' " *VT* 30 (1980) 137-153.
[36] "The teacher's task then is to assure the student that the social reality correctly reflects metaphysical reality . . ." Perdue ("Liminality," 120) citing P. Berger, *The Sacred Canopy* (1969) 22-23. The ideology of the wise king continues to operate in later times. Qoh 1:13 uses different terms to express the same role for the king. See also 3:11; 7:23-25; 8:16-17. R. E. Murphy has raised questions concerning the "search for order" ("Wisdom Theses," *Wisdom and Knowledge* II [J. Papin Festschrift; J. Armenti ed.; Philadelphia: Villanova University] 196-198, and "Wisdom—Theses and Hypotheses," *IW*, 35-36). Murphy

and this is the main point of Proverbs 25 — as it encompasses and pertains to the social order.

Job 28, though coming from a different sphere of the wisdom tradition, illumines the language and meaning of our text. Men search (*ḥqr*, Job 28:3) the uttermost recesses of the cosmos for gold, silver, and gems which are less precious than wisdom; that which is hidden (v 11) man brings to light. But wisdom "is hid (*nʿlmh*) from the eyes of all living, and concealed (*nstrh*) . . ." (vv 20-21). God alone understands and knows its place, for he created and "established it and searched it out (*hkynh* . . . *ḥqrh*" v 27; cf. *kwn* in Prov 25:5). Here, God's transcendence is clearly set forth and the only proper response, in view of man's limits, is that given at the poem's end, whether by an editor or the poet:

Behold, the fear of the Lord, that is wisdom;
and to depart from evil is understanding (Job 28:28).

The God of Prov 25:2 can conceal and thus, by implication, reveal.[37] His hidden wisdom comprises not only his acts of creation but also his plans and judgments in history. Yahweh asks "shall I hide from Abraham what I am about to do" (Gen 18:17)? To God's revelation of his plan Abraham responds by arguing that "the Judge of all the earth" should do right and not destroy the righteous (*ṣdyq*) with the wicked (*ršʿ*; v 25).

The shift from cosmic to historical or judicial concerns as found in Prov 25:2-3 to vv 4-5 is actually a common one.[38] It is a function of the integration of the social order within the cosmic. Thus Job with its stock cosmic imagery for wisdom:[39]

Can you find out the deep things (*hḥqr*) of God? . . .
It is higher than heaven — what can you do?
Deeper (*ʿmqh*) than Sheol — what can you know? . . .
If he [God] . . . calls to judgment, who can hinder him?
(Job 11:7-10, RSV).

The effect of this imagery in Prov 25:2-3 is firmly to set the king within the creation theology of wisdom, and to associate his wisdom with God's.

Similarly, the stereotyped expression, *ʾyn ḥqr*, is used only of God and of

---

correctly points to some problems in current formulations in the construct "search for order." Nonetheless, as virtually all scholars now agree, wisdom concerns world order — however we may struggle to formulate it.

[37] Cf. Deut 29:29; 2 Kgs 4:27; Sir 11:4; 16:21-22.

[38] Exod 15; Jud 5:4-5, 20-21; Job; Pss 72; 82; 89; 93-97; 104:35; 135-136 etc. Jer 31:35-37 is especially interesting in relation to Prov 25; note its use of *šmym*, *ʿrs*, *ḥqr*.

[39] This imagery for God's inscrutable wisdom continues in the Jewish tradition. See Qoh 7:24; Sir 1:1-3; and especially Wisdom 9:16.

his works in creation and judgment[40] except in Prov 25:3 where it is applied to the king's heart. This unites the king's glory and wisdom with that of God, but only with respect to those beneath the king. For "the king's heart is a stream of water in the hand of the Lord; he turns it wherever he will" (21:1). But for those beneath the king, his wisdom is like that of "angel of God" in judgment (2 Sam 14:17, 20; 19:27). It is a measure of the collapse of Saul's royal character that he reveals (*glh,* cf. Prov 18:2) and cannot conceal (*ystr*) any matter (*dbr*) from his son Jonathan (1 Sam 20:2). Jonathan merely has to "sound out" (*ḥqr*) his father (20:12).[41]

But what is the *dbr* that the king's searching penetrates? The answer is to be sought in the immediately following context (Prov 25:4-5, 6-10), but also in the non-contiguous context latent in the language of vv 2-3. For an ancient sage, given to "associative" thinking,[42] such a proverb pair would call to mind such Sayings as 20:5:

> The purpose in a man's mind (*lb*) is like deep (*'mqym*) water,
> but a man of understanding will draw it out (cf.18:4; Ps 64:7)

While the king's heart is inscrutable, his wisdom is revealed by his judicial ability — also found in lesser men — to pentrate the motives and purposes of the human heart (Prov 18:17; Job 29:16). To act as a wise judge is an essential part of the kingly glory,[43] which entails the ability to search out the heart of a matter or conflict (*dbr, ryb*). Thus Solmon's ideal wisdom is revealed in the case of the two harlots:

> And all Israel heard of the judgment . . . and they stood in awe of the king, because they perceived that the wisdom of God was in him, to render justice (1 Kgs 3:28)

---

[40] Isa 40:28; Ps 145:3; Job 5:9; 9:10; cf. 34:24; 36:26 (*l' ḥqr*).

[41] On the "absolute necessity of secrecy" and the "phenomenology of revealing the truth" for the maker of history, see the profound essay of the philosopher and U.N. diplomat C. Malik, "History-Making, History-Writing, History-Interpreting" *Center Journal* 1 (Fall, 1982) 11-42, 24-25.

[42] S. M. Paul, "Mnemonic Devices," *IDBSup,* 600-602. Dov Noy ("The Jewish Versions of the 'Animal Languages' Folktale (AT 670)," *Scripta Hierosolymitana* 22 [1971] 176, 185-188) gives a brilliant analysis of Hebrew folktales which exploit Qoh 11:1 through "associative" thinking. See also Joseph Heineman, "The Proem in the Aggadic Midrashim. A Form Critical Study," *Scripta Hierosolymitana* 22 (1971) 100-122. Boström (*Paronomasi,* 1-15) provides a variety of word and sound associations from the Bible, Midrashim, and non-Hebrew sources. Such associative procedures presuppose a culture with a well-known oral or literary body of traditional materials with a quasi-canonical status. G. B. Caird, *Language and Imagery of the Bible* (Philadelphia: Westminster, 1980) 107-108.

[43] Cf. Ps 72:1-4, 12-14", and n. 54 below. B. Kovacs ("Sociological," 415-418) discusses the "demesne" of the king, set below Yahweh and above his subjects. Cf. Sophocles, "Oedipus Rex," 11. 496-507, 530.

Men are rightly in awe of the king; the evil-doer as well as the seeker after wisdom both know that "nothing is hid from the king" (1 Sam 18:13;, cf. 1 Kgs 10:3); "the king is like the angel of God to discern (šmʿ) good and evil" (2 Sam 14:17). If the following is true of peers (rʿym), how much more so of the king?

He who states his case first seems right (ṣdyq),
until the other comes and examines him (wḥqrw, Prov 18:17).

The texts we have been considering place the king's judicial inquiry (ḥqr dbr) in the context of God's created order and justice wherein his unfathomable wisdom is concealed and revealed. It is not necessary to restrict the meaning of ḥqr dbr to a judicial Sitz; our point is merely that it can have such a setting and that the following verses in Proverbs 25 seem to pull the expression there in this direction. Dbr has many meanings, and ḥqr too is not exclusively a judicial term. Yet, as texts like Prov 18:17 (above, cf. 28:11) and Job 29:16 make clear, the root ḥqr had a specialized judicial function already in the period of Biblical Hebrew. Out of this developed the technical usage of Mishnaic Hebrew.[44] Similarly, already in Biblical Hebrew dbr has a specialized judicial sense[45] which continues into Mishnaic Hebrew.[46] Akkadian, like Hebrew, also has a number of technical legal idioms using "word, matter" (awātum, dbr respectively). The Akkadian expression amātam amāru "to investigate an affair" which is equivalent to dīnam amāru "to investigate a case"[47] provides us with the semantic parallel to ḥqr dbr as a legal phrase.

Against the background of the foregoing, Prov 25:4-5 will be seen to follow quite naturally upon vv 2-3. The judicial concerns implicit in vv 2-3 are elaborated in vv 4-5. These latter verses also spell out the conflict of good and evil which threatens to disrupt good social order unless the king judges rightly. The links with the foregoing verses are reinforced by the repetition of the keyword mlk.

Verse 4 provides the imagery for the thought-core in v 5. The process of refining and the metalworker's craft are stock metaphors for impure social situations which need purification through judgment. The wicked are dross, judgment is the refiner's fire and so on. Typical examples include Isa 1:21-26; Jer

---

[44] ḥqr, ḥqrh, Sanh. 4:1,5; Aboth 1:9 etc.

[45] TDOT III, 108 and BDB 183b give references. See especially Deut 13:15 (English 13:14) with its collocation of dbr and ḥqr.

[46] Gmrw 't hdbr "When they had concluded the case . . ." (Sanh. 3:7) is equivalent in meaning to the passive formulation of Sanh. 6:1, ngmr hdyn, "When the case has been concluded. . . ." The idiom, gmr 't hdbr, has its exact semantic equivalent in Akkadian awātam gamāru, " to make final settlement (of a dispute)" and gummuru "to render a final verdict" (CAD vol. 5, "G," 26-27, 30).

[47] CAD vol. I, pt. II, "A," 19, 20. Note also ḥqr ryb in Job 29:16; cf. 13:8-9. Ringgren³ (100) recognizes the legal connotations of our phrase in Prov 25:2: "d. h. wohl Rechtsachen." Does thqrwn mlyn ("you search out matters") in the ryb context of Job 32:11 provide a parallel to ḥqr dbr?

6:27-30; and Ezek 22:18-22.[48] The imagery in Prov 25:4 is, as in so many sayings, elliptical. The process of purification is a necessary but not a sufficient condition for the goal of a fine artwork. Similarly, in v 5, the removal of the wicked is necessary but not in itself sufficient to secure the throne in righteousness. As Bryce has pointed out, v 4 requires two functions: "the refining of the ore itself and the casting of the vessel."[49] The second function is not mentioned but is implicitly present as the technical operation intended by and made possible by the refining (cf. Exod 32:24; Isa 54:16). In both vv 4 and 5, the end in view is more than a simple result of the act of removal. Thus the parallel protases omit necessary positive steps to the final goal. Furthermore, the stated goals (silver vessel and throne stable in righteousness) have wide ramifications. The silver vessel functions metaphorically as a symbol for that which is pure, beautiful, achieved by hard work and skill, and fit for its purposes (cf. Rom 9:20-23). The throne, itself a symbol of the king's office and functions — especially the judicial (Pss 9:5; 122:5; Isa 16:5) — is prefigured by the silver vessel in v 4. It must be pure and is achieved first of all by the removal of the wicked through judgment. The aesthetic craftsmanship thereof provides a fitting echo of the wise artistry in the silver vessel.[50] In a positive sense, the throne is established by righteous wisdom.[51]

The vocabulary of Prov 25:5b firmly sets the verse within the tradition of Judean Royal Ideology. In its entirety the colon is a stereotyped phrase in which the three key elements (kwn, ks', sdq) can be applied to either the Divine or the Davidic king.[52] While it is not the place of this work to explore the ideology

---

[48] K. H. Singer, *Die Metalle Gold, Silber, Bronze, Kupfer und Eisen im Alten Testament und ihre Symbolik* (Forschung zur Bibel 43, Würzburg: Echter Verlag, 1980) 83-89. Vermeylen, "Le Proto-Isaïe," 38. Cf. Prov 10:20; 27:21; and especially 17:3.

[49] "Structural Analysis," 114.

[50] On the aesthetics of wisdom in Proverbs, see B. Kovacs, "Sociological," 323, 454-456.

[51] The symbolism of 25:5b appears to have a New Kingdom Egyptian background which underscores the cosmic dimensions of the verse. In Egypt, the pedestal of the throne takes the form of the hieroglyph for *maat* (righteousness, world order). So R. J. Williams (" 'A People Come Out of Egypt': An Egyptologist Looks at the Old Testament," *VTSup* 28 [1975] 234) following H. Brunner ("Gerechtigkeit als Fundament des Thrones," *VT* 8 [1958] 426-428). See also O. Keel, *The Symbolism of the Biblical World* (New York: Seabury, 1978) 171.

[52] All three elements appear in the following texts: 1) of Yahweh: Pss 89:15; 2) of the Davidic king: Isa 9:6; 16:5; Prov 20:28 (LXX); 16:12; cf. 29:14. In many important texts from the same tradition complex two elements appear (kwn, ks'): 2 Sam 7:13, 16; 1 Kgs 2:12, 45; Pss 89:5, 37-38; 93:2; 103:19; 1 Chron 17:12, 14; 22:10. On ks' see Whitelam, *Just King*, 31-33; R. de Vaux, *AI* I, 106-107. The stability (kwn) of the throne is based on the stability of the cosmos or world order (Ps 93:1-2; cf. 97:2; 96:10; 104:5; Isa 45:18). This aspect of kwn is developed by Robert W. E. Forrest, "An inquiry into Yahweh's commendation of Job," *SR* 8 (1979) 162-165. J. Vermeylen ("Le proto-Isaïe," 48) concludes his comparison of royal proverbs to Isa 9:1-6a and 11:1-5, of which "la parenté avec la

implicit in 25:5, a few comments are in order. First, we may assume that this ideology provides the worldview parameters which hold for the entire passage, and not just for this Saying, as McKane and others would assume. Since the verse functions as Introduction to the passage in conjunction with vv 2-4, and since it receives an inclusio in v 26, the literary unity of the whole passage requires that we take the verse as implicit background to *all* the Sayings and Admonitions. This should not surprise us since the king is the main stay and support of social order and stability. Secondly, 25:1, in connection with 25:2-5, is to be taken seriously as a declaration of the royal provenance of our passage.[53] Thirdly, the process of removing the wicked is a standard task of the king within Israel and without.[54] Thus the "court apologetic" in 1 Kgs 1-2 which explains Solomon's

---

réflexion sapientielle émanant des milieux intellectuels de la cour de Jérusalem me paraît indéniable."

[53] So R. B. Y. Scott, "Solomon and the Beginnings of Wisdom in Israel," *VTSup* 3 (1953) 273-274. McKane (577), without grounds, weakens Scott's solid conclusions. Most scholars follow Scott. Cf., e.g., Gemser (93), Barucq (193, 201), Whybray (146-147), and Ringgren[3] (100). For the broader cultural context of Proverbs 25-27, see B. O. Obed, "Judah and the Exile," *Israelite and Judaean History* (J. H. Hayes and J. M. Miller, eds.; Philadelphia: Westminster, 1977) 435-451.

[54] Royal justice has two complementary aspects, 1) the protection or liberation of the poor and oppressed, and 2) the removal or destruction of the wicked and the oppressor. P. E. Dion ("Tu feras disparaître le mal du milieu de toi," *RB* 87 [1980] 321-349, 337-339) and I. L. Seeligmann ("Zur Terminologie für das Gerichtsverfahren in Wortschatz des Biblischen Hebräisch," *VTSup* 16 [1967] 274) provide examples. See also, e.g., 2 Sam 4:11; Ps 21:8-14; 45:7-8; 72; 82; Prov 11:21; 16:12; 20:8; 20:26; 24:23-25; and W. Bühlmann, *RR*, 91.

For a general ANE survey (including Israel) of this matter, see Whitelam, *Just King*, 17-37. A. Gamper (*Gott als Richter in Mesopotamien und im Alten Testament* [Innsbruck: Universitätsverlag Wagner, 1966] 45-55) provides early Mesopotamian examples but is to be used with caution.

Cf. the Prologue of Codex Hammurabi:

When lofty Anum . . .
established (*ú-ki-in-nu-šum*) for him [Marduk] . . .
   an enduring kingship,
   whose foundations are as firm as heaven and earth—
at that time Anum and Enlil named me
to promote the welfare of the people . . .
to cause justice (*mi-ša-ra-am*) to prevail in the land
to destroy the wicked and the evil . . . (CH I, 1-35; *ANET*[3], 164).

For the text, see R. Borger, *Babylonisch-assyrische Lesestücke* II (Rome: Pontifical Biblical Institute, 1963) 4-5. Note the sequence of God, king, justice (removal of the wicked), and the reference to cosmic order in the merismus "heaven and earth." See also *Merikare* 45-51 (*AEL* I, 100) and the eighth century Karatepe Inscription.

actions is a perfect instantiation of Prov 25:5. Solomon acts with "wisdom" (1 Kgs 2:6,9), and by the removal of the wicked his throne/kingdom is established (1 Kgs 2:12, 46).[55]

The series of Admonitions (vv 6-10) which follows the "Introduction" (vv 2-5) develops the two thematic axes of the preceding verses: A) the vertical hierarchy of God-king-subjects and B) the horizontal opposition of good and evil. Furthermore, the two axes appear in the same order in the Introduction and Admonitions: A) vv 2-3, B) vv 4-5 , A) vv 6-7, B) vv 7c-10. However, these Admonitions present weakened contrasts in comparison to those of vv 2-5. Verses 6-7 concern not the unbridgeable gaps between God and king or king and subjects, but the relatively close and fluid hierarchy among the king's men. Verses 7c-10 similarly concern legal disputes (*ryb*) among peers (*rʿ*) in which one is declared *ṣdyq* (in the right) and the other *rš'* (in the wrong) — technical legal terms (cf. Prov 17:15, 26; 18:17) which are less absolute than the black and white contrast of v 5. The formal affinities of these three Admonitions have been laid out above (Structure), and their common pattern of negative Precept followed by threatened negative consequence suggests that they must be construed together. This suggestion is confirmed by the detailed analysis in Footnote 3 above. Thus vv 7c-10 as well as vv 6-7 concern the men of the court. Of course this does not exclude the applicability of these Admonitions beyond the court.

---

[55] The scholarly debate whether 1 Kgs 1-2 is for or against Solomon (F. Langlamet, "Pour ou contre Salomon? La rédaction prosalomonienne de 1 Rois I-II," *RB* 83 [1976] 321-379 and 481-529) is resolved when the passage is read as a "court apolgetic" (P. Kyle McCarter Jr., " 'Plots, True or False': the Succession Narrative as Court Apologetic," *Int* 35 [1981] 355-367, especially 360, n. 12) or "Instruction" (Perdue, "Liminality," 123-124). 1 Kgs 1-2 emphasizes that by Solomon's executions his kingdom was established (2:12, 45). In these chapters *ksʾ* is a keyword: 1:13, 17, 20, 24, 27, 30, 35, 37, 46, 47; 2:12, 19, 24, 33, 45. See notes 52, 54 above.

Perdue's view on the Instruction character of David's Testament need not conflict with McCarter's (cf. "Liminality," 119, n. 33). Elsewhere, ("The Testament of David and Egyptian Royal Instructions," *Scripture in Context II: More Essays on the Comparative Method* [W. W. Hallo, J. C. Moyer, and L. G. Perdue eds.; Winona Lake: Eisenbrauns, 1983] 79-96) Perdue makes a crucial point:

> In a court setting ... one wonders if the political executions by Solomon, as expedient as they were, would have been takan as anti-Solomonic? If the document was ... read by a sophisticated, courtly audience ... would not ... the emphasis upon Solomon wisely finding a legal basis upon which to execute dangerous rebels have been admired and appreciated as evidence of a wise king sitting upon the throne? Indeed, modern readers whose ethical sensibilities are shocked by Solomon's executions may be basing their reactions on different ethical standards than those present in a *Gruppenethos* of the court.

Prov 25:4-5 provides further evidence for the ideology described by McCarter and Perdue in 1 Kings 1-2.

Verses 6-7 concern social mobility in the court: the jockeying for power, position, and glory (*hdr* picks up the *kbd* of v 2).[56] Virtually all the imagery and vocabulary of social position in vv 6-7 is spatial (*lpny mlk, bmqwm gdlym, t'md, 'lh hnh, hšpylk, lpny ndyb*). By the horizontal imagery of *presence* (*lpny mlk*, etc.), vv 6-7 are related to v 5, and by the high-low imagery (*'lh, hšpylk*) to v 3a.[57] The negative Precepts of v 6 warn against making too much of oneself, of transgressing spatial/social boundaries. Thus the first Admonition in the series requires recognition of limits, a central concern of wisdom thinking.[58]

Verses 7c-10 form two Admonitions linked by concern for legal disputes among peers. These verses may follow upon the first Admonition partly because, then (2 Sam 15:2-7) as now, success in legal cases can be a stepping stone to political power and position. The imagery of vv 7c-8 is mainly optical (*r'w 'ynyk, hklym*),[59] that of vv 9-10 mainly aural (*šm', dbtk*). Together these Admonitions appear to form a conventional wisdom topos: the avoidance of unnecessary lawsuits and their negative consequences:

Do not frequent a law court,
Do not loiter where there is a dispute,
For in the dispute they will have you as a *testifier*
Then you will be made their witness

---

[56] *Hdr* and *kbd* are a stereotyped word pair. Pss 8:6; 29:2; 96:8-9; 145:5, 12; 1 Chron 16:29. Cf. Prov 14:28 *hdrt mlk* and 29:23 where *špl* (hiph.) is opposed to *kbwd*.

[57] The symbolic representation of social status by physical position appears very early. Cf. Ptahhotep 13 (ll. 220-231) and McKane's comments thereon (commentary, 60-61). Related is Ptahhotep 119-142 on which see E. Würthwein ("Egyptian Wisdom and the Old Testament," *SAIW*, 118 who points out that social order is a matter of *maat* and thus divinely ordained. For Israel see 1 Sam 20:18, 25-29, and M. Weinfeld ("The Counsel of the 'Elders' to Rehoboam and its Implications," *Maarav* 3 [1982] 51-53) with further examples. De Vaux (*AI* I, 107; K. F. Müller, *Das assyrische Ritual* [MVAG 41/3; Leipzig, 1937) presents an Akkadian royal homage ritual which is interesting in this regard. Later examples: "Ankhsheshonq" 13/23 (Lichtheim, *AEL* III, 170); Sir 7:4-7; Sanh. 4:4; Matt 23:6; Luke 14:7-11; James 2:1-7.

[58] Cf. Prov 25:27; 26:1; 27:2. Perdue, "Liminality." G. von Rad *WII*, 97-110. B. Kovacs ("Sociological,") has done the most extensive analysis of the role of social position and authority ("demesne") in Proverbs and the social group which produced Prov 15:28-22:16. Many of his observations apply equally well to Prov 25-27. "The wise evidence in these sayings a symbolic social hierarchy.... Theirs is an ethic and an ethos of propriety.... With propriety goes what we shall call 'demesne,' that realm of experience and action over which one has effective control. To be restrained [i.e., wise] is to recognize the boundaries of one's demesne and observe them. To overreach those limits is to court disaster, the more when it is done with (foolish) confidence" (322-323). "To have a dmesne . . . is also to have limits beyond which one cannot act, certainly not without impunity" (326). Cf. pp. 338-364, 433, 442-446, 458, especially 348 on the wise and the king.

[59] See notes 2, 3 above.

And they will bring you to a lawsuit not your own to affirm.
Should it be a dispute of your own, extinguish the flame!
... They remember what a man forgets and lay the accusation.[60]

In a certain sense, here too (and in Prov 25:7c-10) we have to do with a transgression of limits. The man who hastens to a *ryb* which does not properly concern him is out of his own territory and will suffer for it (Prov 26:17; 27:8).

At first glance 25:11-15 appear quite unrelated to the foregoing themes of king's court and justice, and the disputes which take place under the surveillance of that justice. The sense of a shift is heightened by the switch from Admonition to Saying form. However, a close reading suggests that while these Sayings may indeed be applied outside the court, they are nonetheless of prime concern to the nobility.

Postel has pointed out that

> the series, Yahweh (25:2a), the king (25:2b-7), and speech (25:8-14 and most of vs. 15-18) ... parallels 16:1-33 in topical arrangement (a section Skladny claims is addressed to young officials)."[61]

Postel's observation is broadly correct, but must be more carefully nuanced.

Verses 11-12 form a proverb pair, linked by their common imagery (jewelry//speech), vocabulary (*zhb*), syntax (verb + *'l* + object), form, but also by their use of terms appropriate to the *ryb* setting. The last item provides the point of contact with the foregoing Admonitions. In v 11, the qal participle phrase (*dābār dābur*) is the passive equivalent of the active piel construction of which M. Weinfeld says,

> A thorough examination of all occurences of the idiom *dibber dābār* ... reveals that in general it does not mean simply "to speak a word," but rather "to arrive at a decision through bargaining (usually at a gathering)."[62]

Thus, by analogy, and given its judicial context, the passive phrase in Prov 25:11b most likely refers to a decision which settles a matter of dispute. It is *this* "word spoken" which is as splendid as golden apples in a design of silver. Furthermore, silver (*ksp*) calls forth in the reader's mind the imagery of judgment in v 4, as does the implicit imagery of the silversmith's art found in the jewelry of vv 11-12. Unfortunately, the exact sense of *'pnyw* (v 11) still escapes us.[63]

---

[60] The first line is literally, "Do not go with reference to standing in an assembly (*ina pu-uh-ri*)." Lambert, *BWL* 100-101, "Counsels of Wisdom, 11 31-37, 40 (cf. Prov 26:17; 24:28). Lambert (313) also points to Arabic *Ahiqar*, a passage from Menander the Egyptian, and a prototype of the quoted passage "in *VS* 10.204 rev. v.17-20 = J. J. A. Van Dijk, *La Sagesse*, pp. 103-6."

[61] Postel, "Form and Function," 61-62.

[62] "The Counsel," *Maarav* 3 (1982) 43. Cf. Judg 11:11; 1 Kgs 12:7; Isa 8:10; 58:13; Hos 10:4; 1 Sam 20:23 (= covenant, vv 14-17).

[63] See note 4 above.

The second colon of v 12 strengthens our argument that this couplet is appropriate to a *ryb* setting: *mwkyḥ ḥkm 'l 'zn šm't*. *Šm't* resonates with the legal technical term *šm'* in v 10.[64] Of greater weight, however, is the technical juridical sense of *mwkyḥ*.[65] The picture of healthy justice presented in 25:12 is in sharp contrast to the scene in Amos 5:10: "They hate the arbiter (*mwkyḥ*) in the gate, and detest him whose plea is just" (*JPSV,* cf. Job 9:33). Thus while Prov 25:11-12 may find application beyond the judicial setting (implicitly in the presence of the king 25:5-6),[66] their preceding context in our passage (vv 7c-10) and the primary meaning of their vocabulary requires a judicial undrstanding of these verses.

Verses 13-14 are bound together by weather imagery. These verses return to the courtly hierarchical concern about relations with superiors, first in a positive sense (v 13) and then in the negative sense of failed upward mobility (v 14; cf. 18:16; 19:6; 21:14). It is important to note that in Israel, as in the ANE generally, messengers could possess very high, even courtly, social status.[67]

Finally, v 15 forms a weak verbal[68] but a strong thematic inclusio to the first couplet of Section one of the poem (vv 2-15). It thus serves to summarize the two thematic axes which are elaborated in this section of the poem:

A. v 15a = relation to superior; hierarchy
B. v 15b = conflict (resolved by proper speech).

Thus we can discern a *thematic* pattern to the first section of Prov 25:2-27. The Introduction and Inclusio are parallel while the enclosed Admonitions and Sayings are organized as a chiasmus:

[64] On *šm'* in v 10 see note 3 above. *'zn šm't* need not refer to a judge (Prov 20:12). And it is not clear if the use of *twkyḥ* in 15:31a has legal overtones. But note how McKane (480) parses the syntax here: "an ear which listens to reproof is life."

[65] "In der Tat lässt sich הוכיח durchaus von der Argumentation eines Anklägers verstehen." The semantic development is from the technical juridical to a more generalized usage. I. L. Seeligmann, "Terminologie," *VTSup* 16 (1967) 266-267. Cf. *THAT,* I, s.v. ykḥ for a less assertive portrait of the semantic development.

[66] May one assume for ancient Israel something like the legal fiction which obtains in modern England, namely that all cases are tried in the presence of the king? Cf. J. H. Round, "Court," *Encyclopaedia Britannica* 7 (Eleventh Edition, 1910-11) 322. R. de Vaux, *AI* 1, 151-153. Whitelam (*Just King,* 185-206) convincingly argues for a historical judicial reform by Jehoshaphat which expanded the jurisdiction of the king's courts at the expense of autonomous local institutions. Whitelam also suggests that Absalom took advantage of his father's failure to delegate judicial authority (a *šm'*) in his attempt to usurp the throne, 2 Sam 15:1-6 (140-41). Cf. N. Porteous, "Royal Wisdom," *VTSup* 3 (1953) 247.

[67] A. D. Crown, "Messengers and Scribes: The ספר and מלאך in the Old Testament," *VT* 24 (1974) 366-370, and his "Tidings and Instructions: How News Travelled in the Ancient Near East," *JESHO* 17 (1974) 244-271. See especially pp. 258-263 on the high social status of royal messengers and the reasons therefor. Instructions to messengers appear in Ptahhotep ch. 8 (Lichtheim *AEL* I, 65) and "Satire of Trades," (*AEL* I, 190).

[68] *Mlk/qsyn,* noticed by Bryce ("Wisdom-'Book,' " 151).

Diagram 9

Introduction	A. vv 2-3
	B. vv 4-5
Admonitions	A. vv 6-7
	B. vv 7c-10
Sayings	B. vv 11-12
	A. vv 13-14
Inclusio	A/B v 15

The pair of Admonitions in 25:16-17 opens the second half of the proverb poem. It is bound together by parallels of form, syntax, vocabulary (*pn-šbʻ*), and theme. Verse 16 appeals to the addressee's personal experience (being made sick by too much honey) and so provides an image to help the hearer understand his *neighbor* who may have limits to *his* tolerance for visitation. In excess, even good and friendly visits can become an occasion for conflict between fellows; therefore keep to your rightful *place*. Thus this first Admonition takes up the themes of limits and of conflict among peers (*rʻ*) which we found in the earlier Admonitions (vv 6-10; *rʻ* appears in vv 8, 9). However, while vv 7c-10 concerned themselves with *ryb* in the technical judicial sense, here (vv 16-17) and in the verses which follow (18-24) problems of human conflict in general are explored. Except for the positive Admonition in vv 21-22, human conflict in these verses is always presented negatively, without resolution. Thus the repetition of the letters *rʻ* in every verse from 25:17-21 inclusive has a potent double effect, evoking both *neighbor* and *evil*.[69]

A common misapprehension concerning these verses finds more corruption in the text than is warranted. The abundance of word and sound repetition is seen as evidence for textual problems.[70] It was Boström who pointed out that this phenomenon is due to the poet's artistry and love for word play and is not a sign of textual corruption.[71] We have shown above (n. 30) that such repetition is a characteristic feature of Prov 25-27. Note in 25:18-20 the following examples: *šnwn-šn, rʻ* (4x plus once in v 17), *ʻd-mwʻd-mʻdh, bwgd bywm ṣrh-bgd bywm qrh, šr-bšrym*.[72]

Verse 18 returns us to a judicial referent in the strict sense (cf. vv 7c-10 and their twofold use of *rʻ*) and is an obvious parallel to the Decalogue in its older

---

[69] See note 25 above.

[70] I. L. Seeligmann, "Indications of Editorial Alteration and Adaptation in the Massoretic Text and the Septuagint," *VT* 11 (1961) 204, follwing Hitzig. Similarly, Gemser, Barucq, Ringgren.

[71] *Paronomasi*, 96-97. Boström points out more sound connections than can be discussed here. On the role of aesthetics in the arrangement of Proverbs, see Hermisson, *SIS*, 179-183.

[72] *Šnwn-šn* was noted by Delitzsch, 165. For *rʻ*, compare *ʻr/rʻ* in Prov 13:17-21.

Exod 20:16 version.[73] As Prov 6:19 and 1 Kgs 21:13 make clear, a false witness can *begin* a judicial process as well as join in one already begun.

Like v 18, v 19 concerns relations to one's neighbor (*rʿ*) who proves treacherous in a time of conflict or trouble.

Verse 20 brings up a different problem between peers, namely actions which do damage by violating the wisdom norm of "fittingness" or, to use Kovac's term, "propriety."[74] Taking away something as well as giving something can be unfitting and harmful, depending upon the circumstances (cf. 27:14; 10:26; Sir 22:6). Thus v 20 is related in theme to v 17. Unlike vv 18-19 which portray intentional violence between fellows, vv 17, 20 portray harm done to peer relations through lack of wisdom, the knowledge of fittingness.

The subsequent Admonition (vv 21-22) forms the positive counterpart to the negative admonitory pair in vv 16-17. The links between these two couplets have been laid out above in the section on "Poetics." Whereas "eating" too much causes conflict in vv 16-17, giving to eat resolves conflict in vv 21-22.

Verses 23-24, like vv 16-20, represent conflicts of various sorts, or portray things that *precipitate* conflicts. Unlike vv 4-5, 7c-12, 18, the conflicts here are not of a primarily judicial character, but they do affect everyman, from the courtier to the peasant. There may be a subtle link in the imagery of vv 23-24. Verse 23a pictures bad weather; v 24a portrays a man in a position where he is *exposed* to bad weather—which is better than being exposed to the storms of a tempestuous wife, as in the famous story of Socrates and Xanthippe!

Like its companion Saying in v 13, v 25 initiats the final trio of Sayings in its section. Verses 26, 27 form the important double inclusio to the two opening couplets of the poem (pointed out above in the "poetics" section). The inclusio of *ršʿ—sdq* (vv 5, 26) is reinforced by the appearanc of *mwṭ*, which forms an antithetical word-pair with *kwn* in v 5,[75] and *lpny* which directly echos v 5. Unlike vv 4-5, v 26 portrays the corruption of righteousness and justice; the wicked prevail over the innocent, evil overcomes good. The second half of the poem (vv 16-27) is essentially concerned with conflict and strife brought about by wickedness and the failure of wisdom. Here are portrayed the problems which the king and his men must master by wisdom and justice. As vv 4-5 state the basic duty of the king with regard to righteousness, so v 26 states the inversion of good and evil in the most basic way.

The poetic grounds for taking v 27a as an inclusio to v 16, and v 27b to vv 2-3 have been presented above. The sense of the verse in its context, however,

---

[73] *ʿd šqr* (so also Deut 19:18). Contrast Deut 5:20, *ʿd šwʾ*. M. A. Klopfenstein, *Die Lüge nach den Alten Testament* (Zürich: Gotthelf Verlag, 1964) 18-25. Cf. Prov 6:19; 12:17; 14:5, 25; 19:5. On *ypyh* in these texts, D. Pardee, "*yph* 'witness' in Hebrew and Ugaritic," *VT* 28 (1978) 204-213. "'*d* heisst Zeuge und Ankläger" who hears or sees and then tells (*hgyd*, Prov 12:17) in a court procedure. So I. L. Seeligmann, "Terminologie," *VTSup* 16 (1967) 262-263.

[74] "Sociological," 302, 323.

[75] Isa 40:20; Pss 93:1 = 96:10 = 1 Chron 16:30; Ps 104:5; Prov 12:3. Cf. Ps 112:6-7.

needs some elaboration. That men are limited and must not over-reach their limits is a theme common to wisdom and elsewhere (e.g., Ps 131) in the Hebrew Bible. Sir 3:21-22 well expresses the general thought:

> pl'wt mmk 'l tdrwš/ wmkwsh mmk 'l thqwr
> bmh šhwršyt htbwnn/ w'yn lk 'sq bnstrwt (Ms. A)
> Seek not what is too wonderful for you,
> nor search what is hid from you.
> Reflect on what you can grasp,
> don't be occupied with the hidden (cf. 2 Esdras 4).[76]

As a double inclusio referring back to both vv 2-3 and 16-17, v 27 with v 26) both summarizes and comments upon the two main concerns of the chapter. If vv 4-5 and 26 dealt with righteous order (ṣdqh) and the conflict of good and evil, vv 2-3, 16-17, and 27 concern the wise recognition of limits, both social and prudential. What one may attempt and attain is a function of who he is (eat what is right *for you*) and of circumstancs, both personal (the *kbwd* of others) and impersonal (the "difficult things," *kbdym*,[77] which are beyond one). But life is not just a matter of limits. If one finds the right honey, let him eat it and so attain the *kbwd* that suits him.[78] Such a life is sweet.[79]

---

[76] *APOT* (I, 326, n. 21) provides later allusions to this passage.

[77] While the use of *kbdm* here is uncommon, it is not without semantic parallel. The choice of this expression, rather than a more common word (*npl'wt* or the like) is determined by the desire of the poet to create a powerful inclusio with vv 2-3. We should not forget that *every* word in v 27b is derived from vv 2-3. Furthermore, it gives the poet opportunity to use his beloved device of word-repetition within the poetic unit. See further Van Leeuwen, "Proverbs xxv 27 Once Again."

[78] Prov 8:18; 11:16; 15:33; 18:12; 20:3; 22:4; 29:23; Sir 3:21-24 (vs. Crenshaw, *Old Testament Wisdom*, 35); 7:4-7; 11:1-6.

[79] Prov 25:28 falls outside of the proverb poem just treated. Though its form is congruent with the preceding Sayings, its psychological theme and imagery find no real point of attachment to them. It also lies outside of the careful rhetorical pattern established in vv 2-27. Perhaps this traditional Saying was inserted to make up a required tally in the Hezekiah Collection (Skehan *SIPW*, 17, 22, 44)?

6
Proverbs 26:1-12

Translation

v 1 Like snow in summer, like rain in harvest,
so glory for a fool is not fitting.
v 2 Like a bird in flitting, like a swallow in flying,
so a causeless curse does not alight.
v 3 A whip for the horse, a bridle for the ass,
a rod for the back of fools!

v 4 Do not answer a fool according to his folly,
lest you be like him yourself.
v 5 Do answer a fool according to his folly,
lest he be wise in his own eyes.

v 6 One cutting off his legs, one drinking violence,
one sending messages by the hand of a fool.
v 7 The calves of a lame man which hang (useless),
a proverb in the mouth of fools.
v 8 Like binding a stone in a sling
so is one giving glory to a fool.
v 9 A thorn which comes into (pierces?) the drunkard's hand,
a proverb in the mouth of fools.
v 10 An archer who wounds all,
one who hires a fool or passing drunkard.
v 11 As a dog returns to his vomit,
a fool repeats his folly.

v 12 Have you seen a man wise in his own eyes?
There is more hope for a fool than for him.[2]

---

[1] The LXX of 26:3b misreads *gwy* (nation) for MT *gw* (back) and translates *ethnei* (nation). A similar misreading appears in the LXX of Isaiah. R. C. Van Leeuwen, "Isa 14:12, *Hôlēš 'al gwym* and Gilgamesh XI, 6," *JBL* 99 (1980) 173-84.

[2] The translation of 26:1-12 is fairly straightforward, though vv 8a and 10 remain uncertain. V 9a: J. A. Emerton's suggestion ("Notes on Some Passages in the Book of

Like Prov 25:2-27, the present block of text comprises a proverb poem. In fact, as a literary composition, Prov 26:1-12 is more tightly unified than 25:2-27. In this chapter we hope to substantiate the foregoing claim, employing roughly the same procedures as in the previous chapter.

STRUCTURES

The boundaries of this poem (26:1-12) are obvious. Virtually every commentator has noticed that "fool" (*ksyl*) functions as a keyword in this section, while a new keyword, '*sl*, appears in vv 13-16. *Ksyl* appears in every verse of 26:1-12 but 2. Thus commentators puzzle about the intrusion of this verse into a collection otherwise dedicated to the fool. Closer examination, however, will show that v 2 is essential to the structure and theme of the poem.

The Form-Critical macrostructure of the passage is shown in Diagram 1 below. Prov 26:1-12 has a simpler and more homogeneous form critical structure than Prov 25:2-27. This impression is confirmed when one analyzes the Topic-Comment patterns present in Sayings of the poem (Diagram 2 below).

Diagram 1

Form-Critical (A/S and +/-) Structure of Prov 26:1-12

Verses	Form
	I Introduction
1	S: -/-
2	S: -/-
3	S: -/-
	Section II
4	A: P- ↛ R-
5	A: P+ ↛ R-

Proverbs," *JTS* 20 [1969] 211-214) here is not compelling: "A ring [= *ḥḥ* as in Exod 35:22] which has come into possession of a drunkard...." V 10: *rb* = "archer" with Gemser (95); *škr* = *škr* "drunk" with Syriac and Targum; so Gemser (95) who has noted that *škr* here is a catchword to v 9a. For the martial imagery of 26:10a, cf. Prov 25:18; 26:18. The thought of v 10b is like that of vv 6b, 8b. In v 10 society in general gets hurt, in v 6 the actor himself; v 8a is uncertain but compare v 1.

PROVERBS 26:1-12

                    Section III

        6-11   S: -/-

                    Section IV

        12   S: -/-

                 Diagram 2[3]

        Topic-Comment Analysis of 26:1-12 (Sayings)

          Level 1   *Level 2*

Verses Colon 1 Colon 2   Colon 1   Colon 2

1   FC =   T RT_1 = RT_2 = C = RT_3
2   FC =   T RT_1 = RT_2 = RT_3 = C
3   FC =   T RT_1 = RT_2 = RT_3 (non
                                                 oppositional)

6   FC =   T RT_1 = RT_2 = RT_3
7   FC =   T RT_1 = RT_2
8   FC =   T RT_1 = RT_2
9   FC =   T RT_1 = RT_2
10   FC =   T RT_1 = RT_2
11   FC =   T RT_1 = RT_2 (non
                                                 oppositional)

12   T =   C   [*r'yt*] RT_1 / C = T_2 > RT_1

In this poem, all the Sayings possess the identical T-C pattern on Level 1, except for the complex comparative Saying (v 12) which concludes it. The degree of variation manifested in these Sayings on Level 2 is less diverse than appears at first glance. For the patterns in vv 1, 2, 3, 6 are only slight variants, by chiasmus or ellipsis, of RT_1 = RT_2 = RT_3 = C. Thus the two diagrams above reveal a great deal of paradigmatic unity. However, within the homogeneity of the Sayings, there are some devices which both structure the poem and give it a dynamic such as Prov 25:2-27 as a whole does not possess.

---

[3] The new symbol in this diagram is RT which indicates a "Relational Topic," where the relation of two items composes one complex Topic.

These devices exploit the Level 1 or primary *Topics* of the Sayings which, except for v 12, invariably appear in the second cola of the Sayings (Diagram 2). With this structural pattern, it is not surprising that the keyword *ksyl* also appears in the second colon.[4] Analysis of the Level 1 Saying-Topics of Prov 26:1-12 shows that in every case they are not simple but complex, consisting of a *relation* (i.e., not just "rod" or "fool," but "a rod for the back of fools"). Moreover, each of these complex Topics (except in vv 3, 11) comprises an *oppositional* relation. That is, it consists of opposed or contradictory elements. *The poem as a whole is built up by exploiting these oppositions.* Thus, contrary to most commentators who assume that the theme or "Topic" of the poem is the "fool," *it must be stressed that the poem concerns not just the* ksyl, *but the* ksyl *in his various relations.* To explain the foregoing, closer analysis is needed.

The Sayings in vv 1-3 are congruent structurally, poetically, and thematically. At this stage we are mainly concerned with structure, though all aspects of the Sayings impinge upon one another. Prov 26:1 is a multi-descriptive Saying which is non-oppositional *as a whole* (FC = T). But it consists of three Relational Topics (= RT) which are internally oppositional, followed by a C which is congruent with the internally oppositional Topics: RT_1 (snow in Summer) = RT_2 (rain in harvest) = RT_3 (glory for a fool) = C (is not fitting). This pattern, minus the RTs, appears also in 25:3, 12. Before proceeding to 26:2, it bears repeating that our structural analysis must interact with other types of analysis. On a purely structural (T-C) level, one could not say that any one of the three Topics had precedence over the others. But the form and sense of the Saying (*k. . .k. . .kn*) make it clear that RT_3 with its predicate-Comment is the *core* of the Saying. Hence RT_1 and RT_2 are Figurative Comments upon the second colon.

Prov 26:2 displays the same basic structure and poetic form as v 1: three oppositional RTs receive one negative C: RT_1 (a bird while flitting, = RT_2 (a swallow while flying) = RT_3 (a causelss curse) = C (does not alight). At first glance, 26:2 seems to lack the oppositional, relational type of Topic found in v 1. A closer look, however, shows that the Topics are indeed oppositional, with one of the poles of the relation suppressed. Thus the opposition is implicit and the RTs elliptical.[5]

Prov 26:2 manages to produce this implicit opposition in RT_1 and RT_2 by means of "complementary distribution," a term used by linguists to refer

---

[4] In v 12 the primary Topic (one wise in his own eyes) appears in colon 1 but is resumed by a pronoun in the second colon where it is compared to a *ksyl*. In the Admonitions *ksyl* appears in the first cola and resumptively in the second cola in the form of a pronoun.

[5] As we noted in the preceding chapter with reference to 25:4-5, Sayings are often elliptical in one or another aspect, for artistic reasons (conciseness, form, word-music, the avoidance of monotony in Parallelism etc.) or to provoke thought on the part of the hearer. Cf. A. Berlin, "Grammatical Aspects of Biblical Parallelism," *HUCA* 50 (1979) 20, n. 8.

to linguistic phenomena in binary opposition which are mutually exclusive. Dundes has pointed out this phenomenon in proverbs like "When the cat's away, the mice do play," and "You can't have your cake and eat it too." Dundes notes the antiquity of this sort of opposition by referring to several Sumerian Sayings translated by Kramer:

> If he has meat, he has no lamb,
> if he has a lamb, he has no meat.
> Who builds like a lord, lives like a slave;
> who builds like a slave, lives like a lord.[6]

Only one of the options presented is possible at a time. Hence, where flitting (*nwd*) or flying (*'wp*) is present, anding or coming to rest somewhere is absent. A Sumerian proverb which uses the imagery of the flying sparrow for a different Topic (possessions) provides what is missing in Prov 26:2: "Possessions are sparrows in flight which can find *no place to alight*."[7] Similarly, where a curse is groundless (*hnm*), a legitimate "landing place" for the curse (i.e., a guilty person) is lacking (cf. Ps 109:3 [with object], 17-19, 28). Consequently, as in Prov 26:1, so in v 2 the three RTs are oppositional, with the second term of the relation suppressed, but implied by its complementary opposite. Every part of the Saying interacts to make the whole. The oppositional character of the first two Topics only becomes apparent by comparison with the "groundless curse" and the comment that it does not alight (*l' tb'*). A diagram may help make the oppositions clear.

Diagram 3

RT_1 flitting sparrow	≠	a place to land
RT_2 flying swallow	≠	a place to land
RT_3 causeless curse	≠	a place to land

Though 26:3 drops the simile form, its structure and message are like that of vv 1, 2. Once again we find an ellipsis. In this case the *Comment* is suppressed, though it is easily supplied: a rod for the back of fools is fitting or appropriate.[8] On a grammatical level this Comment need not be expressed since the structure of the nominal sentence as well as the imagery of the horse and ass imply it.

---

[6] "Proverb," 111.

[7] S. N. Kramer, *The Sumerians* (Chicago: University of Chicago, 1963) 225, my emphasis.

[8] Cf 26:1, *n'wh*. The LXX drops *n'wh* (*houtōs ouk estin aphroni timē*), concerning which Cornelius a Lapide (*Commentarii in Sacram Scripturam* vol. 3 [Paris: Pélagaud, 1854, original 1616] 755-56) comments, "*non est,* id est non convenit, non congruit, uti explicat auctor Caten. Graec.*"

Thus, in the structural categories of Dundes, we find in 26:1-3, an introduction comprising three identificational Sayings of identical structure (Diagram 2). Yet, if we look closely at the structure of the second colon in each verse, i.e., at the primary Topic of each Saying, we discover a certain progression of possible relations within the Topics. This progression by means of the opposition of negative (-) and positive (+) can be diagrammed as follows:

Diagram 4

	RELATIONAL TOPIC₃			COMMENT
	Object	Relation	Person	
v 1b	*kbwd* +	misfits	- *ksyl*	*l' n'wh*
v 2b	*qllh* -	misfits	+ innocent (implied)	*l' tb'*
v 3b	*šbṭ* -	befits	- *ksylym*	[*n'wh* (implied)]

In 26:1b something positive is (mis-) applied to someone negative, an inappropriate relation which evokes the negative Comment *l' n'wh*. In v 2b, the relation is reversed. Something bad is misapplied to someone good, again evoking a negative Comment. Though it does not refer to the *ksyl*, v 2 is far from being unnecessary in the poem. For it advances the "argument" by presenting the second of two possible inappropriate applications of good and bad. In the introductory scheme of the poem., v 2 is a logical complement to v 1.

It is only with 26:3 that we encounter a non-oppositional RT: the rod befits the fool. Something negative befits the negative. Logically speaking, there remains the possible fitting relation of positive to positive. The poem, however, does not present this option—both because it is obvious, and because its focus is on the negativity of folly.

Thus far the structure and progression of the poem's "Introduction." For the moment we pass over vv 4-5, since these are Admonitions, and continue with the Sayings in vv 6-11 which are closely connected with vv 1-3. The structural homogeneity of vv 6-11 on Levels 1 and 2 is patent in Diagram 2. As noted, all the RTs in these Sayings are oppositional, except for the last one (v 11). In vv 6-10, something good (*dbrym, mšl, kbwd,* employment) is related to someone negative, the "fool." This produces an oppositional RT such as first appeared in Section I, v 1. Hence, *Section III reveals the same pattern as Section I:* A block of oppositional RTs is finally resolved by a verse (3, 11) in which two negatives form a non-oppositional RT (rod/fool in v 3, fool/folly in v 11). While Section I (vv 1, 2) established the logical possibilities of opposition (Diagram 4), Section III (vv 6-10) is content to use just one pattern of opposition in its Topics: a good object "misfits" a bad person (*ksyl*). Thus, in structural terms, Section III is highly coherent.

Enough evidence has been put forward, I believe, to establish that this "roverb poem" works by means of oppositions both *between* Sayings (vv 1-3; cf. vv 4-5) as well as *within* Sayings to create larger literary units. But there is still more evidence for the use of opposition as a structuring device within this poem. In *every* Saying or Admonition, there is an Actant (= A) implicit or explicit, who acts negatively either *with respect to* a fool (= Relating Actant or RA) or *as* a fool (= Foolish Actant or FA). A possible exception is v 2 which nonetheless has a Negative Actant (= NA). Our point can be made by focusing upon the Level 1 Topic in each case (vv 1b, 2b, 3b, 6b, 7b, 8b, 9b, 10b, 11b; cf. 4a, 5a). Verse 1b implies someone acting, verbally or otherwise,[9] towards a fool. This implicit Actant becomes explicit in the *nwtn* of v 8b. Verse 2b implies someone acting (cursing) inappropriately—the sort of action characteristic of a fool.[10] Verse 3b implies someone acting towards (beating) a fool. Thus in 26:1-3, we have this pattern of Actants:

Diagram 5

v 1	Actant who *Relates* to a fool (= RA).
v 2	Negative Actant (= Fool) (= NA or FA).
v 3	Actant who relates to a fool (= RA)![11]

In Section III, the pattern of RA and FA in alternation most clearly appears, for here the actants are explicitly named. Section IV (v 12) completes the pattern. A diagram provides an overview:

Diagram 6

Verse	Actant
6b	RA (*šlḥ*)
7b	FA (speaking implicit)
8b	RA (*nwtn*)
9b	FA (speaking implicit)
10b	RA (*śkr*)
11b	FA (*šnh*)
12a	RA (*r'yt*)

---

[9] See G. B. Caird (*Language and Imagery*, 7-8, 20-25) on performative language.

[10] Compare the story of Nabal in 1 Samuel 25. While not strictly a curse, Nabal's response to David's men (vv 10, 11) is in opposition to the blessings of David and Abigail, and when his insult (*ḥrph*) comes back upon his own head, it functions very much like a curse (v 39). See also David's response to the cursing of Shimei in 2 Sam 16:12 and Prov 10:18 (*mws' dbh hw' ksyl*, "he who brings out an accusation is a fool").

[11] The Admonitions in vv 4-5 contain a similar pattern of relations: RA (4a)/ FA (4b); RA (5a)/ FA (5b). Prov 26:17-25 will be seen to employ a pattern of Negative Actants and Relating Actants.

Thus far, we have analysed two types of Structure to lay bare certain levels of coherence and arrangement in the poem, particularly in Sections I and III. A few comments on Sections II and IV are in order to complete this section of our study. Section II (vv 4, 5) is form critically a different genre, the Admonition. The two Admonitions are parallel, but contradictory. This contradition constitutes the heart of the poem and is the central problem around which the whole is constructed. For the moment it suffices to make two points. First, the Admonitions, like the rest of the poem, proceed by way of opposition in relation to the fool ("answer not/ answer"). Secondly, the placement of the Admonitions shows that the overall form-critical macro-structure of the poem is identical to that found in 25:2-27: an Introduction composed of Sayings is followed by a body of Admonitions and Sayings (repeated thrice in 25:2-27) which work out the concerns set out in the Introduction.

Section IV (26:12) belongs to a different class than the preceding eleven verses both structurally and form-critically. Here, for the first time, the poem uses a comparative structure where the contrasted elements are not congruent![12] The *r'yt* plays an important role in the Saying and poem. But in terms of proverbial structure it is irrelevant; it merely acts as a frame for the proverbial comparison.

One final point must be made concerning the role and place of Prov 26:12 in the structure of the poem. I have asserted that 26:12 constitutes the end of this section of Proverbs, as many others have done on the ground

---

[12] Dundes ("Structure of Proverbs," 110-110) places this type of Saying in the oppositional class. His analysis of this type is perfunctory and it is better to see it as an intermediate structure.

Place it between strict identification ("Business is business.") and strict opposition ("One swallow does not a summer make."). The relation between the compared elements is not "=" or "≠" but ">" (more or greater than). It is characteristic of this structural type that two Topics are compared with respect to one Comment. "Better late than never": Good = late (T_1) > never (T_2). Similarly, *ṭwbym hšnym mn h'ḥd*, "Two are better than one" (Qoh 4:9).

In Biblical studies, since W. Zimmerli's seminal study ("Zur Struktur der altestamentlichen Weisheit," *ZAW* 51 [1933] 192-95), this comparative form has been commonly called by the form-critical designation, "*Tôb-Spruch.*" This title is nonetheless inaccurate and misleading. The form is not limited to Sayings which employ its most common terms, *ṭwb...mn* (better...than). This is already clear in the Egyptian materials cited by Bryce (" 'Better'-Proverbs: An Historical and Structural Study," *Book of Seminar Papers* [ed. L. L. McGaughy; Missoula: SBL, 1972] 243-54, especially 345-46). In Egypt one finds beside the terms, *3h...r* (better...than) a wide variety of terms to introduce the comparison. Hence it is better to refer to this form as the Comparative Saying as Bryce himself sometimes does.

that it contains the last instance of *ksyl*. There is, however, one more corroborating reason for recognizing 26:12 as the deliberate conclusion of the whole.

In their studies of the "Better-Saying," both Bryce and G. S. Ogden,[13] pointed out that Comparative Sayings often have particular rhetorical functions within blocks of Saying material. In his study, Bryce demonstrated that in the Egyptian Instructions the Comparative Saying is characteristically used to open a literary unit or to close it in a summarizing, often paradoxical way. Bryce further asserted that "in the concatenated series of proverbs in the book of Proverbs more than a third of the *tôb-Sprüche* appear either at the beginning of a chapter (17:1; 19:1; 22:1) or toward the end (16:32; 25:24)."[14] If Bryce had not artificially restricted his study of the Comparative Saying to examples which employ *twb . . . mn*, he would have discovered that 26:12 and 16 are two prime examples of the rhetorical closure of a literary unit by means of the Comparative Saying.

G. S. Ogden's observations on the Comparative Saying in Qoheleth can be helpfully applied to Prov 26:12, 16. Ogden concurs with Bryce's delineation of "two definable rhetorical functions for the T-S—as either an introductory or concluding device." Ogden finally concludes that "the primary use of the T-S made by Qoheleth, apart from the extended poem in which the T-S is the central feature, is to express conclusions drawn from the observations recorded in the pericope."[15] In the "Sense" section below, I hope to show that this is precisely the case with Prov 26:12 and the parallel refrain in 26:16.

POETICS

The main unifying devices used by the poet in 26:1-12 are those of repetition—of sounds, words, and key phrases. He thus enriches the various words and phrases by placing them in varied contexts.[16] The main example of this device in this passage is, of course, the eleven-fold repetition of *ksyl*. This repetition produces both poetic and thematic unity. This unity of sound and sense is intensified throughout the poem by the frequent occurrence of

---

[13] Bryce, "'Better'-Proverbs;" Ogden, "The 'Better-' Proverb (Tob Spruch), Rhetorical Criticism, and Qoheleth," *JBL* 96 (1977) 489-505.

[14] "'Better'-Sayings," 346-48, 352.

[15] "The 'Better'- Proverb," 491, 497. In addition to sharing the comparative form, 26:12 and 16 are linked thematically by repetition of *hkm b'nyw*.

[16] S. Paul, "Amos 1:3-2:3: A Concatenous Literary Pattern," *JBL* 90 (1971) 397-403; and "Mnemonic Devices." J. Muilenburg, "A Study in Hebrew Rhetoric: Repetition and Style," *VTSup* 1 (1953) 97-111. N. H. Ridderbos, *Die Psalmen: Stilistische Verfahren und Aufbau mit besonderer Berücksichtigung von Ps 1-41* (BZAW 117; Berlin: de Gruyter, 1972) 19-46.

sounds which are cognate with the three consonants of *ksyl*.[17] These sounds provide a constant aural echo of *ksyl* since they so frequently appear in prominent places in the sound-structure of the poem: at the beginning of words (alliteration) and at places which pattern the meaning of the poem either formally (*k...k...kn* in vv 1, 2), or poetically (emphatic words at the start or end of lines and subsections: v 1 *kšlg*, v 3 *ksylym*), or thematically (*ksyl* itself). Though the statistic provided in the last note speaks adequately, the point is best made by the reader himself: when the poem is read out loud, the tune is constantly *ksyl*.

More obvious than the sound patterns which echo *ksyl* are the repetitions of entire phrases in the poem. These repetitions serve both to unify the poem and to place its thematic concerns under the illumination of several contexts. In 26:12 *ḥkm b'ynyw* repeats from v 5 (cf. the same phrase in the refrain of 26:13-16). The significance of this expression will appear below in "Sense." At this point we only note its presence in two important locations, the contradictory core of the poem (Section II, v 5) and the paradoxical conclusion of the whole (Section IV, v 12).

The most dramatic phrase repetition (with some variation of verb) appears in the contradictory Admonitions in vv 4a, 5a: *'l t'n/ 'nh ksyl k'wltw*. There is an echo of this phrase in the *ksyl... b'wltw* in v 11. Verses 1 and 8 share the phrase *lksyl kbwd*, while vv 7 and 9 share an entire second colon: *wmšl bpy ksylym*. These repetitions are not instances of a marred text as, for example, seems possible in 10:8b = 10b and 10:6b = 11b. All of the repetitions in 26:1-12 fit their context and must be granted their intensive and cohesive force (see below).

The poem also makes contiguous links between line-units, sometimes in quite striking ways, by means of imagery or verbal artistry. On this level of poetic functioning, units which at first glance seem quite unrelated are found to be connected. Surprising juxtaposition of seemingly dissimilar images, ideas, or sentiments is a common feature of ancient Hebrew poetry. It is left to the reader to discern the connection![18]

Several contiguous links of this sort appear in 26:1-12. In the light of the common tendency to deny v 2 its place in the poem, the devices which cement this verse in place are especially important. We have already noted its place in the pattern of oppositions in the "Introduction" (vv 1-3). Formally and aesthetically, 26:1, 2 are tightly linked. They are structurally and formally identical, even down to the *k...k...kn* simile pattern, which v 3 deletes. In

---

[17] By cognate sounds I refer to the sibilants *š, ś, s*, to the palatal *k*, the velar *q*, and the liquid *l*. These consonants, together with *ksyl* itself, constitute 40.3% of the non-vowel-letter consonants of the poem (112 of 278 consonants). For the theory and praxis of analysis of sound patterns in ancient Hebrew poetry, see L. Alonso-Schökel (*Das Alte Testament als literarisches Kunstwerk* [Köln: Bachem, 1971] 1-76).

[18] N. H. Ridderbos, *Die Psalmen*, 74, 75, 106, 107. Cf. Gemser, 8, 9.

my judgment, however, the strongest device to weld v 2 in place is a chiasmus built upon a punning opposition of the roots *kbd* (heavy) and *qll* (light).[19] This pattern appears in the Topic (second colon) of each verse:

Diagram 7

| v 1b | l' n'wh | kbwd |
| v 2b | qllt | l' tb' |

Besides linking the two verses, this chiasmus accentuates the two reversals of relations that we portrayed above in Diagrams 4 and 5. A further link for v 3 is the animal imagery common to vv 2 and 3 (the only other beast in the poem is the dog of v 11). This common feature is heightened by the rhyme which exists among *ṣpwr, drwr* and *ḥmwr*. In the last chapter we noted this type of linkage between 25:11-12, 13-14. Naturally, the imagery is not the only tie between these units. Yet it does add another bit of cement to the cohesive force of the poem.

Another playful connection exists on the level of imagery between 26:6 and 7. In v 6, the feet (*rglym*) have been "lost," in v 7, the lame man (another example of inability to walk) has only his calves (*sqym*) left to dangle. Of course this is perhaps to exaggerate the "logic" of the association between these verses. But what is certain is the connection between the inability to "walk" and the progression up the leg from *rglym* to *sqym*.[20]

The *ḥms šth* in 26:6 seems to anticipate the drinking theme which appears in vv 9-10. Yet what has passed unnoticed is that v 11 is also strongly bound to vv 9, 10 by the use of images traditionally associated with drinking (*škr*). The associative connections of the root *škr* in 26:9, 10 with v 11 are two. First, drunkenness produces vomit (*q'* or *qy'*). In fact, *every* time the noun "vomit" occurs in the OT, it is associated with *škr* (Isa 19:14; 28:8; Jer 48:26, *qy'*).[21] Secondly, we find that in Isa 56:10-12 the rulers are portrayed as dogs

---

[19] This punning opposition is frequent. M. Tsevat ("The Meaning of the Book of Job," *SAIW* 359) notes its presence in Job 40:2. C. L. Seow ("Hosea 14:10 and the Foolish People Motif," *CBQ* 44 [1982] 212-24) discusses the "parallel pair" *kbwd/qlwn* in Hos 4:7; Prov 3:35; Hab 2:16; and cites Prov 13:18. J. G. Williams ("The Power of Form," 51), following McKane, (428) discusses the play of heavy/light in connection with Prov 11:2 — where it does not occur. A partial list of further examples: Prov 12:9; Isa 3:5; 16:14; 23:9; 1 Sam 2:30; 6:5; 1 Kgs 12:4, 9-11,14. In Deut 27:16 *mqlh 'byw* is in implicit opposition to *kbd* in Deut 5:16 (so *BDB* 885b). The most extended development of this opposition known to me is in Ben Sira 3:6-12 (Hebrew Ms. A). Finally the opposition is found linking Sayings 29 (*yqyr*) and 30 (*qlyl*) in the Aramaic Proverbs of Ahiqar (*APA*, 98-99).

[20] See the order, knees, calves, foot in Deut 28:35. For another brilliant example of the use of commonly associated body parts to link two poetic lines, see the juxtaposition of *byd* and *brglym* in Isa 28:2, 3.

[21] Cf. the use of the verb *qwh* in Jer 25:27. Only in Prov 23:8 and 25:16 does the verb

(*klbym*) who are greedy for strong drink (*škr*). These associations produce a sharp commentary on the drunkard as a sub-type of the fool: as the fool repeats his folly, so the drunk, doglike, returns to his drink (cf. Prov 23:35; 20:1).

Our analysis of the imagery which links 26:9-11 together would suggest that on other levels as well, Section III (vv 6-11) might fall into two smaller parts of three verses each: IIIA (vv 6-8) and IIIB (vv 9-11). In fact this is the case. The poem uses verbal allusion and the alternation of forms to create these smaller groupings. Subsection IIIA ends with the simile form, *k. . .kn,* while Subsection IIIB employs the *k* and dispenses with the *kn* (but note the *k* of *klb*).[22] This use of the simile form brings these two verses into prominence within Section III. Their salience finds its reason in their position at the end of their respective three-verse Subsections, but more importantly in their function as liaison verses which link the various sections of the poem by verbal and thematic allusions. For only these two verses in Section III contain verbal connections with other sections. Verse 8 with its *k. . .kn* formula brings to mind vv 1, 2 of the Introduction. This formulaic echo is reinforced by the repetition of *kn. . .lksyl kbwd* in v 8. Finally, the opening word of v 8 (*ksrwr*) resonates with the opening word of v 2 (*kšpwr*). While the simile in v 8 alludes to Section I, the simile in v 11 alludes to the two verses of Section II (vv 4-5) by means of the *ksyl. . .b'wltw*. At the same time, the *wmšl bpy ksylym* in vv 7 and 9 links IIIA and IIIB.[23]

The foregoing account of structure and poetics is sufficient, I believe, to establish that the units in Prov 26:1-12 must not only be exegeted as independent Sayings and Admonitions, but must be interpreted *together* as parts of a unified conceptual and aesthetic whole. It is indeed probable that some of the units are not traditional, but were composed explicitly for this poem, though traditional material may underlie them.[24] To the task of explicating this proverb poem we now turn.

---

qy' (not the noun) appear without an associated *škr*. In these two cases, the vomiting is a result of eating beyond wise limits.

[22] This phenomenon of tightening the poetic means of expression also occurs in Section I (vv 1-3). Verse 2 drops a *w* and v 3 drops the *k. . .k. . .kn*, as well as the *w* in what is essentially the same form. In the case of v 3, the staccato terseness of expression mimics the imagery of beating.

[23] On the rhetorical technique just described, see S. Paul, "Amos 1:3."

[24] Cf. M. Lichtheim, "Observations on Papyrus Insinger," *SAL,* 287: "It does not appear likely that the more than five-hundred monostichic sayings of Ankhsheshonq were all of them genuine proverbs or widely known maxims; for a large proportion of them look like ad-hoc creations of the author-compiler." The similes of Proverbs 26 "are quite obviously engineered—they are literary products" (McKane, 593).

SENSE

The structural and poetic arguments just presented for the poem's unity must be born out in the interpretation of the whole. My exegetical argument in this section is that Prov 26:1-12 is a proverb poem or "treatise" on the "hermeneutics"[25] of wisdom. It may seem anachronistic to employ a currently fashionable term to describe an ancient text. But I believe that exegesis of Prov 26:1-12 will show it to be carefully constructed to force the reader to confront perennial problems which are properly labelled hermeneutic. That is, how are the proverbs to be used and applied in various, even contradictory life settings? The passage evinces a profound awareness of the interaction of the *proverbs*, which must be interpreted, and *life*, which must be interpreted in terms of the proverbs. This text forces the reader to reflect on the problem of *fittingness*, and on the limits of human understanding, especially of the other (the *ksyl*), of proverbs (*mšlym*, vv 7, 9), and of self (vv 4-5, 12).

Like the opening verses of 25:2-27, so the Introduction of 26:1-12 (vv 1-3) requires close attention, for it reveals the main themes of the poem. Prov 26:1 presupposes the common ANE correlation between cosmic and social order, in this case a world in disorder. The term in v 1 which especially illuminates the idea of order operative here and in the entire poem (vv 1-12) is *n'wh*, "comely, seemly" (*BDB*). The two-fold sense of "comely" and "seemly" find their semantic commonality in the notion of *fittingness* or harmony with some implicit standard or norm. The scope of fittingness ranges from the cosmic to the trivial matters of daily action and domestic relations, all of which demand fitting responses in word or deed. Ultimately that is fitting which corresponds to the divinely instituted order of things. "Not fitting" is that which upsets the order of nature and society (Prov 17:7; 19:10; 26:1).[26] The praise of God is "fitting" (Pss 33:1; 93:5; 147:1) for man. The shapes and contours which "befit" a woman's face and body and make her "comely" or beautiful are "fitting" (*n'wh*; Cant 1:5; 2:14; 4:3; 6:4). *N'wh* is not the order of creation (including society) itself.[27] Rather, *n'wh* seems to designate states of

---

[25] I mean "hermeneutics" in the broad sense developed by H. G. Gadamer (*Wahrheit und Methode* [Tübingen: J. C. Mohr-Siebeck, 1960]): Hermeneutics is the process of undrstanding not only texts but also people, situations, events etc.

[26] To 26:1, compare 1 Sam 12:16-18: no human is "fit" to take Yahweh's place as king. Murphy (*WL*, 66) has recently recognized the *l' n'wh* form in Proverbs as a relative of the *l' twb* form. The *l' n'wh* form is infrequent, occurring only in Prov 17:7; 19:10; 26:1 and Sir 10:18; 14:3; 15:9; 41:16. Murphy does not cite the Ben Sirah texts. *L' twb* appears in Prov 17:26; 18:5; 19:2; 20:23; 25:27; 28:21; this form does not occur in Qoheleth or Ben Sirah (cf. *bl twb* in Prov 24:23 and *l' yhkm* in 20:1). The three occurrences of *l' n'wh* in Proverbs share a common *topos:* the social hierarchy of rulers and officers or subordinates which suffers inversion.

[27] In Hebrew the main designation for cosmic order, corresponding to Egyptian *maat*, is *sdq*. So H. H. Schmid, *Gerechtigkeit*, 60-61. Of course one must take into account the

affairs which are in harmony with the creational standards which hold for them. Thus things may or may not be *n'wh;* they may or may not correspond to the order which (normally) holds for them. Incidentally, this "order" is not an abstract, static Platonic world of eternal and immutable ideas. It includes the aspects of time and place, of contingent situation and context. Thus while what is *n'wh* always befits the order which holds for it, this order itself is no simple thing. It needs to be discerned by the wise.[28]

Against this background we can be fairly succinct in our treatment of 26:1. The Saying correlates disorder in the natural world with disorder in the social world. Things that are in themselves good are misapplied where they are not fitting. As our analysis of the structure of 26:1-12 has shown, the idea of fittingness is the poem's central concern. This concern is essentially a hermeneutical one. Wisdom, to a very large extent, is a matter of interpreting people, events, situations, actions in relation to norms for existence.

---

divergence of Egyptian and Hebrew world views. Schmid (67) follows A. Jepsen's ("צדק und צדקה im Alten Testament," *Gottes Wort und Gottes Land, H. W. Hertzberg . . . dargebracht* [H. Graf Reventlow ed.; Göttingen, 1965] 80) distinction of *sdq* and *sdqh:*

> Das Substantiv צדק bezeichnet ursprünglich die kosmische Ordnung, die sich in Weisheit, Recht usf. konkretisiert und vom König im Rahmen des Irdischen gewährleistet wird, צדקה dementsprechend das in diesem Horizont ordnungsgemässe oder sogar ordnungsschaffende Verhalten oder Handeln.

If this is correct, then *n'wh* and *sdqh* stand in a similar relation to world order (*sdq*): though each has peculiar connotations, they both denote what is in harmony with order.

[28] Cf Kovacs, "Structural-Constraints," 455, 56. The Egyptian term *aḥ* seems to correspond significantly to Hebrew *n'wh.* Like *n'wh, aḥ* includes the notions of comeliness and seemliness. R. O. Faulkner defines *aḥ* as "glorious, splendid," and "beneficial, useful, profitable," and *aḥt* as "what is good, profitable, useful" (*A Concise Dictionary of Middle Egyptian,* [Oxford: Oxford University, 1962] 4). But in discussing Ptahotep 5, H. Frankfort puts the term in a profounder context:

> 'Maat is good and its worth is lasting.' The excellence of the official consisted in his agreement with Maat—justice, truth. . . . The word *akh,* which is translated 'to be good' or 'to be of advantage,' possesses, according to the dictionary, an *'unklare verschwommene Bedeutung.'* But this impression of an obscure and fluid meaning is often caused, not by any lack of clarity in the original, but by the incompatibility of ancient and modern conceptions. Such a discrepancy exists in the case of Maat . . . we should have to render it, at one and the same time, as a social, an ethical, and a cosmological conception. *Akh* seems to be untranslatable for similar reasons; it may mean 'to be agreeable,' 'to be advantageous,' but also 'to be effective, splendid, sacred, transfigured'—*meanings which find their common root in the concept of harmony with the divine order of the universe.*

(*Ancient Egyptian Religion,* 63, 64, my emphasis). H. Gese (*Lehre und Wirklichkeit in der alten Weisheit,* 14, n. 4) follows Frankfort's analysis.

Prov 26:1 judges that glory (*kbwd*) does not befit the fool. *Kbwd* here functions as a catch-word to the *kbd* which began and concluded the previous poem (25:2-27). Thus the function of 26:1-12 in relation to 25:2-27 is to elaborate the wisdom requisite for success in the earlier poem's world with its hierarchy of glory and its conflict of persons. One must have self-knowledge (26:12) in order to avoid tactlessly exalting himself in the presence of the king (25:6-7; cf. 27:2). In dealing with peers (*r'ym*), one must know who is good and who is bad (cf. 17:17-18!) and who is foolish and who wise (26:1-12, *passim;* 25:8, 9, 17, 18). One must not be a fool in speech (26:7, 9; 25:11, 12). A superior must be astute in selecting a servant for the delicate mission of envoy (26:6; 25:13, 25), or for other work (26:10).

Glory (*kbwd*) designates one's place in society.[29] A fool is one who has not the qualifications for public position, power, respect, and responsibility. When such *kbwd* is given to the fool, the consequences are disastrous; the fool harms himself and society by the misuse of his office, just as rain in harvest damages the crop. Such a person is "out of place" and "out of order." The misapplication of public position and power (*kbwd*) is most serious when fools are given the glory of ruling (Qoh 4:13; 10: 5-7; cf. Prov 29:2, 12),[30] but the principle involved is universally applicable.[31] Whenever a fool is trusted with responsibilities beyond his capabilities, harm ensues.

It is the evaluation "not fitting" that raises the hermeneutical problem of judgment and application; for as 26:8 makes plain, someone must "give" the *kbwd* to a fool. Thus this person has either acted perversely or angrily (cf. note 30) or, more to the point, has *misinterpreted* the person and situation in question. Prov 26:1 makes an evaluation of fittingness (negatively formulated) which holds for wise behavior relative to others; v 8 shows that people fail to

---

[29] C. Westermann, *THAT* 1, col. 798. God (Mal 1:6), kings (Ps 21:6), rulers (Gen 45:13), as well as ordinary men and women have a *kbwd* that is proper to them (Prov 3:35; 11:16; 15:33; 18:12; 20:3; 27:18; 29:23; Sir 10:23-24, 27-31; Ps 4:3 etc.). Cf. the Akkadian "Counsels of Wisdom" (*BWL* 102-103, line 66): "Do not honour a slave girl in your house" (*amta ina bīti e tu-kab-bit*). "This whole concept of honour [*kbwd*] can be understood only from the point of view of a religiously based pattern of society. . . . The man who is without honour is the fool (Prov. 26.1, 8), the 'disorderly' man who . . . is unable to adapt himself to that order which is imposed on all men" (von Rad, *WII* 83).

[30] When Pre is angry with a land he makes justice (*maat*) cease in it. . . .
When Pre is angry with a land he makes great its humble people and humbles its great people.
When Pre is angry with a land he sets the fools over the wise.
When Pre is angry with a land he orders its ruler to mistreat its people.
When Pre is angry with a land he appoints its scribe to rule it.
When Pre is angry with a land he appoints its washerman as chief of police.
Ankhsheshonq 5.1 in Lichtheim, *AEL* 3 (1980) 163-64.

[31] Cf. the modern "Peter Principle:" A man is promoted to his level of incompetence.

fulfill this norm. A concrete example of the issues involved in 26:1 is the folly of Rehoboam who gave the *kbwd* of counselor to the young men instead of the elders to whom it was due (1 Kgs 12:1-20; cf. Prov 20:29; 16:31).[32]

As the analysis of structure and poetics has shown, Prov 26:2 is intimately tied to its textual surround. As good can be unfittingly given to a bad man (v 1), so evil can be given to a good man (v 2).[33] The main function of verse 2 seems to further the logic of oppositions with regard to fittingness, as shown above. Moreover, there is perhaps an implicit reminder that Yahweh sets limits to unfitting human activity, for he is the understood guarantor of the curse.[34] Here the freedom of God to set limits to the action of man is presupposed.[35]

Finally, in v 3, we are told what is fitting for the fool: a rod for his back. Both the imagery and message of this verse are commonplace. The fool needs a rod because he will not listen (17:10 10:13; 19:29; 18:6; 27:22; Ps 32:9; Sir 33:24).[36]

Thus the dialectic of oppositions in 26:1-3 arrives at a widely accepted conclusion. It perfectly introduces the *first* of the two Admonitions which follow: since the fool will not listen (the point of v 3), do not answer him on his terms (v 4).[37] This Admonition at one and the same time utters a wisdom cliché (v 4a) and *begins* to pull the rug from under the feet of the smug, self-assured sage (v 4b) — a rug pulling completed with a vicious yank in v 5a! The distinction between fool and wiseman is not absolute; precisely when one has "mastered" the conventional wisdom (as in 26:3, 4), he is in danger of becoming foolish. For

---

[32] Gray hair in Prov 16:31; 20:29 is wisdom. A. Caquot, "Israelite Perceptions of Wisdom and Strength in the Light of the Ras Shamra Texts," *IW*, 27.

[33] Ironically, even the praise of God by a bad man is not fitting: *l' n'th tlhlh bpy rš'* (Sir 15:9 [Ms. A]; cf. Prov 15:8; 21:27).

[34] For the imagery of 26:2, compare the divinely ordained flying curse which comes to is proper object (*b'h 'l*) in Zech 5:1-4. Contrary to some of the older interpretations of curse in the OT, it does not have a "magical" force inherent in itself, but depends upon the deity for effectiveness. So O. Keel (*Symbolism of the Biblical World*, 96-97) with ANE references. J. W. Rogerson (*Anthropology*, 46-53) provides a corrective to older theories of magic which still influence OT studies. See also J. Scharbart (*TDOT* II, 303) and C. A. Keller (*THAT* 2, 646). Even McKane admits the "religious" character of v 2 (594, 600: "the theological point"). Cf. Aramaic Ahiqar, lines 123-124 in *APA*.

[35] On Yahweh as the "limit" of human wisdom and action see von Rad (*WII*, 97-110) and J. J. Collins ("Proverbial Wisdom," 10-12). For this problem in Egypt see H. Brunner, "Der freie Wille Gottes in der aegyptischen Weisheit," *SPOA*, 103-120.

[36] "Another's instruction does not enter the heart of a fool; what is in his heart is in his heart" (Ankhsheshonq 27:10; *AEL* III, 180). "Thoth has placed the stick on earth in order to teach the fool by it" (P Insinger 9:6; cf. 14:6-7, 11, 16; *AEL* III, 192, 196). "Thou [Ishtar] didst love the horse, magnificent in battle. (Yet) thou hast decreed for him the whip, the spur, and the thong" (Gilgamesh VI, 153-54; A. Heidel, *The Gilgamesh Epic and Old Testament Parallels* [Chicago: University of Chicago, 1963] 51).

[37] Note how the Syriac tried to resolve the "contradiction" by modifying v 5a: "Answer a fool according to your wisdom. . . ."

if v 4 tells you *not* to answer the fool to avoid becoming one yourself, v 5 insists that there may be a time when higher wisdom and different circumstances dictate the abrogation of conventional wisdom (v 4). So, to avoid folly, do you or do you not address a fool according to his folly?[38]

We must note that these Admonitions contain absolutely no criteria by which to decide the matter. Here wisdom, the knowledge of what is fitting, is pushed to its limits: the wise man must evaluate the fool and the situation to rightly decide his course of action, but the Admonitions themselves leave him devoid of guidance. The juxtapositions of the Admonitory pair both makes clear what wisdom requires (knowledge of what is fitting) and that humans often cannot attain to that knowledge.[39]

Thus Prov 26:4-5 takes the problem of fittingness (vv 1-3), which the wise man is ordinarily expected to master, and formulates it in a contradictory way which exposes the *limits* of wisdom. Anyone who thinks he has a infallible answer to the dilemma is himself "wise in his own eyes." This last phrase must be taken up again (v 12).[40]

Having put the problem in an insoluble form (vv 4-5), the poet turns to several life situations where evaluative judgments must be made:

---

[38] The most important ANE parallel to Prov 26:4-5 is the Akkadian "Dialogue of Pessimism" with its *sic et non*. "The Dialogue of Pessimism emerges as an intellectual manifesto of the kaleidoscopic ideal of wisdom. Its scope is to know the pro and con of every aspect of reality . . ." (G. Buccellati, "Tre Saggi Sulla Sapienza Mesopotamica-II. Il Dialogo del Pessimismo: La Scienza degli Opposti come Ideale Sapienziale," *OA* 11 [1972] 94, my translation). It is this humanly unattainable ideal of wisdom which leads in Mesopotamia to the pessimism of the dialogue and in Israel to the warning, do not be "wise in your own eyes." The tacit converse of this last phrase is "fear the LORD" (Prov 3:7).

[39] "The wise man is not a perfect man, because one or another of his virtues may fail him under certain conditions. . . . The wise man's salvation lies in his piety, for it enables him to 'consult with the god'. . . . For instance, his 'trust' (*nḥt*) in God makes him 'patient' (*'w-ḥ3.t*) in 'misfortune' (*stb*). Conversely, the 'arrogance' of the fool prevents him from turning to God and leads him into 'crime' (*btw*) and 'evil-doing' (*why*)" (Lichtheim, "Observations," 292).

[40] As we shall argue at the conclusion of this section, Yahweh's wisdom is in implicit contrast to the limited wisdom of man. The shadow of Prov 25:2 would seem also to impinge on 26:1-12. He is the hidden limiter and judge of human competence. Prov 16:1, 2 make explicit this tacit opposition. In 26:4-5, the dilemma is "what is the right response (*'nh*) to a fool"; Prov 16:1 declares, "The plans of the mind belong to man, but the answer (*m'nh*) of the tongue is from the LORD." In 26:5, 12, a man is *ḥkm b'ynyw*, in 16:2, "All the ways of a man are pure in his own eyes (*zk b'ynyw*), but the LORD weighs the spirit" (cf. 21:2).

the sending of an envoy (v 6)
the speaking of a proverb (vv 7, 9)
the giving of *kbwd* (vv 1, 8)
the hiring of workers (v 10).[41]

In this subsection, vv 7, 9 give an explicitly hermeneutic coloring to the whole. In the close proximity of the contradictory *mšlym* of vv 4-5, the reader of vv 7, 9 is forced to see that knowledge of a stock of proverbs does not ensure their wise application.[42] Verse 11 prepares the reader for v 12 in the same way v 3 prepares for v 4. The hopeless character of the fool is portrayed in his doglike return to folly. But v 12 paradoxically presents a folly even more hopeless: the man "wise in his own eyes."

Verse 12 is in a class by itself (= Section IV) in terms of form and structure, and because it acts as a conclusion and refrain to the entire poem. It also seems to sum up the pattern of AR and AF which appeared in diagram 6 above. The reader is the AR in the Saying ("Have *you* seen . . .") just as he is in the Admonitions (vv 4, 5). His *action* is his visual and mental perception of the irremediable fool, "one wise in his own eyes" (AF). This idiomatic phrase[43] provides an ironic

---

[41] It is not necessary for our argument—which rests largely on the other grounds—to solve all the difficulties which attend the imagery and text of the FCs in vv 6, 8, 10. Even where not clear in very detail, the negative character and general import of the images is plain. See note 2 above.

[42] There is he who has not been taught,
yet he knows how to instruct another.
There is he who knows the instruction,
yet he does not know how to live by it.
(P. Insinger 9:16-17; *AEL* III, 192). Cf. Sir 21:20; 15:9-10.

[43] The idiom *X b'yny P* ("X in the eyes of P") is used in Hebrew to denote a person's subjective evaluation of things in implicit, paradigmatic opposition to some *other's* evaluation (*X b'yny Q*). The "X" slot in the idiom can be filled by various evaluative adjectives (e. g. *twb, yšr, hkm, r', špl, gdwl, zk*) or their verbal equivalents. The implicit oppositum (the P/Q slot) must always be taken into account in reading the idiom. This "other" can sometimes be other people (Prov 12:15; 28:11), but most importantly it is some higher judge of what is right or wise. When in Judges each man does *hyšr b'ynyw* (17:6; 21:25), it is because there is no king who ensures that what is right in *his* eyes is done. The human king is in turn accountable to the divine king (cf. 1 Kgs 11:33, 38; Prov 25:2-3). The folly of being wise in one's own eyes is parallel to the notion of relying on one's own heart as seen in the Proverb Pair in 28:25b-26 and in 3:5, 7:
He who trusts in the LORD (*bwṭḥ 'l yhwh*) will be enriched.
He who trusts in his own mind (*bwṭḥ blbw*) is a fool (*ksyl*);
but he who walks in wisdom will be delivered (28:25b-26).
Trust in the Lord (*bṭḥ 'l yhwh*) with all your heart,
and do not rely on your own insight. . . .
Be not wise in your own eyes;
fear the Lord, and turn from evil (3:5, 7).

dialectic in the Saying. As the viewer looks at the other, the other is himself engaged in a fatal act of self-perception (=AF). It is finally the failure of self-knowledge that defines the fool. Because such a person does not know himself, he is prone to seeking *kbwd* which is beyond his limits (cf. chapter 25 and 26:1, 8). Whatever a man's rank, and no matter how wise he may be, he is always in danger of transgressing the limits of the "fitting," of assuming mastery of demesnes beyond his control and so becoming "wise in his own eyes." Even the king is limited by God (25:2; 21:1)! Prov 26:12 is thus a dangerous Saying, in the same way that Nathan's parable to David after the death of Uriah is dangerous (2 Sam 12:1-4). Even as "you" look down upon the fool whose self-perception is awry, you yourself may be "wise in your own eyes" (cf. vv 4b, 5b).

We may sum up the hermeneutical concerns of this passage as follows. First, implicitly portrayed in every verse is the universal fact of interpretation—of people, proverbs, things, events, situations, and times. Secondly, it is by inescapable acts of interpretation that a man defines himself as wise or foolish. Humanity, which has no lack of fools, forces a person to judge and act wisely over against the fool—or to be counted one with him (26:4). Thirdly, the *sine qua non* of wise judgment is a sense of fittingness, of how the *realia* of life are good only when properly applied. That is, the wise person perceives the larger, tacit context of norms and circumstances in terms of which persons, a saying (vv 7, 9), a word (v 2b), a rod (v 3) a message (v 6), status (v 1, 8), or a job (v 10b) are fitting.[44] Prov 26:1-12 is also profoundly aware that the relationships in which

---

McKane (*Prophets and Wise Men* 66; Commentary, 17-18) attempts to distinguish between a secular (Prov 26:5, 12, 16; 28:11) and a religious usage (Prov 3:7; Isa 5:21) of *hkm bʿynyw*. But McKane imposes a modern dichotomy on the texts which is foreign to them. For example, the folly of a rich man's being "wise in his own eyes" (28:11) is exposed in the Proverb Pair 18:10-11:
The name of the LORD is a strong (ʿz) tower;
The righteous man runs into it and is safe (wnśgb).
A rich man's wealth is his strong (ʿzw) city,
and like a high (nśgbh) wall in his imagination (RSV marg.).

[44] Without proper appreciation of propriety or fittingness, ancient wisdom cannot be understood. See Prov 25:20 discussed in the preceding chapter. Kovacs, "Structural," 302, 323, 455-56, 542. G. von Rad's discussion of "The Doctrine of the Proper Time," (*WII*, 138-143; cf. Schmid, *WGW*, 23-24, 33-34) focuses upon only one aspect of the larger problem of fittingness. Nonetheless, von Rad's work as a whole shows awareness of man's need to *fit into* or harmonize with the cosmic order (78).

Among the multitude of propriety sayings in the ANE, Ankhsheshonq has some that are very sharp:

> There is no good deed except a good deed which you have done for him who has need of it (15:6).
> If you are sent to get chaff and you find wheat, do not buy [it] (15:21).
> If you trade in straw when it is wanted, you should not go around with wheat (15:22; *AEL* III, 171).

humans stand provide the context for judging others and ourselves as wise or foolish, and our words, deeds, and thoughts as fitting or unfitting.[45] Finally, Prov 26:1-12 is conscious of the limits of human wisdom (vv 4-5, 12). The context of understanding is ultimately beyond the grasp of man. For its scope is reality in its expanse and in its hiddenness (25:2-3). And if man were able to grasp it all, it is yet beyond his power to control. God and world are the ultimate context of meaning and limit of wisdom (21:30-31).[46]

---

[45] Peter Seitel "Proverbs: a Social Use of Metaphor," *Genre* 2 [1969] 143-161; reprinted in W. Mieder and A. Dundes, eds., *The Wisdom of Many* [New York and London: Garland, 1981 122-139; and in Dan Ben-Amos, *Folklore Genres* [Austin and London: University of Texas, 1976] 125-143) has provided a fundamental analysis of the relation of the proverb to the social situation or personal context in which the meaning of a proverb is actualized.

[46] Kovacs, "Structural," 456-57.

7
Proverbs 26:13-16

Translation

v 13 A sluggard says, "There's a great cat on the street, a lion in the squares."

v 14 The door turns on its hinge,
and the sluggard on his bed.

v 15 The sluggard buries his hand in the bowl,
he is too weary[1] to return it to his mouth.

v 16 The sluggard is wiser in his own eyes
than seven[2] who return a judicious answer.[3]

Prov 26:13-16 is a poem focusing on the sluggard (*'ṣl*). It is one of three such poems in the book (cf. 6:6-11; 24:30-34) in addition to many single proverbs which employ the term *'ṣl* or treat the theme.[4] The sluggard-poems in chapters 6 and 24 share a quasi-narrative style and an identical refrain of two lines (6:10-11 = 24:33-34). Unlike the two other poems, 26:13-16 tells no story. Rather it achieves its unity mainly in the manner of 26:1-12; that is, by the repetition in each line of the keyword (*ksyl*, *'ṣl*). Moreover, 26:16 forms a refrain with 26:12 formally by its comparative structure and thematically by its repetition of *ḥkm*

---

[1] R. Gordis (*The Book of Job: Commentary, New Translation, Special Studies* [New York: Jewish Theological Seminary of America, 1978] 46) argues that *l'h* always means "be unable." Cf. *HALAT* (487) on the hiphil.

[2] Is there here an echo of the tradition of the "seven sages"? E. Reiner, "The Etiological Myth of the 'Seven Sages,'" *Or* 30 (1961) 1-11.

[3] For *hšyb t'm*, cf. *dny'l htyb 't' wt'm l'rywk* "Daniel replied with counsel and discretion to Arioch ..." (Dan 2:14). The semantic range of *t'm* is quite wide, including "decree" (Jon 3:7) and in the Aramaic and Akkadian cognates, the meaning "instruction." Cf. P. E. Dion, "La Lettre Araméenne Pass-Partout et ses sous-espèces," *RB* 89 (1982) 528-575, 558, No. 10 and n. 171.

[4] *'ṣl* (noun) occurs fourteen times in Proverbs (6:6, 9; 10:26; 13:4; 15:19; 19:24; 20:4; 21:25; 22:13; 24:30; 26:13, 14, 15, 16). Prov 19:24//26:15 and 22:13//26:13 with slight variations. *'ṣlh* appears once (Prov 19:15); *'ṣlwt* once (31:27) and *'ṣltym* in Qoh 10:18. The verb *'ṣl* occurs in Judg 18:9.

b'ynyw. Though 26:13-16 is not as complex in its organisation as 26:1-12 (it is after all only four lines long), these features suggest it was compiled by the same hand as 26:1-12.

The rationale for this small *'ṣl* poem in the larger collection 25-27 is not hard to seek. Laziness can thwart talent, position, wealth, and power. Laziness is thus a particularly pernicious form of folly (26:12).[5] These Sayings are of universal applicability, but in the context of 25:1-27 and 26:1-12, we may assume that their primary address is to young men of the uppermost class. Along with 26:1-12, the Sayings warn young courtiers of obstacles to legitimate success and *kbwd*—things which the offspring of the elite sometimes assume come with their birthright.

STRUCTURE

The brevity of this section entails that the poetic means required to bind the Sayings together need not be elaborate (contrast 25:23-27). Form-critically, we have a solid block of Sayings without Admonitions. All the Sayings are negative. This compares with the homogeneity of Sayings in 26:1-12.

Diagram 1

Form-critical (A/S and +/-) Structure of Prov 26:13-16

Verses	Form
13-16	S: -/-

The T-C structure of 26:13-16, on the other hand, is marvelously varied—in contrast to 26:1-12 and 25:2-27 which only vary at beginnings or ends of sections. The obvious unity of 26:13-16 on form-critical and thematic grounds means that the poet is free to vary his T-C structures, since uniformity on this level is not needed to reinforce the unity of the disparate Sayings.

Diagram 2

T-C Analysis of 26:13-16

Verses	Level 1		Level 2	
	Colon 1	Colon 2	Colon 1	Colon 2
13	See Diagram 3			
14	FC = T		T_1 = C = T_2 = C (modified)	
15	T = C		T = C_1 = [T] = C_2	
16	C = T_1 > T_2			

[5] The sluggard needs wisdom (6:6); he does not obey the order of the seasons (20:4; 6:6) in contrast to the wise son (10:4-5); he rejects reality (22:13; 26:13). In 26:12, 16 and 26:6; 10:26, *ksyl* and *'ṣl* occupy identical semantic slots.

The T-C structure of Prov 26:13 is so complex that it is best presented in the form of a "phrase marker" tree:

Diagram 3

T-C Analysis of Prov 26:13

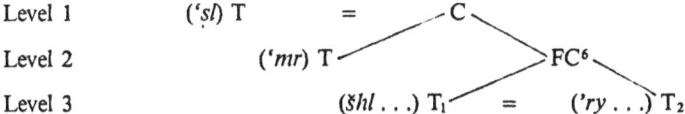

Level 1   ('sl) T   =   C
Level 2   ('mr) T   FC⁶
Level 3   (šhl ...) T₁   =   ('ry ...) T₂

Prov 26:13, like 26:12, is a *Frame Saying*. That is, it employs a Saying within a Saying (cf. 20:9, 14; 22:29). In the type of Frame Saying found in 26:12, 13 contrast 20:14), the Frame element (r'yt, 'mr 'sl) has an important role in the sense of the Saying, and can be incorporated into the T-C analysis: The sluggard (T) = says there is a ... (C). In the case of 26:12, however, we put the Frame Element [r'yt] in brackets since the remainder was able to function as an independent Saying. But in v 13, each part is indispensable to the working of the whole. On Level 3, we find a marvelously elliptical subsaying of the form T₁ = T₂: the reader, given the knowledge that a sluggard is speaking, is left to surmise the point of "a lion in the street." The unstated Comment on this Level is supplied by the parallel Saying in 22:13, ['mr 'sl]: 'ry bḥws (T) = btwk rḥbwt 'rṣḥ (C), "The fool says, 'There is a lion outside, I'll be killed in the streets.' "

Verse 14 reverts to the T-C pattern of choice in 25:2-27 and 26:1-12. Verse 16 uses the comparative form which also concludes 26:1-12 (cf. 25:24). The comparison in 26:16 (where *ḥkm* is the comment) is utterly ironic since it is seen through the eyes of the sluggard.

POETICS

Because of its relative brevity and the powerful binding force of the repeated *'sl*, we may expect the repertoire of unifying poetic devices in 26:13-16 to be modest. There are nonetheless a number which give delight and further the ironic mockery of sloth in the poem. One such connective device is the repetition of *šwb* hiphil) in vv 15, 16. The connection created is reinforced by the play on *ṭmn*, "He buries," and *ṭ'm*, "taste," in the same two lines. Thus a mocking irony is produced: Because the sluggard buries (*ṭmn*) his hand, he "cannot even taste food because he is too lazy to put food into his mouth (v 15); yet he claims a 'taste' (*ṭ'm*) for wisdom more acute than 'the seven (great sages)' (v 16)."⁷

---

⁶ It may be helpful to recall that since the direct discourse functions as a semantic modifier of the verb ('mr), it relates to the verb as C to T.

⁷ A. R. Ceresko, private communication. I am here indebted to Professor Ceresko for several observations on the ironic imagery of the Poem.

There are further ironies on the level of imagery. Basic to these is the continuity of place: Having made his excuse not to go out of the house (v 13), the sluggard doesn't even get out of bed (v 14). He turns on his bed like a door, but won't open the door—for fear of a cat. Verses 15 and 16 find him still at home, stuck to his table and feeling complacently wise.

SENSE

These Sayings are quite straightforward and need little exegesis. They portray the obvious by means of wonderfully unobvious images: lion in the street, a door on the hinge, hand in the dish. The sluggard is not wise because he refuses to face up to reality and its demands: the world order requires work in season (10:4-5) for survival and success. Prov 26:16 sums up the absurdity of laziness by its claim that the sluggard thinks himself wise.

8
Proverbs 26:17-28

Translation

v 17 One grabbing the ears of a passing dog,¹
       one mingling in a quarrel not his own.
v 18 Like a madman shooting missiles, arrows, and death,
v 19 so is a man who deceives his neighbour
       and says, "Wasn't I just joking?"

v 20 By lack of wood the fire fails,
       without a slanderer² the quarrel ceases.
v 21 Charcoal for coals, wood for fire,
       and a quarreler for kindling conflict.
v 22 Words of a slanderer are like tasty bits,
       they too go down to the "chambers" of the belly.

v 23 Impure silver³ glazed on clay,
       burning⁴ lips and a wicked heart.

---

¹ Read, with many commentators, *'br* as modifying *klb*.

² *Nrgn* is often translated "backbiter" (cf. *BDB* 920), but a survey of the instances of the verb *rgn* (Deut 1:27; Isa 29:24; Pss 106:25; Prov 16:28; 18:8 [= 26:22]; 26:20) suggests that more is connoted than mere malicious gossip (though this is not excluded). *Rgn* connotes the attempt, by verbal calumny, to wrongfully attack the rights, reputation, or authority of another to secure one's own will. From Isa 29:24 it appears that the subject of this verb lacks wisdom (*bynh, lqh*).

³ The unusual phrase *ksp sygym* ("silver of dross")in 26:23 must be understood in some such sense: what seems to be silver is actually impure. So Toy (479). Cf. R. L. Harris, "A Mention of Pottery Glazing in Proverbs," *JAOS* 60 (1940) 268-69. The point is simply that what appears as silver is corrupt and covers what is base. The famous suggestion of H. L. Ginsberg and W. F. Albright, now almost universally accepted by scholars, that *ksp sygym* is related to Ugaritic *spsg* ("glaze") has recently been dealt a death blow by M. Dietrich and O. Loretz ("Die angebliche Ug.—He. Parallele SPSG // SPS(J)G(JM)," *UF* 8 (1976) 37-40.

⁴ Though the emendation *hlqym*, suggested by the LXX and preferred by most commentators, is tempting, the MT *lectio difficilior, dlqym,* is to be read. The imagery of "fiery lips" finds its parallel in the proverb Pair (cf. McKane, 493-494) or triplet (cf. Gemser 73)

v 24   With his lips a hater dissimulates,
       while inside he sets deceit;
v 25   (if his voice speaks kindly, don't believe him,
       for seven abominations are in his heart).

v 26   Hate conceals by guile;
       its evil will be exposed in the assembly.
v 27   One digging a pit falls therein;
       one rolling a stone, it turns on him.
v 28   A false tongue hates those it crushes,[5]

---

of 16:27-28/29. In 16:27b the *'yš bly'l* has burning fire on his lips (*w'l śptyw k'š srbt*); in 16:28 the *'yš thpkwt* (who is parallel to both the *'yš bly'l* and the *nrgn*) incites conflict (*yšlh mdwn*). The congruence of vocabulary, imagery, and theme between 26:20-23 and 16:27-28 is evident. Gispen (II, 257) cited 16:27 but failed to note the connection with 16:28. Within the context of 26:17-28, *dlqym* nicely reinforces the imagery of fire in vv 20-21, and is suitable to the heat-using technologies of metallurgy and ceramics implicit in v 23a. Finally, *dlqym* makes a nice play on the more frequent expressions using the organs of speech and *hlq*. It is the proximity of one of these in v 28b (*ph hlq*) which probably led to the LXX *leia* in v 23b.

[5] Vs 28 is difficult. *Dkyw* in Proverbs 26:28a was misunderstood already by the LXX (*alētheian*, cf. Syriac, Targum, Vulgate and the *BHS* apparatus) and much scholarly ingenuity has been expended on the word since then. Toy (480) sums up the traditional arguments against *dkyw*:

   a false tongue hates its afflicted ones is improbable . . . the tongue is said in OT. [sic]
   to speak and smite and pierce, but never to hate or crush a person.

However, the imagery of v 28a is not so unusual as Toy and many scholars imagine, as is evident when it is seen that *dk*, "crushed, oppressed" (*BDB* [194], only in Prov 26:28; Pss 9:10; 10:18; 74:21) is not to be related to the metaphorical root *dkh* but to the metaphorical usage of *dk'*. For example, Prov 22:22: *w'l tdk' 'ny bš'r* "Don't *crush* the poor in the gate" (i.e., in a lawsuit; Job 5:4 is similar: *ydk' bš'r*). Further metaphorical use of *dk'* in a juridical context occurs in Ps 72:4; 94:5-6; and Lam 3:34. It is perhaps pushing the evidence to insist upon a juridical *Sitz* for Prov 26:28, but the use of *lšwn šqr*, in my judgment, makes such a setting most probable (cf. v 26, *qhl*). Nor is Toy's attempt to separate "hate" and "tongue" convincing as becomes apparent when Prov 26:24a, 26a, 28a, are juxtaposed with 10:12 (*śn'h t'wrr mdnym/ w'l kl pš'ym tksh 'hbh*) and 10:18a: "He who conceals hate with lying lips . . . (*mksh śn'h śpty šqr*)." Cf. M. A. Klopfenstein [*Die Lüge*, 165, 411, n. 718) who also retains *dkyw* in 26:28. As to Toy's objection that the tongue does not "crush" in the OT, we may note that the tongue is a metaphor for speech or words which indeed *can* "crush," as Job 19:2 makes plain: "How long will you torment my soul, and crush me with words (*wtdk'wnny bmlym*)?" Toy also seeks to disqualify the parallel in Prov 25:15b: "a soft tongue breaks bones (*wlšwn rkh tšbr grm*). But cf. Aramaic Ahiqar, Saying 23 (*APA*, 91); Sir 28:17; and note the false bravado of the modern children's ditty: "Sticks and stones may break my bones, but words will never hurt me!"

Barucq (200) and Gladson ("Retributive," 159) are similar to our interpretation. For the suggestions of G. R. Driver, see Gemser (94) and McKane (600).

yet a slick[6] mouth works (its own) calamity.

While some critics are content to find only smaller groupings and individual Sayings in Prov 26:17-28,[7] the majority of scholars judge that at least vv 20-28 comprise a thematic unit.[8] McKane, who usually treats proverbs as discrete units having no mutual interconnection, expresses the majority view:

> Verses . . . 20-28 [have to do] with malevolent, anti-social behaviour. It is a question whether vv 17-19 should also be attached to vv 20-28.[9]

In this chapter, our thesis is that the literary unit extends from vv 17-28,[10] and that this section of Proverbs 25-27 develops themes taken from Chapter 25, concluding them with an affirmation of the act-consequence schema in which evil deeds carry within them their own consequences.[11] Further, the section is divided into four subsections of three lines each.[12]

STRUCTURE

The form-critical structure of 26:17-28, arranged in four groups of three lines, appears below. Justification for this arrangement will appear in the sections on Poetics and Sense.

---

[6] The rendering of *hlq* here as "flattering" (RSV) unnecessarily narrows its semantic content in light of the parallelism with *lšwn šqr* and the consequence entailed by *mdhh*. The principal denotation of the root is smoothness or slickness. N. M. Waldman ("Excessive Speech," 144-145) has noted that *hlq* and *kzb* "overlap in meaning." The roots *hlq* and *dhh* form a semantic pair. Retribution is expressed by their collocation in Jer 23:12; Pss 5:10-11; 35:5-6. Cf. Prov 7:21. In Prov 14:32, *dhh* alone appears in a retributive setting. In Prov 29:5, *hlq* does.

[7] Gispen (II, 252-260) for example, does not deal with the question of the larger unit(s) in this section. Van der Ploeg (91-92) groups vv 17-22, 23-26, and 27-28. Delitzsch (190-98) groups vv 17-19, 20-22, and 23-28 on thematic grounds.

[8] This conclusion is generally based on thematic considerations. So Gemser (95); Whybray (153); Ringgren (103); R. E. Murphy (*WL*, 78). J. A. Gladson ("Retributive Paradoxes in Proverbs 10-29," [Vanderbilt Ph.D. Dissertation, 1978] 160, cf. 164) sees the thematic unity as running from v 18 through v 28. As we shall argue below, v 17 also belongs to the larger unit.

[9] McKane (595). McKane is "inclined to opt for" separating vv 17-19 from 20-28.

[10] Barucq (197) sees the thematic unit ("sur le querelleur") as comprising vv 17-26.

[11] K. Koch, "Gibt es ein Vergeltungsdogma im Alten Testament?" *ZTHK* 52 (1955) 1-42; reprinted in *Um das Prinzip der Vergeltung in Religon und Recht des Alten Testaments* (Darmstadt: Wissenschaftliche Buchgesellschaft, 1972) 130-180; translated as "Is There a Doctrine of Retribution in the Old Tstament?" (J. L. Crenshaw, ed.; *Theodicy in the Old Testament;* Philadelphia: Fortress, 1983) 57-87.

[12] Earlier triplets in the Hezekian collection include 25:18-20; 26:1-3, 6-9, 9-11, 13-15. Scholars who divide 26:17-28 into three-line segments include Ewald (230-31), who also notes the connections among the subsections; Delitzsch (190-98), who, however, joins vv 23-28 together; and Gladson (159-164). For the most part, these divisions are made intuitively, without explicit analysis. None of these scholars sees the equal segments as running from v 17 to 28 inclusive.

Diagram 1

Form-Critical (A/S and +/-) Structure of Prov 26:17-28

Verses	Form
17	S: -/-
18	S: -/-
19	S: -/-
20	S: ∅ /∅
21	S: -/-
22	S: -/-
23	S: -/-
24	S: -/-
25	(a: p-/ms-)
26	S: - → -
27	S:- → -/ - → -
28	S: - → -

Form-critically, Diagram 1 contains a consistent pattern of negative Sayings scarcely broken by the Admonition in vv 24-25 of which only v 25a can be distinguished from its context of Sayings. This Admonition is not of the Consequential type which has appeared exclusively up to this point in chapters 25-26.[13] Rather it is an Admonition of the *Explanatory* type,[14] where the motivation for the Precept appears as a clause or Saying which grounds the Precept in an aspect of reality—human nature or divine justice, for example. The subsidiary Admonition in 26:25 fits in very well with its surrounding Sayings, for it merely draws out the implications of v 24.

The last three Sayings of this passage (vv 26-28) are of a Consequential type used to express the pattern of act and consequence,[15] in contrast to the foregoing Sayings which are non-consequential. The Admonition (vv 24-25) thus helps accentuate the transition from the block of non-consequential Sayings

---

[13] We should note that Prov 25:6-7 is a mixed form. Its logic is that of the negative Consequential Admonition with a Result (v 7b) to be avoided. At the same time it employs a MS (Motive Saying) of the Comparative type which makes it appear like an Explanatory motivation. See the following note.

[14] For rferences to the form critical analysis of Motive Clauses, see note 14 in Chapter 4 above.

[15] Koch ("Doctrine," 59, 62) mentions 26:27, 28 as examples of the "Action-Consequences-Construct" in which "one who acts is going to experience the consequences of one's own actions."

(vv 17-23/24) to the final consequential group (vv 26-28), and to mark the boundary of the third three-line unit.

Diagram 1 shows further that this section of Proverbs consistently portrays matters which receive a negative evaluation. Even in v 20, the only exception to this pattern, we find not a positive state of affairs but merely the *absence* of the negative (*mdwn*, cf. v 21).

Analysis of the T-C structures employed in Prov 26:17-28 reveals that these play a much smaller role in the unity of the passage than in 25:2-27 and 26:1-12. The coherence found in 26:(17-19) 20-28 by many scholars is created by other, mostly thematic, means.

Diagram 2
Topic-Comment Analysis of 26:17-28

Verses	Level 1 Colon 1	Colon 2	Level 2 Colon 1	Colon 2
17	FC =	T		
18	FC =			
19		T		
20	FC =	T	$T_1 = C_1$	$= T_2 = C_2$
21	FC =	T	$T_1 = T_2$	$= T_3$[16]
22	T =	FC	$T_1 = FC_1$	$= T_1 = FC_2$
23	FC =	T	$T_1 = C_1$	$= T_2 = C_2$
24	T =	C	$C_1 = T$	$= C_2$
25	[Admonition]			
26	T ≠	C	$C_1 = T_1$	$\rightarrow C_2 = T_2$
27	FS =	FS	$T_1 \rightarrow C_1$	$= T_2 \rightarrow C_2$
28	T →	C	$T_1 = C_1$	$\rightarrow T_2 = C_2$

The foregoing T-C analysis shows less uniformity than appeared in the form critical overview found in Diagram 1. Yet one may note several predominant patterns. For example, vv 17-21, 23 share the FC = T pattern which helps bind subsections 1 (vv 17-19) and 2 (vv 20-22) together. On Level 1 the T = C pattern appears in vv 24, 26 (cf. v 28 [T → C]), and the T = FC pattern in v 22. Subsection 4 (vv 26-28) is strongly uniform due to the T → C pattern, whether on Level 1 (vv 26, 28) or Level 2 (v 27). Furthermore, on Level 2, the pattern $T_1 = C_1 = T_2 = C_2$ is employed, with some slight variations, in vv 20, 22, 23, 27, and 28.

---

[16] On Level 3, each of the three topics may be further broken down in to a T-C.

The FC = T structure employed on Level 1 of Subsection 1 (vv 17-19) is familiar from chapters 25 and 26:1-12. In vv 18-19 this pattern spans two lines, forming a couplet (cf. 25:4-5, 16-17). Subsection two (vv 20-22) uses the same FC = T structure in each line of its couplet (vv 20-21) but concludes with T = FC. The third Subsection (vv 23-25) also begins with FC = T, but ends with a T = C Saying cum subsidiary Admonition. The fourth Subsection brings a new structure, the Consequential Saying, in which one finds consequences which follow upon earlier actions. Here the "Deed-Consequence" pattern may be diagrammed, "T → C." In vv 26 and 28, this structure encompasses the two cola of the line. In v 27, the pattern appears complete in each colon so that we must speak of two, mutually illuminating Figurative Sayings (= FS).[17] These FSs have no explicit literal referent; such a referent must be inferred from the context.

POETICS

In the following section on "Sense," I will argue that the themes of Prov 26:17-18 are derived from chapter 25. Such themes are made visible and organized by poetic and structural devices. Patterns of sense and patterns of form are, of course, always mutually interactive in a fine literary composition.[18]

Prov 26:17-28 is unusual in that it employs regular sub-units of three proverbs or "triplets."[19] These sub-units have strong *internal* cohesion thematically, a cohesion which also manifests itself on the poetic level principally by means of word repetition and the devices of parallelism.

Before turning to the triplets and then to the coherence *among* them, the building blocks of the three-line "triplets" must be mentioned. Excepting the final consequential subsection 4 (vv 26-28), each of the triplets comprises an obvious couplet[20] plus an additional line. The arrangement of couplets and lines appears in Diagram 3.

---

[17] Thus the two *cola* of 26:27 have the same structural relationship as the two *lines* of 21.

[18] According to N. H. Ridderbos (*Die Psalmen* 63, 66), thought units or themes (our "sense" level) have a greater role in structuring most BH poetry than do "purely" formal schemes like that of the English Sonnet. Ridderbos admits, however, that the form/content distinction is not an entirely happy one. One might rather say that in poetry thought is incarnate in form.

[19] Regular strophes (e.g., Ps 119) are infrequent in BH poetry. See Ridderbos, *Die Psalmen*, 65-69.

[20] The couplets in 18-19 and 24-25 are obviously defined by their forms (*k . . . kn* simile, two-line Admonition in which the suffixes of *qwlw* and *bw* need an antecedent from v 24). The couplet in vv 20-21 is obvious on grounds of theme, word repetition, and devices like assonance and alliteration.

Diagram 3

Couplet/Line Organization of 26:17-25

Subsection	Verse	Unit	
1.	17	line	A
	18–19	couplet	B
2.	20–21	couplet	B
	22	line	A
3.	23	line	A
	24–25	couplet	B

Such a grouping of lines and couplets might lead one to construe couplets and lines as independent units. However, both poetic devices and thematic patterns (see "Sense" below) operate together to bind the proverbs into groups of three, and to weld these triplets into a larger, more complex poem.

In this section on Poetics, we will only focus upon the more important devices. First, we need to note the construction of internal cohesion among the units within the triplet subsections. The poet consistently uses the simple but effective device of inclusio to mark the boundary lines of each subsection in 26:17-28. These inclusiones appear as follows.

Diagram 4

Inclusiones of Subsections in 26:17-28

Subsection	Verses	Word or Root
1.	17, 19	l'[21]
2.	20, 22	$nrgn$
3.	23, 25	lb[22]
4.	26, 28	$śn'$[23]

Within the subsections the following prominent instances of word repetition appear, linking contiguous lines: $'s$, $'š$, $mdwn$ (vv 20-21); $śph$ (vv 23-24, not a couplet). Since v 27 does not at first glance seem to fit in subsection 4, it is worth pointing out a couple of poetic binders. First, the play of $tglh$ (v 26) and gll

---

[21] This is the weakest of the subsection inclusiones in the poem since l' does not have significant thematic content. However, one should note that l' in v 17 is made emphatic by its juxtaposition with lw. Furthermore, ryb (v 17) and r' (v 19) function as a virtual thematic word-pair, taken from 25:7c-10. See our argument in Sense below.

[22] Thematically, this is the inner pole of the inner-outer opposition which dominates this subsection.

[23] The root $śn'$ also appears in v 24, strengthening the ties between subsections 3 and 4.

(v 27). Secondly, there is an alliterative string (discounting prefixes) that binds these two verses together:

v 26   t*k*sh *śn*'h *bmś*'wn/ tglh . . .
v 27   *k*rh *ś*ḥt *b*h ypl/ wgll . . .

In addition to the strong binders of word repetition, there is a variety of lesser binders within the subsections. For instance, while v 25 does not mention *śph* as do vv 23-24, it does mention the *qwl* which is a parallel term. Similarly, v 24 does not have the *lb* of vv 23, 25, but it does have the counterpart, *qrb*. And v 21 lacks *nrgn* (vv 20, 21) but has an *'yš mdwnym* (cf. 16:27-28). Along with the thematic considerations adduced in "Sense" below, the foregoing items should be sufficient to establish that 26:17-28 comprises four three-proverb triplets.

The same device of word repetition, especially of important words, is used in the poem to link contiguous subsections. S. M. Paul has described this technique of linking similar units in a study of the first chapters of Amos.[24] As in Amos, the word repetitions in Prov 26:17-28 link only contiguous sections. Furthermore, this device links subsection 1 only to subsection 2 and subsection 3 only to subsection 4.[25] As we shall see in a moment, the transition from subsection 2 to 3 is made by v 22.

The greatest number of such concatenous word repetitions function to bind subsection 1 and 2 together. By ignoring such clues, some scholars have missed the place and role of Subsection 1 (vv 17-19) in the poem as a whole.[26] The most powerful repetition is that of the key word *ryb* (vv 17 and 21) which is reinforced by the parallel term *mdwn* in vv 20, 21. As *ryb* links the single Saying of v 17 to Subsection 2, so the repetition of *'yš* (vv 19, 21) and the partial homophones *mtlhlh* (v 18) and *mtlhmym* (v 22) serve to bind the couplet of subsection 1 to the second triplet.

Subsections 3 and 4 are linked by two strong thematic repetitions of *r'* (evil; vv 23, 26) and *śn'* (hate; vv 24, 26, 28).[27] Finally there are parallel terms which reinforce the instances of pure repetition. Thus *lśwn* and *ph* in v 28 ties in with *śph* (vv 23, 24) and *qwl* (v 25) of subsection 3 to continue its theme of false speech. And, as noted, *mdwn* (vv 20 21) reinforces the repetition of *ryb* (vv 17,

---

[24] "Amos 1:3-2:3: A Concatenous Literary Pattern," *JBL* 90 (1971) 397-403. This device is characterized by "the concatenation of similar catch words, phrases, or ideas common to only the two units contiguous to one another" (401).

[25] *Rmh* in v 19 and *mrmh* in v 24 is a possible exception, but other than reinforcing the general thematic coherence of the passage, this does not seem to be a strong poetic link. This repetition is at some distance and does not appear in the strong beginning-end positions as does an inclusio.

[26] See note 9 above, with accompanying text.

[27] One may recall the important role of *śn* in the chiasmus linking the Admonitions in 25:16-17 and 25:21-22.

21). Similarly, *bṭn* in v 22 anticipates the terms for the inner man in vv 23-25 (*lb, qrb, lb*).

SENSE

Before pursuing the details of sense in Prov 26:17-28, it is wise to present a brief overview of the thought-progression of the poem — the forest before the trees, so to speak.

The first triplet (vv 17-19) introduces the poem as a whole, embodying two related themes taken from chapter 25: *ryb* (v 17; cf. 25:7c-10) and the *verbal wounder* (vv 18-19; cf. 25:18). The second subsection (vv 20-22) develops the two themes just introduced: the verbal wounder (*nrgn, 'yš mdwnyn*) can *start* (v 26:21; cf. 25:18) or *maintain* (26:20; cf. 25:18) conflict. The wicked power of the *nrgn* is explained in v 22: his words penetrate to the inner being of a person, that hidden core of the self which determines external action.[28] Subsection 3 (vv 23-25) picks up this theme of inner and outer and uses it to warn the reader concerning the duplicitous character of a verbal wounder. The final triplet (vv 26-28) is a series of Sayings which affirm the act-consequence scheme and provide implicit warning to the wicked described in the poem.

While Prov 25:2-27 began with an introduction of thematic concerns encompassing two couplets (four lines), the following poems began with three line units: 26:1-3 forms an introduction to vv 4-12; and 26:13-15 forms a unit in itself, concluded with the comparative refrain of 26:16. Prov 26:17-28 also employs a three line "introduction" to present its main thematic concerns.

What is noteworthy about this last introduction, however, is that its themes are derived from the poem which opens the Hezekian collection in 25:2-27. Taken as a whole, 26:17-19 resumes the complementary themes of *ryb* and *rʿ* which are first found in 25:7c-10. In a more precise way, v 26:17 alludes to 25:7c-8, 9-10 and 26:18-19 alludes to 25:18. The purpose of these allusions is to resume main themes from the earlier poem and to develop them further in the following Sayings and Admonition.

The Admonitions in chapter 25:7c-10 express the theme of social conflict (*ryb*) between peers (*rʿ*). The term *ryb* appears three times in 25:7c-10 and then not again in the Hezekian collection until 26:17 (for *rʿ* see below). Moreover, 26:17 and 25:7c-10 share the same proverb message; their common thrust is that it is dangerous to get involved in a conflict (*ryb*) which is not one's own business.

The couplet in 26:18-19 forms an even more obvious allusion to 25:18. The two units share not only imagery but even key vocabulary: *ḥṣ, 'yš . . . rʿhw*. Whereas 25:18 compares weapons to a man bearing false (*šqr*) witness against his neighbor (*rʿhw*), 26:17-19 compares the shooting of weapons to a man deceiving[29] his neighbor (*rʿ*). Moreover, the harm done to the neighbor is

---

[28] Cf. H. W. Wolff's discussion (*Anthropology of the Old Testament* [Philadelphia: Fortress, 1974] 43-44) on *lb*, and on *bṭn* and *qrb* (63-64).

[29] The roots *šqr* and *rmh* form frequent parallel word pairs. To give a few examples: Jer

accomplished by *verbal* means. It is this nuance of 25:18 which 26:17-18 especially develops. The key term in this allusion is *rʻ*. This word appears twice in 25:7c-10, naturally enough since the *ryb* is directed against the neighbor. But as was pointed out in our treatment of 25:2-27 above, *rʻ* is the key word whose sound pattern (evoking *evil* and *neighbor*) appears in every verse from 25:17 to 25:21—the immediate context of 25:18 to which 26:18 alludes.

Thus, 26:17-19 forms the thematic introduction to vv 20-28. As allusive echoes of key themes and vocabulary from chapter 25, these verses announce to the reader that the writer is resuming some of his concerns from the earlier poem (negative speech which harms the other and causes social conflict). Moreover, as he develops these themes, he incorporates the key lesson of 26:1-12: one must not only avoid *being* a negative person (fool, and by implication, sluggard, false witness, etc.), but in interpersonal relations one must also wisely evaluate and deal with such harmful characters.

We also find that the two units of subsection 1 (vv 17, 18-19) together with subsections 2 and 3 employ a thematic pattern such as is found in 26:1-12. When discussing Prov 26:6-12, we noted the alternation of the RA (Relating Actant, one who acts in relation to a fool) and the FA (Foolish Actant) as a organizing device. Something similar appears in the subsections of Prov 26:17-28. Here, however, we deal not with the FA, but with NA (Negative Actant) and the RA who acts in relation to some negative other, not necessarily a fool.

In the "Introduction," v 17 implicitly issues a warning about how one should relate to a quarreling "dog" who passes by: don't get involved. Thus the figurative and literal Topics of v 17 (*mḥzyq* . . . /*mtʻbr*) concern the one who relates to (an)other, negative person(s) or situation. Thus we use the sign RA to designate the Topics of this verse. Verses 18-19 of this same "Introduction," on the other hand, simply represent an NA, the mad shooter, and allows the reader to draw his own conclusions.

Subsections 2 and 3 (vv 20-22 and 23-25) may be distinguished by the same criterion. In subsection 2 (vv 20-22)[30] the subject or Topic is the *nrgn* (slanderer, v 20, 22) or the *ʼyš mdwnym* ("man of quarrels," v 21). This subsection simply portrays the wicked *nrgn* as one who kindles conflict (*ryb, mdwn*) and, like vv 18-19, allows the reader to draw his own conclusions. Subsection 3 (vv 23-25), on the other hand, portrays the wicked in order to warn the reader (RA): "don't believe him" (v 25a). On this level of meaning, therefore, the following pattern obtains:

23:26; Amos 8:5; Mic 6:12; Pss 109:2; 119:118; 120:2; Prov 12:17.

[30] Gladson ("Retributive," 161) terms these verses the "first movement of 20-28" and sees in v 22 the climax of the movement which "leads to a more explicit consideration of deceptive speech."

Diagram 5

Negative Actant (NA)/ Relating Actant (RA) in 26:17-25

Subsection	Verses	Actant	
1. (Introduction)	17	RA	A.
	18-19	NA	B.
2.	20-22	RA	A.
3.	23-25	NA	B.

To treat with the negative persons portrayed here is to be "embroiled" in a dispute where one is sure to be burnt (vv 20-21), bitten (v 17), or wounded (vv 18-19).

The concluding verse (22) in the second subsection anticipates the contrast of inner and outer developed in the next subsection (vv 23-25): evil words are the outside of an inner-outer dialectic. Such words have a profound impact upon the innermost self of the hearer (v 22). But they can also appear externally well-meaning while concealing evil inner intent (vv 23-25).

The contrast of wicked inner person (*lb r'; bqrbw yšyt mrmh; šb' tw'bwt blbw*) and deceitful outer expression (*śptym dlqym; bśptyw [qere] ynkr; ky yhnn qwlw*)[31] dominates subsection 3 (vv 23-25).[32] Young courtiers as well as ordinary people need to be aware of this mysterious incongruity in human beings ("All is not gold that glitters") and learn to relate wisely to people whose lips belie the evil in their hearts.

The final subsection (vv 26-28) provides and affirms the act-consequence schema with regard to the wicked described in the preceding subsections. Especially the "hater," and those who use their organs of speech to harm the neighbor will themselves suffer the evil they intended for their neighbor. This Subsection serves both to characterize the end of the evil-doer as well as to warn the young person not to be such a person, lest he too suffer such consequences.

This concluding triplet is tied to the foregoing sections by the emphasis on hate (*śn'*, vv 24, 26, 28), dissimulating speech (v 24a and 26a), and the bringing-into-the-open (*tglh*, v 24b) of what dissimulation had hidden. The movement of thought is nicely paralleled by Ps 28:3-4 (*RSV*):

> Take me not off with the wicked, with those who are workers of evil, who speak peace with their neighbors, while mischief is in their hearts. Requite them according to their work, and according to the evil of their deeds; requite them according to the work of their hands; render them their due reward.

---

[31] Cf. Matt 23:25-28 where the outer-inner contrast is explicitly employed for similar analysis of wicked persons.

[32] Gladson ("Retributive," 162) calls vv 23-25 a "six-line [i.e., three-line in our terms] proverb."

It is worthwhile to briefly explore the thematic unity of this final subsection,[33] since it contains some difficulties. Some of the structural and poetic features which hold these three Sayings together have been pointed out in the relevant sections above. On the level of sense, the most powerful cohesive force rests in the common consequential message, in each Saying, that one who plots evil against another will himself suffer evil. In v 26 the verbal dissimulator who meant to hurt another by his falsehood, is himself hurt by it.[34] He stands exposed in the assembly; the hidden is revealed.[35] The next Saying twice follows the same pattern, using conventional imagery: the pit is dug for another's harm (Jer 18:20, 22; Pss 7: 16-17; 9:16-17; Qoh 10:8; Dan 6:24-25 [23-24 Eng.]; Sir 27:29); and presumably the stone which returns upon its roller's head was also intended for another.[36] It is this pattern (harm — intended for the other — turning to hurt the hurter) which provides aid in solving the difficulties of v 28.[37] That verse may be translated:

A false tongue hates those it crushes,
yet a slick mouth works (its own) calamity.

Thus the organs of speech which hate and crush the weak (v 28a) shall cause their own calamity (v 28b).[38]

In sum, this proverb poem presents the Negative Actants (NA) who cause strife and hurt by verbal violence and deception. It warns the reader not to be one such, gives advice in relating to them (RA), and concludes with the act-consequence declaration that the harm they do returns upon themselves.

---

[33] On these verses, see Gladson, "Retributive," 162-163.
[34] A judicial assembly seems most likly (so Toy, 480; cf. Gladson, "Retributive," 162, n. 4 with reference to R. de Vaux, *AI* I, 155-157; against McKane, 604-605).
[35] *Tkśh sn'h,* "hate covers," is an example of "abstract noun balanced by concrete noun" (M. Dahood [*Psalms* III AB 17A; Garden City: Doubleday, 1970] 411-412); the person implicit in *śn'h* is picked up by the suffix of *r'tw*.
[36] Cf. Sir 27:25, 27; Sap Sal 11:16 (Gemser [95]). The leap in imagery from a "pit" to "rolling a stone" was perhaps not so great for the ancient Israelites, since the two can be associated in ordinary life (cf. Gen 29: 3, 8, 10; Josh 10:18).
[37] See the old debate between Ewald and Delitzsch on these verses.
[38] A similar use of body imagery to communicate act-consequence is 21:13, "He who closes his ear to the cry of the poor, will himself cry out and not be heard."

9
Proverbs 27:1-22

Translation

v 1 Do not boast about tomorrow,
for you do not know what a day gives birth to.
v 2 Let another praise you, but not your own mouth
a stranger, but not your own lips!¹

v 3 Stone is heavy and sand a burden,²
but a fool's provocation is heavier than both.
v 4 Wrath is cruel and anger a flood,²
but who can stand before jealousy?

v 5 Better is open rebuke/ than hidden love.
v 6 Faithful are the wounds of a friend,
false³ are the kisses of an enemy.

v 7 A satisfied "soul"⁴ tramples honey,
a hungry "soul" finds even the bitter sweet.
v 8 As a bird wandering from its nest,
so a man wandering from his place.

---

¹ Take *'l* as a rare, but not unique (cf. 12:28), equivalent of *l'*; cf. Toy (485). Thus v 2a,b appears to be a positive Precept ("Let another praise you. . . ."), while the accent actually falls upon not praising oneself. Another's praise is proper while self-praise is unfitting, a point similar to 26:12 on being "wise in one's own eyes," and to 25:6. Hence I take 27:2 as P-/-. The grammatical variety here (*l'* / *'l*) keeps the parallelism from being monotonous. Cf. A. Berlin, "Grammatical Aspects of Biblical Parallelism," *HUCA* 50 (1979) 17-43.

² The construct chains are so rendered here the better to fit English idiom.

³ For the semantic background of this connotation of *n'trwt*, "excessive," see Nahum M. Waldman, "A Note on Excessive Speech and Falsehood," *JQR* 67 (1976-77) 142-45.

⁴ On *npš* see H. W. Wolff, *Anthropology of the Old Testament* (Philadelphia: Fortress, 1974) 10-25.

v 9   Oil and incense gladden the heart,
      a friend's sweetness (gladdens) more than one's own counsel.[5]
v 10 Your friend and your father's friend forsake not,
      but do not enter your brother's house when you have trouble;[6]
      better is a near neighbor than a distant brother.

v 11 Be wise, my son, and gladden my heart,
      and I will have a retort for him who taunts me.
v 12 The prudent saw trouble and hid,
      the simple passed by and paid the price.

v 13 Take his cloak, for he stood surety for a stranger,
      on account of a foreigner, hold him (to his pledge).
v 14 Who blesses his neighbor with a loud voice,
      rising early in the morning,
      will have it considered as cursing.[7]

v 15 A perpetual drip on a day of drizzle
      and a quarrelsome wife are alike;
v 16 who hides her hides the wind,[8]
      his right hand grabs oil.

v 17 Iron sharpens iron/ a man sharpens his friend.[9]
v 18 Who tends a fig tree eats its fruit,
      who guards his master is honored.

---

[5] The translation of v 9b is difficult. I follow *JPSV* but read *śmh* as a double-duty verb. See also the discussion of Delitzsch (204-206). "Sweetness" is used figuratively to refer to the conversation of friends (Ps 55:15), to speech (Prov 16:21, 24), and to wisdom (24:13-14). In Ps 19 a series of terms parallel to *twrh* (vv 8-11) includes "testimony" (*'dwt*) which gives wisdom (v 8b) and the *mšpṭy yhwh* which are sweeter than honey. In Prov 27:9b, the reference seems to be to the sweetness of wisdom (//*'sh*) with a contrast between friend and solitary self (*npš*). *Npš* here functions pronominally, but retains connotations of the inner self; cf. Wolff, *Anthropology*, 23-25. If this reading is correct, the imagery of oil and gladness in v 9a may be compared to that in Psalm 133.

[6] Cf. Prov 25:17.

[7] The proverb message concerns unfittingness; cf. 25:20 and 26:1-12.

[8] Verse 16 is obscure. But note *rwḥ ṣpwn* in 25:23 follwed by a Saying on the *'št mdwnym*.

[9] Read with the versions, Gemser, McKane and others: *yuḥād* (hoph. of *ḥdd*; literally, "is sharpened by") and *yāḥēd* (hiph. of *ḥdd*) respectively. *Pny r'hw* is difficult; cf. McKane, 615.

v 19   As water: face to face,/ so man's heart to man's heart![10]
v 20   Sheol and Abaddon are never satisfied,
       and man's eyes are never satisfied.

v 21   Crucible for silver and furnace for gold . . .
       a man is tested by his praise![11]
v 22   If you crush a fool with a pestle . . .
       his folly will not depart from him![12]

In marked contrast to the preceding sections of Proverbs, 27:1-22 is a loose collection structurally, poetically, and thematically. Instead of a proverb poem, one must call it a proverb miscellany or collection. Its appearance at the end of the first half of the Hezekian collection offers an excellent negative control on the methods employed earlier. The patterns, coherences, and unities which appeared on various levels in the earlier sections break down in 27:1-22. One may therefore legitimately conclude that the high degree of literary unity which prevailed in the earlier sections was a result of determined purpose and superlative artistry, especially considering the formidable difficulty of welding the diverse smaller units (S and A) into larger wholes.

Though the collector of 27:1-22 did not essay the feat of creating a genuine proverb poem, his composition employs one consistent means of construction. Where possible, the collection is built up of proverb Pairs or couplets. Long ago Delitzsch[13] pointed out that the proverbs of 27:1-10 form couplets linked by thematic concerns and/or poetic devices. In my judgment, the entire passage consists of two-line pairs with diverse degrees of cohesion, connected by a variety of means, except for vv 13, 14, 17, 18, 21, 22. Since these residue verses fall out from among the couplets in two line segments, it is proper to diagram the passage as two line (= verse) blocks. Our argument for the couplets appears

---

[10] The idea is of water as a mirror: man comes to self-knowledge through confrontation with the other; so Gemser. The same concerns and form appear in v 17; vv 9 and 21 may also be thematically related.

[11] Verse 21b: I follow the rendering *ad sensum* of the *JPSV*.

[12] Either we have a three-cola Saying or the line is overloaded with *bmktš btwk hrypwt*. The sense remains unaffected.

[13] Pp. 198-204. "In the group 1-6 of this chapter [27] every two proverbs form a pair." But on page 202, Delitzsch also sees vv 7-8 as forming a pair on stylistic grounds: each Saying has a doubled word *beginning* (read thus for the translator's "terminating") with *n* (*npš* and *ndd*). And on page 204, he notes that vv 9-10 are bound by a catchword (*rʻ*) and common theme.

McKane also observes various connections among the proverbs: vv 1-2 (p. 608); 3-4 (same form, p. 611); 5-6 (theme, p. 610); 9-10 (friendship, p. 612); perhaps 15-16 (pp. 616-17).

Barucq (197) mentions the theme of friendship in vv 5-10, except for v 7.

below. A second and related feature characteristic of 27:1-22 is the frequency of repetition of words or roots both within proverbs and between the two units of a proverb pair.[14]

STRUCTURE

The form critical structure of this passage has no discernable pattern or order such as was found in the proverb poems previously analyzed.

Diagram 1

Form-Critical (A/S, +/-) Structure of Prov 27:1-22

Verses	Form
1	A: P-/MS-
2	A: P-/P[15]
3	S: -/-
4	S: -/-
5	S: + +
6	S: +/-
7	S: ∅/∅
8	S: -/-
9	S: +/+(?)
10	A: P+/P-/MS:+ >-(?)
11	A: P+ →R+
12	S: +/-
13	A: P-,MS-/MS-,P-
14	S: -/-
15	S: -/-
16	S: -/-
17	S: +/+
18	S: +/+

---

[14] See above "Prov 25:2-27," note 30, for the data.
[15] See note 1 above.

19	S: +/+
20	S: -/-
21	S: +/+
22	S: -/-/- (?)[16]

While the Topic-Comment analysis of this passage shows a high number of FC = T Sayings on Level 1, no clear pattern or structural unity is established.

Diagram 2

T-C Analysis of Prov 27:1-22 (Sayings only)

Verses	Level 1		Level 2	
	Colon 1	Colon 2	Colon 1	Colon 2
3	FC <	T	$T_1 = T_2 / T_3 = C > (T_1, T_2)$	
4	FC <	T^{17}	$T_1 = T_2 = C < T_3$	
5	$C_1 = T_1$	T_2	....	
6	$S_1 \neq$	S_2	$C_1 = T_1 \neq C_2 = T_2$	
7	$S_1 \neq$	S_2	$T_1 = C_1 \neq T_2 = C_2$	
8	FC =	T	$T_1 = T_2$	
9	Uncertain		$T_1 = C_1$ / Uncertain	
12	$S_1 \neq$	S_2	$T_1 = C_1 \neq T_2 = C_2$	
14	T =	C	....	
15	FC =	T	$T_1 = T_2$	
16	$T = FC_1 =$	$FC_2(?)$	....	
17	FC =	T	$T_1 = C_1 = T_2 = C_2$	
18	FC =	T	$T_1 = C_1 = T_2 = C_2$	
19	FC =	T	....	
20	FC =	T	$T_1 = C_1 = T_2 = C_1$	
21	FC =	T	$RT_1 = RT_2 = RT_3$	
22	Pr+ →	R-	....	

POETICS

There are few poetic devices in 27:1-22 beyond those within individual sayings (which are frequent) and those used to tie couplets together with varying

---

[16] See note 12 above.

[17] Though there is here no adjective plus *mn* comparative construction, McKane (607, 611) is correct in seeing v 4 as a comparative Saying like v 3. The comparison and its Comment work by subtle innuendo: while anger and wrath are difficult to stand up under, the rage of jealousy is virtually impossible. The rhetorical question, *my y'md*, evokes the implicit negative answer, "no one." Stated less indirectly, the Comment would be "cannot be withstood."

degrees of cohesiveness. A number of the latter devices are simple catchwords which have more or less reinforcement on the level of sense.

Verses 1 and 2 share the verb *hll*. Though the verbs are used differently and appear in different stems one may yet say that the two Sayings have in common a focus on the limitations of the individual self with respect to the cosmos and God (v 1)[18] or to the other (v 2). This common focus is emphasized through the repetition of *hll* (cf. 25:6-7).

The second couplet (vv 3-4) is rather tightly linked by a sequence of terms for emotions (*k's, ḥmh, 'p, qn'h*) and by an intensification of the comparative form in th second line: a fool's vexation is heavier than "stone" or "sand," but jealousy in action is the *most* unbearable of emotions, for no one can withstand it.

Verses 5 and 6 are linked by the catchword *'hb* and by the use of paradoxical Topics: open rebuke and hidden love; faithful wounds and false kisses. The paradoxes heighten awareness of the mysterious nature of true love or friendship.

As mentioned, Delitzsch pointed out the stylistic commonality of vv 7-8: verse 7 repeats *npš* and verse 8 *nwdd*. This fondness for alliterative *nuns*, however, seems to have no non-aesthetic function.

The catchword and theme of vv 9-10 is the *r'*, "friend."

Verses 11-12 seem to be linked by the sense parallelism of their respective initial words, *ḥkm* and *'rwm*.

I see no connection between vv 13 and 14. Yet v 13 does echo the opposition of *ẓr* and *nkry* found in v 2.

The next two verses form a couplet since they are linked (if the text is not corrupt) by the pronominal suffix in *špnyh*.

Little connection exists between vv 17-18, though the *pr* of *pry* forms an echo with the *br* of *brzl* in the previous line.

Verses 19-20 share the catchword *'dm*. They also both employ visual imagery to illumine human nature. But v 19 has more formal and thematic affinities with v 17 than with its immediate neighbor.

The final pair of verses (21-22) employ similar imagery (the testing, refining, or removing what is useless by a technical process) and apply it to man.

In a few instances, there appear to be links between lines which are not contiguous, or are in the next couplet. Verses 9 and 11 both share the phrase *śmḥ lb* and, if the translation is correct, concern the joy which the other (friend or son) can bring. As noted above, vv 17-19 are related as to form and theme.

It is possible that the compiler of this section intends the last couplet (vv 21-22) to be an inclusio to the first (vv 1-2), employing the root *hll*.[19] In any

---

[18] Most commentators are agreed that in v 1 the demesne of the future belongs to God, as in Egyptian Wisdom. Cf. Gemser (96) and McKane (607-8) for references.

[19] McKane (607-9) treats vv 1, 2, 21 together. Note also the repetition of the root *'wl* in vv 3, 22.

case, the boundaries of 27:1-22 are clearly marked by the end of the preceding proverb poem (26:17-28) and the beginning of the agricultural poem in 27:23-27.

SENSE

Because there is no overarching thematic concern in 27:1-22, one finds less significant interaction among the proverb units than elsewhere in chapters 25-27. The number of philological uncertainties in the passage renders the larger interpretative task difficult. At best, one finds certain thematic areas represented, sometimes in a cluster, sometimes separated. The couplet connections have been mentioned above. Friendship is the theme to which the greatest number of proverbs are devoted: vv 5-6, 9 (?)-10, 17, 19. A number of verses are complete or partial doublets of proverbs found in Skladny's collection B (27:12//22:3; 27:13//20:16; 27:15//19:13). By these Sayings, the reader is drawn into a wider proverbial context.

But for the most part, it must be admitted that the aphoristic, somewhat isolated nature of the Sayings and Admonitions of this chapter makes them difficult of interpretation. They remain shafts of light in the dark, provoking the reader to ponder what is obscure about the topics they address.

10
Proverbs 27:23-27

Translation

v 23 Know well the condition of your flock,
      bestow your care upon your[1] herds;
v 24 for wealth is not forever,
      nor a crown to all generations.
v 25 [When] the grass passes, the new growth appears,
      the green on the mountains is gathered,
v 26 [there will be] lambs for your clothing,
      he goats for the price of a field,
v 27 enough goat's milk for your food,
      food for your house, and victuals for your maids.

Unlike the sections of Proverbs treated previously in this study our present text is not an Admonition or Saying comprising two lines at most, nor a proverb poem or miscellany composed of such smaller units. Rather, we have a short admonitory poem. Accordingly, the questions and methods which the poem evokes are, in part, different. Since we do not have to establish that a poetic unit lies before us, we may proceed directly to the basic question, What does the poem mean? But this question is less obvious than it seems, entailing yet further questions. What is the genre and setting of the poem? What are its referents? And why did the compiler place it here in the book?

For Skladny and others, this was obviously an agricultural poem and one of the key factors leading him to describe the larger Sammlung C (25-27) as a *Bauernspiegel*, a collection for simple, rustic folk.[2] But R. E. Murphy has rightly pointed out the fallacy of proceeding directly from wisdom imagery to conclusions about genre and Sitz:

---

[1] Emendation not necessary; the second person suffix is double duty.
[2] *ASI*, 56-57. G. von Rad (*WII*, 141 n. 5) expresses the general view on Prov 27:23-27 well: "This didactic poem is not nearly so artistically fashioned as that in Isa. 28.23ff. It is not so ambitious from the point of view of content either. It approximates more to a rule for honest farmers: Do not be slack in your farm work."

The wisdom literature gives evidence of a certain indifference to the specific association between form and life setting. The two are only loosely associated. . . . What is the life setting of the Old Testament wisdom saying? It is a teaching situation, but this tells us little—that of parents, clan elder, court instructor, or religious teacher? . . . a given saying may have a long history; it may have traveled from one given life setting to another without any real change. . . . Agricultural metaphors are not to be restricted to folk wisdom, nor are 'king' proverbs the interest of the court alone. If anything, the wide circle of interests which appears in Prv 10-29 suggests an educated literary circle of the court as a most likely group with universal interests who would have cultivated such sayings.[3]

In the case of Prov 27:23-27, the *origin* of its primary themes in the world of agriculture and animal husbandry is beyond dispute. But the present use of these themes is another matter, as we shall see below. As an admonitory poem in the bucolic mode, our text's primary themes have many parallels, a few of which may be cited.[4]

Already in the oldest known Egyptian Instruction (Prince Hardjedef), the anticipation of death motivates agricultural Precepts which will insure that the funerary priest will provide "life" for the dead by cultic means:

Given that death humbles us,
Given that life exalts us,
The house of death is for life.
Seek for yourself well-watered fields,
— — — — —
Choose for him [a funerary priest] a plot among your fields,
Well-watered every year.
He profits you more than your own son. . . .[5]

Here we have an agricultural admonition in a royal *cum* cultic setting. The motive of the admonition is that the reliable produce of the fields will provide a secure future in the realm of death since it is a defense against the transitoriness of human life: the funerary priest will be reliably provisioned.

A similar motive, though in a different religious milieu, for bucolic Precepts is found in the fragmentary Akkadian text, "Counsels of Pessimism." While

---

[3] "Form Criticism and Wisdom Literature," *CBQ* 31 (1969) 481. Murphy is followed by J. L. Crenshaw, "Wisdom" in *Old Testament Form Criticism,* 236. See also J. Bright, "The Apodictic Prohibition: Some Observations," *JBL* 92 (1973) 185-204.

[4] Toy (493) mentions "Aristotle, Theophrastus, Cato, Varro, Virgil, and others," but suprisingly overlooks Hesiod's *Erga* which contains some important parallels to Prov 25:23-27 as well as to Proverbs as a whole. Cf. *Erga* 230-237, 299-309; the former of these passages establishes the connection of "doing true justice" and the productivity of flocks and fields. A similar connection appears in Psalm 72 to which M. L. West (*Hesiod: Works and Days* [Oxford: Clarendon, 1978] 141) refers while discussing the Proem of the *Erga*. On the setting of the *Erga* in the context of ANE wisdom, see West, 27-30.

[5] *AEL I,* 58-59. The text is dated by Lichtheim in the Fifth Dynasty.

Gemser (97) has pointed to it as a parallel to Prov 27:23-27, he did not mention that the Akkadian text includes both the agricultural Precept and the motivation (that goods and wealth are transitory) which we find in Prov 27:23-27:

8   [... does not] continue for eternity,
9   [Whatever] men do does not last forever,
10 Mankind and their achievements alike come to an end. ...
14 Take thought for your livestock, remember the planting.[6]

Similar bucolic Admonitions or Admonitory poems are widespread,[7] as are Sayings and other types of agricultural lore and wisdom.[8]

Yet, there are two factors, one external and one internal, which militate against taking Prov 27:23-27 as simply a bucolic admonitory poem, set against the backdrop of the evanescence of life. First, contrary to Skladny, there are only three tangential references to farming (rather than to "nature" in general[9]) in all of 25:1-27:22. In 25:13 and 26:1, we have references to the time of harvest ($qsyr$), but the focus is elsewhere. In 27:18, the tending of the fig tree is a metaphor (Figurative Comment) for the servant-master relation. Thus rather than reinforcing the assumption that 27:23-27 is merely agricultural, the non-farming context in Sammlung C (25-27) raises the question, Why should a bucolic admonitory poem have this *Sitz im Buch?*[10]

One may correctly reply that in ancient Israel even the men of the court lived close to the land![11] And thus 27:23-27 would seem to make sense as straightforward farming advice even to royal or courtly persons.

[6] *BWL*, 108-109. Lines 11-13 contain cultic precepts.

[7] See the Sumerian "Farmer's Almanac" from about 1700 B.C. translated and discussed by S. N. Kramer (*The Sumerians* [Chicago: University of Chicago, 1963] 104-109, 340-342. In Egypt, the Theban private correspondence of Heka-nakht from the Eleventh Dynasty is full of agricultural admonitions similar to those in various wisdom traditions. T. G. Henry James, *The Hekanakhte Papers, and Other Early Middle Kingdom Documents* (Publications of the Metropolitan Museum of Art Egyptian Expedition 19; New York: Metropolitan Museum, 1962); a partial translation is found in John A. Wilson, *The Culture of Ancient Egypt* (Chicago: University of Chicago, 1951) 128-130. Aramaic Ahiqar, Saying 40; *APA*, 120.

[8] Prov 6:8; 10:5; 12:10-11; 14:4; 24:27, 30-31; 28:19; 31:16; Isa 28:23-29. This last text is structured by the sequence of planting (ploughing and sowing) and harvest (threshing). See also the "Gezer Calendar" in J. C. L. Gibson, *Textbook of Syrian Semitic Inscriptions Vol. I*, (Oxford: Clarendon, 1971) 1-4. The periodization of the year in the "Gezer Calendar" finds its extended counterpart in such works as Hesiod's *Erga*, 414-617, and the "Farmer's Almanac" cited in the previous note.

[9] See Gemser, 101.

[10] Whybray (158): "This theme appears somewhat strange in a book mainly addressed to the courtiers of Jerusalem."

[11] So Whybray (158) with reference to 2 Sam 13:23. Cf. R. de Vaux (*AI I*, 103). Contrast Toy (493) who thought " 'princely dignity' ... inappropriate to the condition of such a person as is here [in Prov 27:23-27] described." Toy is adequately refuted by Whybray. It must be noted that this was the *only* reason adduced by Toy for his widely accepted emendation of *nzr*, "crown," to *'sr*, "treasure." See below.

But there is an internal datum in the poem which militates against reading it *only* on the bucolic level, though this level has its validity, just as the Parable of the Sower (Mark 4:3-8) can be read as a story about farming: the bucolic reading is legitimate but incomplete. It cannot account for the presence of *nzr*, "crown," in v 24. Conversely, if, with Toy and most moderns, one *assumes* a purely bucolic sense for the poem, *nzr* is indeed awkward. In non-priestly contexts *nzr* "is always the mark of royal, and generally of princely dignity, and here [Prov 27:24] denotes, *per meton. signi pro re signata*, that dignity itself."[12] Thus most modern commentators, following Toy, have emended *nzr* to *'sr*, "treasure," without further reflection.[13] Whybray, however, has adduced a further reason for this widespread emendation:

> This section can hardly be addressed to the king or to a royal prince, as were some wisdom books, since the statement *nor will a crown endure to endless generations* flatly contradicts the firmly held belief that the Judaean dynasty of descendants of David would last for ever![14]

Interestingly, Toy's only substantive argument for his popular emendation has been destroyed by Whybray (see above). That leaves only the question-begging suggestion that *hsn* and *nzr* are "inappropriate" as parallel terms (Oesterley), and the argument of Whybray just quoted. But the belief that David's house would last forver did not long survive the vicissitudes of Judah's history. Jeremiah's attack on this score is an obvious example.[15] But already in Hezekiah's reign (cf. Prov 25:1) Micah spoke in terms which are compatible with Whybray's understanding of the unemended text of Prov 27:24b:

> Zion shall be plowed as a field;
> Jerusalem shall become a heap of ruins,
> and the mountain of the house a wooded height (Mic 3:12)[16]

---

[12] Delitzsch, 219. So also de Vaux, *AI I*, 103 and Whybray, 159. Some of de Vaux's citations, however, contain *'trh* rather than *nzr*.

[13] See note 11 above. Toy's position of 1899 is followed by Oesterley, Gemser, Scott, McKane, Ringgren³, and Whybray. Among post-Toy commentators, Cohen, van der Ploeg, Gispen, and Barucq maintain *nzr*. Cohen and Gispen attempt to resolve the difficulty by making *nzr* a symbol of wealth, which is to force upon it an otherwise unattested sense.

[14] Whybray, 159. Whybray puts this forward as the reason for Toy's emendation of *nzr* to *'sr*. Surprisingly, contrary to Whybray's assertion, neither Toy nor any of his followers advance this argument.

[15] On Jeremiah, see our discussion in Sense below. Cf. also Ps 89:40b: "you have defiled his crown in the dust" (*hllt l'rs nzrw*).

[16] J. L. Mays points out that there is debate "whether the full-fledged 'Zion theology' of the hymns of Zion (Pss. 46, 48, 84, 87) was already present among the leading circles in the late eighth century (*Micah* [Philadelphia: Westminster, 1976] 91 with references to von Rad, G. Wanke and J. J. M. Roberts).

Destruction of the city and the temple of the royal cult would seem to entail the failure of the dynasty. In the days of Jeremiah, this oracle of Micah was recalled by "certain elders of the land" along with Hezekiah's penitent response to the prophetic word of judgment (Jer 26:16-19). One may also ask whether the response of Isaiah to the embassy of Merodach Baladan (Marduk-apal-iddina) of Babylon[17] preserved in Isaiah 39 (2 Kgs 20) does not contain an echo of a prophetic qualification of the Davidic Zion theology.

In any case, while one may argue about the date when this "firmly held belief" came under attack in circles with access to the king, one cannot question, *pace* Whybray, that such attack did occur.

In the light of the foregoing, it is appropriate to pursue the meaning of the poem as it stands, with *nzr*. To the question of date, we shall return.

STRUCTURE

Diagram 1

v 23	P +/+
v 24	MS -/-
v 25	MS +/+/+ →
v 26	R +/+
v 27	R +/+/+

The poem consists of an extended Admonition or Instruction containing Precepts (v 23), a negative Motive Saying (MS), followed by a complex MS (vv 25-27). The extended MS in vv 25-27 consists of circumstantial clauses (v 25) based on the agricultural rhythms of creation followed by the positive Results (vv 26-27) of these rhythms when coupled with obedience to the Precepts in v 23. The Precepts (v 23) admonish the care of "flock" and "herds" precisely because wealth and "crown" are transitory (v 24). Nonetheless, when the fruits of the earth are gathered (v 25), one's herds and flock will provide what is needful (vv 26-27) for him and his "house."[18]

The Topic-Comment structure of the poem's Sayings strongly contrasts with the discrete structures found in the relatively independent Sayings studied in Prov 25:2-27:22. In 27:24-27 only v 24 functions as a self-sufficient MS:

---

[17] The historicity of the embassy is generally acknowledged though the prophetic judgment on Hezekiah's offspring is widely considered an elaboration in the light of the Babylonian exile. See J. Bright, *History of Israel*[3] (Philadelphia: Westminster, 1981) 284-285 and the commentaries.

[18] Most commentators follow Delitzsch (219-220) in seeing v 25 as the antecedent to vv 26-27. Verses 25-27 as a whole function as a complex consequential motive for Precepts in v 23.

Diagram 2

T-C Analysis of 27:24-27

v 24	$C_1 = T_1 / T_2 = C_2$
v 25	$T_1 = T_2 = T_3$
v 26, 27aα	$C_1 = C_2 = C_3$ (Result)
v 27aβb	$C_4 = C_5$ (Result)

As noted above, the circumstantial Topics in v 25 when coupled with obedience to the Precepts lead to the Results set forth in vv 26-27. Hence we have an set of T-C relations extending over several verses. The relation of C_3 to C_4 and C_5 requires special note since the latter two Comments are simply an expansion of the sub-Comment within C_3: Goat's milk (T) ... *enough for your food* (C). It will be argued below that v 27aβb (Comments C_4 and C_5) cannot be broken up. But the affinities of these final Comments to Prov 31:15 lead us to redactional questions which can only be touched upon in this study.

POETICS

Because of the common opinion concerning our poem's integrity, it is not necessary for our purposes to closely analyse its stylistic features such as the alliteration of *lamed* found in vv 23b, 24, 26a, 27. But one literary device merits attention, namely the use of the foliage imagery in v 25 to effect the transition from the negative Motive Saying in v 24 to the positive motivational Results in vv 26-27. Verse 24 establishes the transitoriness of wealth and crown. Verse 25, *at first reading* (i.e., without awarenss of its sequel) seems to continue the theme of transitoriness, by using the traditional image of perishing grass.[19] But the reader is then surprised to find that the very passing (and replenishment) of the grass, which seems to echo the passing of wealth and the generations, has become the foundation for life (vv 26-27).

SENSE

From the foregoing it is clear that I am not content with a merely bucolic reading of 27:23-27. Of course, it "makes sense" on this level — for the most part (*nzr!*) just as "Strike while the iron is hot" makes sense in the smithy. But this latter saying is commonly used metaphorically to refer to situations outside the smithy.

My thesis is that Prov 27:23-27 is not only susceptible to a metaphorical reading, but that its *Sitz im Buch* and internal details are best accounted for

---

[19] Job 8:12; Pss 37:2; 90:5; 103:15; 129:6; Isa 37:27 (= 2 Kgs 19:26); 40:6, 7; 51:12.

when the text is so read, as addressed to the king (and his court) as "shepherd" of his people.[20]

The metaphor of king as "shepherd"[21] of the "sheep"[22] was a widespread commonplace in the ANE and Mediterranean. In connection with Prov 27:23-27 it may be noted that the metaphor was employed in relation to the king's wisdom, his exercise of justice, and his promotion of the well-being of his people.[23] These motifs appear throughout the Prologue and Epilogue of Codex Hammurabi[24] and are nicely summarized in the Epilogue.[25]

In ancient Israel the shepherd metaphor is also frequently applied to the (divine or human) king, though it is never used as a royal title in the manner of the Mesopotamian kings.[26] It is particularly striking that when the (pre-) exilic prophets Jeremiah and Ezekiel attack the degenerate ruler and his court or their successors, they accuse them of being bad shepherds of the flock (Jer 2:8; 10:21; 23:1-6; 25:34, 36; 50:6; Ezekiel 34)[27] and assert that Yahweh will replace them with a new David as shephard (Jer 23:5-6; Ezek 34:23). Significantly, in contrast to the bad shepherds, the new David will act *"wisely,* and shall execute justice

---

[20] Such a reading was current in the Seventeenth Century. See M. Poole, *Synopsis Criticorum* vol. II, (London: Cornelius Bee, 1671) col. 1757. Poole cites Menochius. Bede had applied our text to the *pastores ecclesiae.*

[21] The metaphor has been extensively documented. See especially G. J Botterweck, "Hirt und Herde im alten Testament und im alten Orient," in Wilhelm Corsten et al. (eds.), *Die Kirche und ihre Aemter und Stände. Festgabe ... Joseph Kardinal Frings,* (Köln: Bachem, 1960) 339-352. Further literature in J. A. Soggin, "r'h," (*THAT II*) 791-794, and note 26 below.

[22] Botterweck, "Hirt," 347. Robert M. Good (*The Sheep of His Pasture: a Study of the Hebrew Noun 'am(m) and its Semitic Cognates* [Chico: Scholars, 1983]) argues that *'am* is originally a pastoral term parallel in sense to "flock" (see pp. 52-54 and Nah 3:18).

[23] See the Prologue of Lipit-Ishtar (*ANET*, 159c) where the king is called "the wise shepherd" whose task is to establish "justice in the land . . . to bring well-being to the Sumerians and Akkadians." See further Botterweck, "Hirt," 349-350). I. Seibert, *Hirt-Herde-König* (1969) has not been seen by me. For Egypt, D. Müller, "Der gute Hirte. Ein Beitrag zur Geschichte ägyptischer Bildrede," *ZÄS* 86 (1961) 126-144. See also *THAT II,* 794.

[24] On the function of the Prologue and Epilogue, see S. M. Paul, *Studies in the Book of the Covenant in the Light of Cuneiform and Biblical Law* (Leiden: Brill, 1970) 11-26, especially 25-26, with reference to the king as "faithful shepherd" and *šar mēšārim,* "king of justice."

[25] See *ANET* 178a, rev. xxiv 28-61.

[26] J. Jeremias, "poimen" in *TDNT VI,* 487-88, and *THAT II,* 793-94, with literature.

[27] "Shepherds" in Jer 2:8 refers to "die weltlichen Lenker Israels, also König und Aristokratie," so Botterweck ("Hirt," 346). For the dating of Jer 23:1-6 (excluding v 3), in the time of Zedekiah, see W. Rudolph, (*Jeremias*² [HAT; Tübingen: JCB Mohr, 1958] 134-137).

and righteousness in the land" (whśkyl w'śh mšpt wsdqh b'rs, Jer 23:5). Thus also in Israel the goodness of the shepherd-king consists of wisdom manifest in the exrcise of justice and righteousness.[28]

Against the background of the pervasive use of the shepherd-sheep metaphor for king and people, it is not surprising that in the judicial parable which Nathan uses to expose David's crime against Uriah, he refers to the rich man's (i. e. David's) "flocks and herds" (2 Sam 12:2, 4) Similarly, that the bucolic admonition of Prov 27:23-27 functions as a metaphor for kingship is on the face of it eminently plausible, especially in the context of a collection primarily dedicated to the court.[29]

To demonstrate that the poem is a metaphor for kingship requires that we present a reading of it which does justice to the whole and its details. That is, one must read the poem in the light of our exegetical *assumption* and see if the poem is more satisfactorily accounted for by means of this, rather than some other, exegetical assumption.

How then does the poem read, given our assumption? In itself the first line (v 23) is quite ambiguous, and at first glance seems to be merely straightforward agricultural admonition. But as we have noted above in connection with "Strike while the iron is hot," short Sayings and Admonitions have a metaphoric tendency. With regard to v 23 (yd' td'), compare the following:

12:10	A righteous man knows the need (npš) of his beast, but the mercy of the wicked is cruel.
12:11	He who tills his land will have plenty of bread, but he who follows worthless pursuits has no sense (cf. 28:19).

Of course a good man cares for his animals, but the point of the Saying applies much more significantly to people, as another related Saying shows:

29:7	A righteous man knows the rights (dyn) of the poor, a wicked man does not understand such knowldge (d't).[30]

Our assumption for the Precept in 27:23 is that the implicit addressee(s) are the king and court and the "flock" and "herds" are their subjects, the people of the land.

---

[28] See also the shepherd-wisdom imagery in Jer 3:15 and Ps 78:70-72 (cf. Ezek 34:16). Note the metaphoric use of grazing in connection with justice in Isa 5:16-17.

[29] See Whybray quoted above in note 10.

[30] Both 12:10 and 29:7 begin with the participial phrase, ywd' sdyq. Here, as in 27:23, yd' means "be concerned for." See McKane, 424, 452, 642, and Jer 22:15-16, where the king's duty of judging the case (dyn) of the poor and needy is set forth in terms of the "knowledge" (d't) of God.

In v 24, a negative Motive is given for the preceding Precept: Wealth and crown do not last forever. Verse 24a allows one to continue the bucolic reading: in view of the instability of wealth, one must be all the more careful with that which is in one's charge, i.e., the "sheep." But a merely agricultural interpretation of the poem is shattered by the appearance of the "crown" (*nzr*) in v 24b. As noted above, a crown pertains only to royalty, and the royal position is based not so much on agriculture—though this may not be neglected—as it is on the populace, the human "sheep" who are the royal subjects and objects of his care.

The "logic" which connects the Motive Saying in v 24 to the Precept in v 23 is not far to find:

Prov 14:28 A numerous people is the glory of a king,
without a nation a ruler is ruined (*JPSV*).

Thus the king must "know" (care for) his "flock"; without them he is nothing. They are his "glory" as a good wife is the "crown" (*'trh*) or "glory" (*doxa*) of her husband (Prov 12:4; 1 Cor 11:7 respectively).[31] These passages suggest that there is a meaningful connection in Prov 27:23-24 between the crown as emblem of the king's glory or office and his care of the "sheep" who are also his "glory" and the basis of his royal wealth. Zech 9:16-17 provides a final parallel to this idea complex:

On that day the Lord their God will save them
for they are the flock of his people;
for like the jewels of a crown (*nzr*)
they shall shine on his land.
Yea how good and fair it shall be!
Grain shall make the young men flourish,
and new wine the maidens.[32]

---

[31] For a further instance of the symbolic equivalence of "crown" and "glory," cf. Prov 16:31, "a splendid crown is grey hair" (*'trt tp'rt śybh*) and 20:29, "The splendor of young men is their strength, but the glory of old men is their grey hair (*tp'rt bhwrym khm whdr zqnyn śybh*). On the equation of "grey hair" and "wisdom," see A. Caquot, "Israelite Perceptions of Wisdom and Strength in the Light of the Ras Shamra Texts," *IW*, 25-33. See also Prov 4:9; 17:6; Isa 62:3; Jer 13:18; Ezek 16:12; 23:42. *'trh*, unlike *nzr*, need not apply only to the king's crown in a non-priestly context. In Exod 28:2, 40, the priestly garments emblemize the priestly glory and splendour (*lkbwd wltp'rt*). In Isa 28:1, 3-4, the city Samaria is the "proud crown" (*'trt g'wt*), the "splendor" (*tp'rt*) of the drunkards of Ephraim. Cf. the discussion of W. H. Irwin (*Isaiah 28-33. Translation with Philological Notes* [Rome: Biblical Institute, 1977] 4-7).

[32] RSV. The Text is not without difficulties—but the general sense is not as intractable as suggested by some commentators: "das Bild von der Herde ist auch ohne jede Beziehung zu dem folgenden von den Edelstein." So W. Rudolph, *Sacharja 1-8* (KAT XIII₄; Gütersloh: Gerd Mohn, 1976) 185. The relation, as follows from the texts noted above is thus: flock = people = king's crown/glory. The fluid movement of the agricultural images

As noted above in the section on Poetics, Prov 27:25 serves as a pivot from the negative Motive Saying in v 24 to the positive Motives in vv 25-27. The transitoriness of grass (Isa 40:6-8 etc.) becomes the foundation for the stable life of the flock and shepherd, people and king. The kingdom, as it were, rests ultimately upon the reliability of the fruitful earth.[33] In vv 26-27 the poem returns to its beginning concern with flocks and herds. Here they are particularized and become the basis for the entire economy of the "house," providing clothing, capital for real estate, enough food and provisions for the "house" and its "maidens."

It would seem at this point that we are pretty well finished with what this short poem has to offer. However, the place of the poem in the book and its somewhat peculiar language force reconsideration.

Delitzsch (221) had termed Prov 27:23-27 a "boundary [which] . . . forms the conclusion of the foregoing series of proverbs." Barucq has refined Delitzsch's perception:

> Le developpement XXVII, 23-27, qui interrompt la série des distiques, pourrait bien être l'indice d'une fin de section. Il s'intéresse curieusement à l'économie domestique (souci inconnu du rest du livret) tout comme XXXI, 10-31, qui clôt le livre.[34]

Barucq's remarks contain two seeds which bear fruit upon cultivation. First, both 27:23-27 and 31:10-31 function to close off a section and/or the book itself. They appear to be two of several short poems which have a boundary-marking function in the last third of the book.[35] This suggests that the placement of 27:23-27 is connected with the redaction of 22:17-31:31, or that the redactor of 22:17-31:31 took 25-27 as a model to emulate. The redactor of this part of Proverbs employs brief poems (three of which have agricultural themes) to mark the end of subsections or smaller collections.

---

comes full circle when grain and wine cause the young men and women to "bear fruit" (*ynwbb*). Note also in the continuation of this passage (Zech 10:1-5) the mélange of agricultural, pastoral, and other metaphors.

[33] Cf. the many associations among kingship, wisdom, justice, and a fruitful earth both within and without Israel. H. H. Schmid, *GAW,* 14-57. See especially Ps 72:1-4, 6, 16.

[34] "Proverbes (Livre des)," *DBSup* 8 (1972) col. 1402. See also his commentary, 18, 193, 217.

[35] Prov 23:29-35 closes the section beginning with 22:17. Chapter 24:1-22 is a new subsection (inclusio *qn'/r'h* in vv 1, 19 and other, especially thematic, features) bounded by the poem in 23:29-35 and the title in 24:23. Chapter 24:30-34 ends the section beginning in 24:23. The placement of this "sluggard poem" is clearly due to a redactional stage of the book as a whole since it employs a refrain (24:33-34) found also in 6:10-11. Chapter 27:23-27 marks the end of Skladny's Collection C. Prov 31:10-31 ends the entire book and is tied to 31:1-9 as M. H. Lichtenstein has shown ("Chiasm: and Symmetry," 202-211). The LXX accents the courtly focus of Chapters 25-29 by inserting 31:1-9 at their head.

The second seed planted by Barucq is to call attention to the common interest in 27:23-27 and 31:10-31 in "l'économie domestique." This common concern, however, is much more precise in content than suggested by Barucq. One may argue that the poems betray the touch of a common hand, and that the domestic, agricultural, and economic concerns serve largely the same purposes in each.

The two poems share some tell-tale phrases and concerns. Two primary foci of activity of the 'št ḥyl in 31:10-31 are to provide food (*lḥm*, vv 14, 27, cf. 15, 16) and clothing (*lbwš*, vv 21, 22, 25)[36] for her "house" (*byt*, vv 15, 21 [twice], 27). The wise woman considers a field (*śdh*) and buys it (v 16). In 27:23-27 these same main concerns appear: bread (*lḥm*) for the house (*byt*), requisite clothing (*lbwš*), and the possibility of buying a field (*śdh*, v 26b). In 31:15b, the "valiant wife" supplies *ṭrp lbyth wḥq ln'rtyh* ("provisions for her household, the daily fare of her maids").[37]

The phrases just quoted from 31:15b appear to be a redactional connection between Prov 31:10-31 and 27:23-27. In spite of the length of the lines in question, neither *wḥq ln'rtyh* in 31:15b nor *lḥm bytk* in 27:27aβ, are to be deleted *metri causa*. In the first place, *ṭrp* and *ḥq* form the "breakup of a stereotype word pair," as is shown by 30:8b (note 37). Secondly, *byt* and *n'rwt* form another word pair common to 27:27 and 31:15b. Thirdly, in 27:27 as a whole (*wdy ḥlb 'zym llḥmk llḥm bytk whyym ln'rwtyk* "enough goat's milk for your food, food for your house, and victuals for your maids"), the idea of wise or adequate allotment (31:15b, *ḥq*, not too much, nor too little) is captured by *dy*, "enough," which qualifies all the Comments in 27:27 (cf. 25:16, 27a). Finally, the concluding phrases of these two lines are especially noteworthy and their parallelism too precise to be happenstance, for each item is an exact counterpart to its fellow:

31:15b	*ṭrp lbyth wḥq ln'rtyh*
27:27b	*llḥm bytk whyym ln'rwtyk*

In the one case the sense of multivalent *ḥyym* (victuals) depends upon the preceding *lḥm*, in the other *ḥq* depends upon the preceding *ṭrp*. For these reasons, we would argue that neither 31:15b nor 27:27aβb may be broken up. Prov 27:27aβb as a whole might be a redactional addition to 27:23-27aα which could form a complete unit. But if the phrases in question may not be broken, then 31:15 must stand as a whole.

---

[36] See the clothing imagery and concerns in 31:13, 17, 19, 22, 24, 25.

[37] Thus *JPSV* rightly against Scott (185), *RSV* and others who take *ḥq* as "instructions" or "tasks" for the maids. *Ṭrp* and *ḥq* form the "break up of a stereotype phrase." Cf. Prov 30:8 *hṭrypny lḥm ḥqy*, "feed me with my alloted bread" (and Matt 6:11?). The reference is to the alloted portion or ration which servants and underlings receive. E. Z. Melamed, "Break-up of Stereotype Phrases as an Artistic Device in Biblical Poetry," *Studies in the Bible*, ed. C. Rabin (Scripta Hierosolymitana 8; Jerusalem, 1961) 115-153.

In 27:27, the appearance of *n'rwt,* "maids," in parallel to house seems at first glance quite unmotivated. Though a king or wealthy landowner will have both *n'rym* and *n'rwt,* as does Boaz (Ruth 2:8, 22, 23; 3:2), why should the poet in this short bucolic poem choose maids over menservants? It can only be that he is influenced by the feminine embodiment of wisdom in 31:10-31, whose servants are naturally female.[38]

These parallels betwen 27:23-27 and 31:10-31 cannot be accidental and in the light of recent research confirm our suggestion that the two poems have a similar function and message: kings and rulers must carry out their office with wisdom. M. H. Lichtenstein has shown that

> The juxtaposition of the two poems of Proverbs 31, as it now stands in the Hebrew text, and however it may have come about, has effected a most happy and fitting union. Indeed, Lemuel's mother has been provided with a most appropriate daughter-in-law, in more ways than one.[39]

The connection between the wise, "valiant woman" in 31:10-31 and the queen mother's advice to King Lemuel in vv 1-9 is further reinforced in view of the significant role of the queen mother in ancient Israel.[40] As the "valiant woman" embodies the essentials of wisdom, including concern for the poor and needy (v 20), so must kings (vv 5, 9); for it is by Lady Wisdom that Kings rule and decree (*yḥqqw*) what is just (8:15-16).

Prov 27:23-27 has a similar relation to kingship. In a parabolic fashion, it urges the king to execute his task wisely by caring for his flock. Positively, such wisdom produces prosperity (cf. 8:18; 31:10, 31), and continuity of the dynasty.

If this interpretation of Prov 27:23-27 is correct, what is the date of this section, and how does it relate to Proverbs 25-27 as a whole? I would suggest the following, but in the nature of the case these matters are uncertain. Chapters 25 and 26 stem from the court of Hezekiah, late eighth century, as most scholars agree. Chapter 27:1-22 is extremely hard to date. Its character as a proverb miscellany sets it apart from the "proverb poems" in 25-26, though it does have thematic affinities with them. Basically two reasons may be suggested to account for this. 1) Chapter 27:1-22 arises in the same Hezekian circle which created 25-26. But in 27:1-22, the individual author did not attempt, or was unable, to achieve the higher literary unity found in the subsections of 25 and 26. 2) Chapter 27:1-22 is quite unrelated to 25-26; it stems from another time and setting which we are unable to establish. Of these two options, I am inclined toward the first.

---

[38] In Proverbs, *n'rh* only appears in the plural, 9:3; 27:27; 31:15. Cf. 1 Sam 25:42 where Abigail, an archetypically wise wife (vv 3, 33) appears with her five *n'rwt.* In Prov 27:27, the immediate connection is with 31:15, but the parallel with wisdom and her *n'rwt* in 9:3 further illuminates the motivation for *n'rwt* in 27:27.

[39] "Chiasm and Symmetry," (221).

[40] Niels-Erik A. Andreasen, "The Role of the Queen Mother in Israelite Society," *CBQ* 45 (1983) 179-94.

Finally, 27:23-27 also has two possible settings. 1) It is a parable on kingship which was written in the post-exilic period. Though Israel has no king, it does have rulers and "shepherds." The post-exilic writers continue to use the imagery and categories of kingship when discussing government, as can be seen from the prophetic texts discussed above (cf. also Zech 11:4-15; 13:7). 2) It is a Hezekian composition (as far as 27:23-27aα) designed to act as an end-marker to the first half of chapters 25-29. In this case, 27:27aβb is a late redactorial gloss designed to create links with Proverbs 31 and chapters 1-9.

The affinities of 27:23-27 with the poem in 31:10-31 argue for a similar date and *Sitz*. My suggestion is that we have to do with the final redaction of the book. For the place of 31:10-31 must be seen in relation to Lady Wisdom in chapters 1-9, to whom the "valiant woman" forms a thematic inclusio. To date 31:10-31 is extremely difficult, but there appears to be a clue in the presence of a bilingual Hebrew-Greek pun. In v 27 *swpyh* is a perfect Hebrew transliteration of Greek *sophia*, "wisdom." Only in this verse does the poet break his regular pattern of perfect verbs with a participle.[41] The pun suggests a time early in the Hellenistic period.

---

[41] Al Wolters "*Sôpîyyâ* (Prov 31:27) as Hymnic Participle and Play on *Sophia*," *JBL* 104 (1985) 577-587.

11
Recapitulation and Reflections

In the preceding chapters, we have presented a problem, developed some methods to deal with it, and proceeded to analyze a body of text (Proverbs 25-27) in terms of the problem and our methods.

The problem is that of literary context among the Sayings and Admonitions in the Book of Proverbs. Do these small wisdom units exist only in random, non-significant juxtaposition, at best linked by mnemonic catch-words, or do they form larger units of meaning, encompassing a number of the smaller units in patterned, significant wholes?

After noting that there have been two main lines of research (Chapters I, II), corresponding to the alternative views implied in the questions just asked, we laid out the heuristic assumptions (Chapter III) which would make possible the perception of larger literary units built out of the relatively discrete and independent basic units, Sayings and Admonitions. These assumptions are 1) that synchronic analysis has a necessary logical and hence methodological priority over diachronic analysis, 2) that meaning in literary units is built up by a process of accretion, 3) that the nature of the unity in a literary composition is a function of its genre, in our case the "proverb poem."

In Chapter IV we set forth our methods of analysis. We desired methods that would expose genuine coherences of meaning, but which would also discriminate among the various patterns and devices employed to create different proverb poems, and most important, which would discriminate between the *degrees* of cohesion in different segments of text.

Three methods of approach to the text were explained. First was a twofold structural analysis. By structural analysis we mean a method employing key concepts developed by post-Saussurian linguistics. In particular, the notion of paradigmatic options arranged to create syntagmatic patterns or blocks of Sayings and Admonitions was put forward as a means of dealing with the peculiar genre of the proverb poem, which does not develop its meaning in a narrative syntagmatic way.

The two types of structural analysis complement one another. The first is based upon the well-known contrast of Admonitions and Sayings in combination with the explicit or implicit valuations of positive (+) or negative (-) which pervade Proverbs. The second structural method applies only to the Sayings and is based upon the Topic-Comment analysis of proverbs developed by Allan

Dundes and others. Here patterns of Topic-Comment structure within individual Sayings function as paradigmatic options which the writer of a proverb poem can employ to create syntagmatic patterns or blocks by similarity and dissimilarity.

The second method applied to the text is poetic analysis. It is comparable to what is often called "rhetorical criticism" among Old Testament scholars. Our assumption is that the same poetic devices common to clearly unified poems such as Psalms or prophetic pericopes will be found to operate among the small wisdom units to build proverb poems.

The third approach to the text is a "semantic" one. This is not so much a "method" per se, but is the attempt to listen carefully to our texts while paying close attention to the patterns, parts, and details which create larger significant units. Here we must penetrate not only the forms and patterns which the texts embody, but also the larger ideational patterns which are the "sense" of the poem. Chapters V through X provide translations and analyses of the subsections of Proverbs 25-27. The subsections are 25:2-27; 26:1-12, 13-16, 17-28; 27:1-22, 23-27 (Prov 25:28 fits into no larger pattern and seems an addition). The first four of these subsections may be properly described as "proverb poems" in that they employ Admonitions and Sayings to create larger patterns and blocks of meaning. These subsections share some common techniques in terms of structure, poetics, and sense, but each possesses its own individuality. Prov 27:1-22 on the other hand must be termed a "proverb miscellany," for it lacks an organized and coherent macrostructure, though its poetic devices serve fairly consistently to link Sayings or Admonitions into couplets. Nor does 27:1-22 possess any overarching theme to bind it together semantically. Prov 27:23-27 is a bucolic parable to admonish the king or, by extension, any ruler or shepherd of the people.

The four proverb poems (25:2-26:28) reveal the following semantic or thematic concerns. Prov 25:2-27 is united by two main concerns: 1) social hierarchy, rank, or position (God-king-subjects) and 2) social conflict and its resolution. Its primary address is to the young men of the royal court. Prov 26:1-12 is linked to the preceding poem by the catchword root *kbd* (25:2 [bis], 27 [bis]; 26:1) and by a worry about status wrongly given (26:1, 8). But its main interest is in the problem of the correct understanding and application of proverbs (*mšlym*, vv 7, 9) to various situations, and in evaluating and dealing with the negative other, typified by the fool (*ksyl*). Prov 26:13-16 is built upon a similar pattern of word repetition (*'ṣl*) as 26:1-12 (*ksyl*) and shares with the latter a refrain phrase (*ḥkm b'ynyw*; vv 12, 16). Prov 26:17-28 is thematically based upon the theme of social conflict (*ryb*) taken from chapter 25:2-27 and develops this theme particularly in terms of the verbal wounder. Prov 27:1-22 is only a proverb miscellany and does not possess the semantic coherence of the preceding poems, yet its content is quite compatible with them, and there are thematic echoes (e.g., 25:6-7, 26:1, 8, 27:2; 25:20, 27:14).

Prov 27:23-27, a bucolic admonitory parable, we argue, is addressed to a king or to ruling "shepherds." Yet this parable raises questions that lead us beyond the scope of the present work. Our primary focus has been on the individual subunits, with occasional hints as to their interrelatedness in the larger grouping of chapters 25-27. Prov 27:23-27, however, raises the redactional problem with particular acuteness. For not only does it appear as one of several poems which mark the end of sections in the Book of Proverbs, it employs a phrase which is to be linked with Proverbs 31, in what seems to be part of the book's final redaction.

Hence the present work opens up two avenues for future research. The first, which is a prerequisite to the second, is to apply the methods here developed to all the proverbial sections in chapters 10-29. This would achieve a more reliable identification and description of the individual proverbs as well as of the various sections of the book than has hitherto occurred. The second is to investigate the redactional relations obtaining among the various sections analyzed, rather than treating redaction as a matter of individual Sayings and Admonitions only.

Bibliography

Important recent bibliographies include those of J. L. Crenshaw (1974, 1976) and F. Vattioni (1972). Abbreviations not found in the *Journal of Biblical Literature* or *Catholic Biblical Quarterly* style sheets may be found in the Table of Abbreviations.

Commentaries

Cornelius a Lapide, *Commentarii in Sacram Scripturam* vol. 3 (Paris: Pélagaud, 1854, original 1616).

A. Barucq, *Le Livre des Proverbes* (Sources Bibliques; Paris: Galbada, 1964).

A. Cohen, *Proverbs* (London: Soncino, 1946).

F. Delitzsch, *The Book of Proverbs* (Commentary on the Old Testament in Ten Volumes by C. F. Keil and F. Delitzsch, VI; Grand Rapids: Eerdmans, 1975 [German original 1873]).

H. Ewald, *Die Salomonischen Schriften* (Die Dichter des Alten Bundes, II; Göttingen: Vandenhoeck and Ruprecht: 1867).

B. Gemser, *Sprüche Salomos* (HAT 16; Tübingen: Mohr, 1963^2).

W. H. Gispen, *Spreuken I, II* (KV; Kampen: Kok, 1952, 1954).

D. Kidner, *Proverbs: an Introduction and Commentary* (Tyndale Old Testament Commentaries; Leicester: Tyndale, 1964).

W. McKane, *Proverbs: A New Approach* (Old Testament Library; Philadelphia: Westminster, 1970).

W. O. E. Oesterley, *The Book of Proverbs* (London: Methuen, 1929).

M. Poole, *Synopsis Criticorum aliorumque S. Scripturae Interpretum*, vol. 2 (London: Cornelius Bee, 1671).

H. Ringgren, *Sprüche* (ATD 16; third edition; Göttingen: Vandenhoeck und Ruprecht, 1981).

R. B. Y. Scott, *Proverbs and Ecclesiastes* (AB 18; Garden City: Doubleday, 1965).

C. H. Toy, *The Book of Proverbs* (ICC; New York: Scribner's, 1902).

J. van der Ploeg, *Spreuken* (De Boeken van het Oude Testament; Roermond en Maaseik: Romen, 1952).

R. N. Whybray, *The Book of Proverbs* (Cambridge Bible Commentary; Cambridge: Cambridge University, 1972).

Other Secondary Sources

M. H. Abrams, *The Mirror and the Lamp: Romantic Theory and the Critical Tradition* (London: Oxford University, 1953).

W. F. Albright, "A New Hebrew Word for 'Glaze' in Proverbs 26:23," *BASOR* 98 (1945) 24-25.

L. Alonso-Schökel, *Das Alte Testament als literarisches Kunstwerk* (Köln: Bachem, 1971).

L. Alonso-Schökel, cf. A. Schökel.

R. Alter, *The Art of Biblical Narrative* (New York: Basic Books, 1981).

B. Alster, *The Instructions of Suruppak: A Sumerian Proverb Collection* (Mesopotamia 3; Copenhagen: Akademisk, 1974)

———, *Studies in Sumerian Proverbs* (Mesopotamia 2; Copenhagen: Akademisk, 1975)

N. A. Andreasen, "The Role of the Queen Mother in Israelite Society," *CBQ* (1983) 179-194.

A. Austin, *T. S. Eliot, The Literary and Social Criticism* (Bloomington: Indiana University, 1971).

S. E. Balentine, "Description of the Semantic Field of Hebrew Words for 'Hide,'" *VT* 30 (1980) 137-153.

A. Barucq, "Livre des Proverbes," *DBSup* 8 (1972) coll. 1395-1476.

J. Barton, "Natural Law and Poetic Justice in the Old Testament," *JTS* 30 (1979) 1-14.

A. Berlin, "Grammatical Aspects of Biblical Parallelism," *HUCA* 50 (1979) 17-43.

R. Borger, *Babylonisch-assyrische Lesestücke* (Rome: Pontifical Biblical Institute, 1963).

G. Boström, *Paronomasi i den äldre hebreiska Maschallitteraturen* (Acta Universitatis Lundensis, Nova Series; Lunds Universitets Årsskrift, Ny Föld, Avdelningen 1, vol. 23, no. 8; Lund: Gleerup, 1928).

G. J. Botterweck, "Hirt und Herde im alten Tastament und im alten Orient," *Die Kirche und ihre Aemter und Stände. Festgabe . . . Joseph Kardinal Frings,* (Köln: Bachem, 1960) 339-352.

J. Bright, "The Apodictic Prohibition: Some Observations," *JBL* 92 (1973) 185-204.

———, *History of Israel*³ (Philadelphia: Westminster, 1981).

H. Brunner, "Der freie Wille Gottes in der aegyptischen Weisheit," *SPOA*, 103-120.

———, "Gerechtigkeit als Fundament des Thrones," *VT* 8 (1958) 426-428.

J. H. Brunvand, *The Study of American Folklore* (second ed.; New York: Norton, 1978).

G. E. Bryce, "Another Wisdom 'Book' in Proverbs," *JBL* 91 (1972) 145-157.

———, " 'Better'-Proverbs: An Historical and Structural Study," *Book of Seminar Papers* 2 (L. C. McGaughy, ed.; Missoula: SBL, 1972) 343-354.

———, *A Legacy of Wisdom: the Egyptian Contribution to the Wisdom of Israel* (Lewisburg: Bucknell University, 1979).

———, "The Structural Analysis of Didactic Texts," *Biblical and Near Eastern Studies* (La Sor Festschrift; ed. G. A. Tuttle; Grand Rapids: Eerdmans, 1978) 107-21.

G. Buccellati, "Tre Saggi sulla Sapienza Mesopotamica —II. Il Dialogo del pessimismo: La Scienza degli Opposti come Ideale Sapienziale," *Oriens Antiquus* 11 (1972) 81-100.

———, "Wisdom and Not: The Case of Mesopotamia," *JAOS* 101 (1981) 35-47.

W. Bühlmann, *Vom Rechten Reden und Schweigen: Studien zu Proverbien 10-31* (Göttingen: Vandenhoeck und Ruprecht, 1976).

W. Bühlmann and K. Scherer, *Stilfiguren der Bibel* (Fribourg: Schweizerisches Katholisches Bibelwerk, 1973).

M. J. Buss, "The Idea of *Sitz im Leben*—History and Critique," *ZAW* 90 (1978) 157-170.

G. B. Caird, *Language and Imagery of the Bible* (Philadelphia: Westminster, 1980).

A. Caquot, "Israelite Perceptions of Wisdom and Strength in the Light of the Ras Shamra Texts," *IW*, 25-33.

C. E. Carlston, "Proverbs, Maxims, and the Historical Jesus," *JBL* 99 (1980) 87-105.

U. Cassuto, "The Sequence and Arrangement of the Biblical Sections" (1947), *Biblical and Oriental Studies* I (Jerusalem: Magnes, 1973) 1-6.

H. Cazelles, "A Propos d'une phrase de H. H. Rowley," *VTSupp* 3 (1955) 26-32.

B. S. Childs, *Introduction to the Old Testament as Scripture* (Philadelphia: Fortress, 1979).

R. E. Clements, "The Unity of the Book of Isaiah," *Int* 36 (1982) 117-129.

D. J. A. Clines, "Story and Poem: The Old Testament as Literature and Scripture," *Int* 34 (1980) 115-127.

D. J. A. Clines and D. M. Gunn, " 'You tried to persuade me' and 'Violence! Outrage!' in Jeremiah XX 7-8," *VT* 28 (1978) 20-27.

R. G. Collingwood, *The Idea of History* (Oxford: Clarendon, 1946).

J. J. Collins, "Proverbial Wisdom and the Yahwist Vision," *Semeia* 17 (1980) 1-17.

J. L. Crenshaw, *Old Testament Wisdom: An Introduction* (Atlanta: John Knox, 1981).

———, "Prolegomenon," *Studies in Ancient Israelite Wisdom* (New York: Ktav, 1976) 1-60.

———, "Wisdom," *Old Testament Form Criticism* (J. H. Hayes, ed.; Trinity University Monograph Series 2; San Antonio: Trinity University, 1974) 225-264.

A. D. Crown, "Messengers and Scribes: The ספר and מלאך in the Old Testament," *VT* 24 (1974) 366-370.

———, "Tidings and Instructions: How News Travelled in the Ancient Near East," *JESHO* 17 (1974) 244-271.

J. Culler, *Structuralist Poetics: Structuralism, Linguistics, and the Study of Literature* (Ithaca: Cornell University, 1975).

M. Dahood, "Hebrew Poetry," *IDBSup* (1976) 669-672.

———, *Psalms* III (AB; Garden City: Doubleday, 1970).

———, "Two Pauline Quotations From the Old Testament," *CBQ* 17 (1955) 19-24.

F. Daneš, "Functional Sentence Perspective and the Organization of the Text," *Janua Linguarum* (Series Minor 147, *Papers on Functional Sentence Perspective*; Prague: Academia and The Hague: Mouton, 1974) 106-128.

R. de Vaux, *Ancient Israel* I, II (New York: McGraw-Hill, 1961).

J. de Waard, "The Chiastic Structure of Amos V 1-17," *VT* 27 (1977) 170-177.

M. Dietrich, O. Loretz, and J. Sanmartin, "Die angebliche ug.-he. Parallele spsg//sps(j)g(jm)," *UF* 8 (1976) 37-40.

P. E. Dion, "La Lettre Araméenne Passe-Partout et ses sous-espèces," *RB* 89 (1982) 528-575.

———, "Tu feras disparaître le mal du milieu de toi," *RB* 87 (1980) 321-349.

S. R. Driver, *Introduction to the Literature of the Old Testament* (9th ed. [1913]; reprinted Gloucester, Mass.: Peter Smith 1972).

A. Dundes, "On the Structure of the Proverb," *Analytic Essays in Folklore* (A. Dundes, ed.; Studies in Folklore 2; The Hague/Paris: Mouton, 1975) 103-118.

A. Dundes and R. A. Georges, "Toward a Structural Definition of the Riddle," *Analytic Essays in Folklore* (A. Dundes, ed.; Studies in Folklore 2; The Hague/Paris: Mouton, 1975) 95-102.

O. Eissfeldt, *The Old Testament: An Introduction* (New York: Harper and Row, 1965).

J. A. Emerton, "Notes on Some Passages in the Book of Proverbs," *JTS* N.S. 20 (1969) 202-220.

———, "Wisdom," *Tradition and Interpretation* (Ed. G. W. Anderson; Oxford: Clarendon, 1979) 214-237.

R. O. Faulkner, *A Concise Dictionary of Middle Egyptian* (Oxford: Oxford University, 1962).

J. Fichtner, *Die altorientalische Weisheit in ihrer israelitisch-jüdischen Ausprägung: Eine Studie zur Nationalisiering der Weisheit in Israel* (BZAW 62; Giessen: Töpelmann, 1933).

G. Fohrer, "Remarks on the Modern Interpretation of the Prophets," *JBL* 80 (1961) 309-319.

C. R. Fontaine, *Traditional Sayings in the Old Testament* (Sheffield: Almond, 1982).

R. W. E. Forrest, "An Inquiry into Yahweh's Commendation of Job," *SR* 8 (1979) 159-168.

M. V. Fox, "Aspects of the Religion of the Book of Proverbs," *HUCA* 39 (1968) 55-69.

———, "Two Decades of Research in Egyptian Wisdom Literature," *ZÄS* 107 (1980) 120-135.

H. Frankfort, *Ancient Egyptian Religion: An Interpretation* (New York: Harper, 1948).

H. G. Gadamer, *Wahrheit und Methode: Grundzüge einer philosophischen Hermeneutik* (Tübingen: Mohr, 1975⁴).

J. G. Gammie et al., eds., *Israelite Wisdom: Theological and Literary Essays in Honor of Samuel Terrien* (Missoula: Scholars, 1978).

A. Gamper, *Gott als Richter in Mesopotamien und im Alten Testament* (Innsbruck: Universitätsverlag Wagner, 1966).

B. Gemser, "Gedachtenassociaties in het Spreukenboek, een middel tot tekstfixering," *Onder Eigen Vaandel* 2 (1927) 137-151.

———, "The Importance of the Motive Clause in Old Testament Law," *VTSup* 1 (1953) 50-66.

———, "The Spiritual Structure of Biblical Aphoristic Wisdom," *SAIW*, 208-219.

H. Gese, *Lehre und Wirklichkeit in der Alten Weisheit* (Tübingen: Mohr, 1958).

J. C. L. Gibson, *Textbook of Syrian Semitic Inscriptions Vol. I. Hebrew and Moabite Inscriptions* (Oxford: Clarendon, 1971).

M. Gilbert, ed., *La Sagesse de l'Ancien Testament*, (BETL 51; Gembloux: Leuven University, 1979).

J. A. Gladson, "Retributive Paradoxes in Proverbs 10-29," (Ph.D. diss. Vanderbilt; Ann Arbor: University Microfilms International, 1978).

E. M. Good, *Irony in the Old Testament* (Philadelphia: Westminster, 1965).

———, "The Unfilled Sea: Style and Meaning in Ecclesiastes 1:2-11," *IW* (1978) 59-73.

J. Goody, *The Domestication of the Savage Mind* (Cambridge: Cambridge University, 1977).

R. Gordis, *The Book of Job: Commentary, New Translation, and Special Studies* (Moreshet 2; New York: Jewish Theological Seminary of America, 1978).

E. I. Gordon and T. Jacobsen, *Sumerian Proverbs* (Philadelphia: University Museum of the University of Pennsylvania, 1959).

R. L. Harris, "A Mention of Pottery Glazing in Proverbs," *JAOS* 60 (1940) 268-269.

Susan E. Haviland and H. H. Clark, "What's New? Acquiring New Information as a Process in Comprehension," *Journal of Verbal Learning and Verbal Behavior* 13 (1974) 512-521.

T. Hawkes, *Structuralism and Semiotics* (Berkeley and Los Angeles: University of California, 1977).

A. Heidel, *The Gilgamesh Epic and Old Testament Parallels* (Chicago: University of Chicago, 1946).

J. Heineman, "The Proem in the Aggadic Midrashim. A Form Critical Study," *Scripta Hierosolymitana* 22 (1971) 110-122.

H. J. Hermisson, "Observations on the Creation Theology in Wisdom," *IW* 43-57.

———, *Studien zur israelitischen Spruchweisheit* (WMANT 28; Neukirchen-Vluyn: Neukirchener, 1968).

E. Hornung and O. Keel eds., *Studien zu altägyptischen Lebenslehren* (OBO 28; Freiburg: Universitätsverlag, 1979).

W. L. Humphreys, "The Motif of the Wise Courtier in the Book of Proverbs," *IW,* 177-90.

W. H. Irwin, *Isaiah 28-33. Translation with Philological Notes* (Rome: Biblical Institute, 1977).

J. H. Jackson and N. Kessler, eds., *Rhetorical Criticism, Essays in Honor of James Muilenburg* (Pittsburgh: Pickwick, 1974).

R. Jakobson, "Grammatical Parallelism and its Russian Facet," *Language* 42 (1966) 399-429.

E. Jenni, *Das hebräische Pi'el* (Zürich: EVZ Verlag, 1968).

C. A. Keller, "Zum sogenannten Vergeltungsglauben im Proverbienbuch," *Beiträge zur alttestamentlichen Theologie* (W. Zimmerli Festschrift; ed. H. Donner et al; Göttingen: Vandenhoeck and Ruprecht, 1977) 223-238.

O. Keel, *The Symbolism of the Biblical World* (New York: Seabury, 1978).

H. Kenner, *Das Phänomen der verkehrten Welt in der griechisch-römischen Antike* (Klagenfurt: Geschichtsverein für Kärnten, 1970).

M. A. Klopfenstein, *Die Lüge nach dan Alten Testament* (Zürich: Gotthelf Verlag, 1964).

———, *Scham und Schande nach dem Alten Testament* (ATANT 62; Zürich: Theologischer Verlag, 1972).

K. Koch, "Gibt es ein Vergeltungsdogma im AT?" *ZThK* 52 (1955) 1-44.

———, *The Growth of the Biblical Tradition* (New York: Scribner's, 1969).

K. Koch, ed., *Um das Prinzip der Vergeltung in Religion und Recht des Alten Testaments* (Wege der Forschung 125; Darmstadt: Wissenschaftliche Buchgesellschaft, 1972).

B. Kovacs, "Sociological-Structural Constraints Upon Wisdom: The Spatial and Temporal Matrix of Proverbs 15:28-22:16" (Ph.D. diss.; Vanderbilt; Ann Arbor: University Microfilms International, 1978).

S. N. Kramer, *The Sumerians* (Chicago: University of Chicago, 1963).

J. L. Kugel, *The Idea of Biblical Poetry* (New Haven: Yale, 1982).

D. Kunzle, "The World Upside Down: The Iconography of a European Broadsheet Type," *The Reversible World: Symbolic Inversion in Art and Society* (B. A. Babcock, ed.; Ithaca: Cornell University, 1978).

T. O. Lambdin, *Introduction to Biblical Hebrew* (New York: Scribner's, 1971).

W. G. Lambert, *Babylonian Wisdom Literature* (Oxford: Clarendon, 1960).

B. Lang, "Vorläufer von Speiseeis in Bibel und Orient. Eine Untersuchung von Spr 25, 13," *Mélanges bibliques et orientaux en l'honneur de M. Henri Cazelles* (A. Caquot and M. Delcor, eds.; AOAT 212; Neukirchen-Vluyn: Neukirchener Verlag, 1981).

F. Langlemet, "Pour ou Contre Salomon? La rédaction prosalomonienne de 1 Rois, I-II," *RB* 83 (1976) 321-379, 481-529.

M. Lichtheim, *Ancient Egyptian Literature: Vols, I, II, III* (Berkeley: University of California, 1973-1980).

———, "Observations on Papyrus Insinger," *Studien zu altägyptischen Lebenslehren* (OBO 28; Freiburg: Universitätsverlag, 1979) 284-305.

C. Lévi-Strauss, *The Savage Mind* (London: Weidenfeld and Nicolson, 1972).

———, "The Story of Asdiwal," *The Structural Study of Myth and Totemism* (ed. E. Leach; London: Tavistock, 1967) 1-47.

M. H. Lichtenstein, "Chiasm and Symmetry in Proverbs 31," *CBQ* 44 (1982) 202-211.

J. M. Lindenberger, *The Aramaic Proverbs of Ahiqar* (Baltimore: Johns Hopkins University, 1983).

J. Lyons, *Introduction to Theoretical Linguistics* (London: Cambridge University, 1968).

———, "Linguistics," *Encyclopaedia Britannica, Macropaedia* Vol. 10 (fifteenth edition, 1978) 998-1103.

A. A. MacIntosh, "A Note on Proverbs xxv 27," *VT* 20 (1970) 112-114.

C. Malik, "History-Making, History-Writing, History-Interpreting," *Center Journal* 1 (Fall, 1982) 11-42.

J. L. Mays, *Micah* (OTL; Philadelphia: Westminster, 1976).

P. K. McCarter Jr., " 'Plots, True or False,' the Succession Narrative as Court Apologetic," *Interp* 35 (1981) 355-367.

W. McKane, *Prophets and Wise Men* (Studies in Biblical Theology 44; Naperville, Ill.: Alec R. Allanson, 1965)

E. Z. Melamed, "Break-up of Stereotype Phrases as an Artistic Device in Biblical Poetry," *Studies in the Bible* (C. Rabin, ed.; Scripta Hierosolymitana 8; Jerusalem, 1961) 115-153.

W. Mieder, "The Essence of Literary Proverb Study," New York Folklore Quarterly 30 (1974) 66-76.

L. T. Milic, *Style and Stylistics: an Analytic Bibliography* (New York: The Free Press, 1967).

S. Morenz, "Feurige Kohlen auf dem Haupt," *ThLZ* 78 (1953) coll. 187-192.

J. Muilenburg, "A Study in Hebrew Rhetoric: Repetition and Style." *VTSup* 1 (1953) 97-111.

D. Müller, "Der gute Hirte. Ein Beitrag zur Geschichte ägyptischer Bildrede," *ZÄS* 86 (1961) 126-144.

K. F. Müller, *Das assyrische Ritual* (MVAG 41/3; Leipzig, 1937).

T. Munro, *Form and Style in the Arts: An Introduction to Aesthetic Morphology* (Cleveland: Case Western Reserve University, 1970).

R. E. Murphy, "Form Criticism and Wisdom Literature," *CBQ* 31 (1969) 475-483.

———, "Hebrew Wisdom," *JAOS* 101 (1981) 21-34.

———, *Wisdom Literature* (FOTL 13; Grand Rapids: Eerdmans, 1981).

———, "Wisdom Theses," *Wisdom and Knowledge II* (J. Papin Festschrift; J. Armenti, ed.; Philadelphia: Villanova University, 1976) 187-200.

———, "Wisdom—Theses and Hypotheses," *IW*, 35-42.

P. J. Nel, *The Structure and Ethos of the Wisdom Admonitions in Proverbs* (BZAW 158; Berlin: de Gruyter, 1982).

M. Noth and D. W. Thomas eds., *Wisdom in Israel and in the Ancient Near East* (H. H. Rowly Festschrift) *VTSup* 3 (1955).

D. Noy, "The Jewish Versions of the 'Animal Languages' Folktale (AT 670)," *Scripta Hierosolymitana* 22 (1971) 171-207.

M. O'Conner, *Hebrew Verse Structure* (Winona Lake: Eisenbraun's, 1980).

G. S. Ogden, "The 'Better' Proverb (*Tôb-Spruch*), Rhetorical Criticism and Qoheleth," *JBL* 96 (1977) 489-505.

Z. Palkova and B. Palek, "Functional Sentence Perspective and Textlinguistics," *Current Trends in Textlinguistics* (Research in Text Theory 2; ed. W. Dressler; Berlin: de Gruyter, 1977) 212-227.

D. Pardee, *Handbook of Ancient Hebrew Letters* (SBL Sources for Biblical Study 15; Chico: Scholars, 1982).

———, "Types and Distribution of Parallelism in Ugaritic and Hebrew Poetry" (Unpublished Communication Prepared for the Annual Meeting of the Society of Biblical Literature, New York, December 21, 1982).

———, "*yph* 'witness' in Hebrew and Ugaritic," *VT* 28 (1978) 204-213.

D. Patte, *What is Structural Exegesis?* (Philadelphia: Fortress, 1976).

S. Paul, "A Literary Reinvestigation of the Oracles against the Nations of Amos," *De La Tôrah au Messie. Mélanges Henri Cazelles* (ed. J. Doré, P. Grelot, and M. Carrez; Paris: Desclée, 1981) 189-204.

———, "Amos 1:3-2:3: A Concatenous Literary Pattern," *JBL* 90 (1971) 397-403.

———, "Mnemonic Devices," *IDBSup* 600-602.

———, *Studies in the Book of the Covenant in the Light of Cuneiform and Biblical Law* (Leiden: Brill, 1970).

L. G. Perdue, "Liminality as a Social Setting for Wisdom Instructions," *ZAW* 93 (1981) 114-126.

———, "The Testament of David and Egyptian Royal Instructions," *Scripture in Context II: More Essays on the Comparative Method* (W. W. Hallo, J. C. Moyer, and L. G. Perdue, eds.; Winona Lake: Eisenbrauns, 1983) 79-96.

———, *Wisdom and Cult* (SBLDS 30; Missoula/Chico: Scholars, 1977).

O. Plöger, "Zur Auslegung der Sentenzensammlungen des Proverbiabuches," *Probleme biblischer Theologie. Gerhard von Rad zum 70. Geburtstag* (ed. H. W. Wolff; Munich: C. Kaiser, 1971) 402-416.

N. Porteous, "Royal Wisdom," *VTSup* 3 (1953) 247-261.

H. J. Postel, "The Form and Function of the Motive Clause in Proverbs 10-29" (Ph. D. Dissertation; University of Iowa, 1976).

H. D. Preuss, "Das Gottesbild der älteren Weisheit Israels, " *VTSup* 23 (1972) 117-45.

———, "Erwägungen zum theologischen Ort alttestamentlicher Weisheitsliteratur," *EvT* 30 (1970) 393-417.

J. B. Pritchard, ed., *Ancient Near Eastern Texts Relating to the Old Testament* (Third ed. with Supplement; Princeton: Princeton University, 1969).

L. Ramaroson, " 'Charbons ardents': 'sur la tête' ou 'pour le feu'?" *Bib* 51 (1970) 230-234.

E. Reiner, "The Etiological Myth of the Seven Sages" *Or* 30 (1961) 1-11.

W. Richter, *Exegese als Literaturwissenschaft: Entwurf einer alttestamentlichen Literaturtheorie und Methodologie* (Göttingen: Vandenhoeck and Ruprecht, 1972).

———, *Recht und Ethos: Versuch einer Ortung des Weisheitlichen Mahnspruches* (Munich: Kösel, 1966).

N. H. Ridderbos, *Die Psalmen: Stilistische Verfahren und Aufbau, mit besonderer Berücksichtigung von Ps. 1-41* (BZAW 117; Berlin: de Gruyter, 1972).

J. W. Rogerson, *Anthropology and the Old Testament* (Atlanta: John Knox, 1979).

L. Röhrich and W. Mieder, *Sprichwort* (Stuttgart: Metzler, 1977).

J. H. Round, "Court," *Encyclopaedia Britannica* 7 (11th Ed.; New York: Encyclopaedia Britannica, 1910-11) 322-324.

H. Rücker, *Die Begründungen Jahwes im Pentatauch* (Erfurter Theologische Studien 30; Leipzig: St. Benno, 1973).

Les Sagesses du Proche-Orient Ancien: Colloque de Strasbourg 17-19 mai 1962 (Bibliothque des Centres d'Etudes Supérieures spécialisés; Paris: Presses Universitaires de France, 1963).

H. H. Schmid, *Gerechtigkeit als Weltordnung* (BHT 40; Tübingen: Mohr, 1968).

———, *Wesen und Geschichte der Weisheit* (BZAW 101 Berlin: Töpelmann, 1966).

A. Schökel (= L. Alonso-Schökel), "Poésie hébraïque," *DBSup* 8 (1972) coll. 47-90.

C. T. Scott, "On Defining the Riddle: The Problem of a Structural Unit," *Folklore Genres* (ed. D. Ben-Amos; Austin: University of Texas, 1976) 77-90.

R. B. Y. Scott, "Solomon and the Beginnings of Wisdom in Israel," *VTSup* 3 (1953) 262-279.

R. B. Y. Scott, "Wise and Foolish, Righteous and Wicked," *VTSup* 23 (1972) 146-65.

P. Seitel, "Proverbs: A Social Use of Metaphor," *Genre* 2 (1969) 143-61. Repr. in *Folklore Genres* (D. Ben-Amos ed.; Austin: University of Texas, 1976) 125-43.

I. L. Seeligmann, "Indications of Editorial Alteration and Adaptation in the Massoretic Text and the Septuagint," *VT* 11, (1961) 201-221.

———, "Zur Terminologie für das Gerichtsverfahren im Wortschatz des Biblischen Hebräisch," *VTSup* 16 (1967) 251-278.

C. L. Seow, "Hosea 14:10 and the Foolish People Motif," *CBQ* 44 (1982) 212-224.

W. K. Simpson, *The Literature of Ancient Egypt* (New Haven: Yale University, 1973).

K. H. Singer, *Die Metalle Gold, Silber, Bronze, Kupfer und Eisen im Alten Testament und ihre Symbolik* (Forschung zur Bibel 43, Würzburg: Echter, 1980).

P. W. Skehan, "A Single Editor for the Whole Book of Proverbs," *SIPW*, 15-26.

———, *Studies in Israelite Poetry and Wisdom* (CBQMS 1; Washington: Catholic Biblical Association of America, 1971).

———, "Wisdom's House," *SIPW*, 27-45.

U. Skladny, *Die ältesten Spruchsammlungen in Israel*, (Göttingen; Vandenhoeck und Ruprecht, 1962).

R. Sonsino, *Motive Clauses in Hebrew Law: Biblical Forms and Near Eastern Parallels* (SBLDS 45; Chico: Scholars, 1980).

J. H. Stek, "The Stylistics of Hebrew Poetry," *CTJ* 9 (1974) 15-30.

A. Taylor, *The Proverb* (Cambridge, Mass.: Harvard, 1931).

J. M. Thompson, *The Form and Function of Proverbs in Ancient Israel* (The Hague/Paris: Mouton, 1974).

M. Tsevat, "The Meaning of the Book of Job," *SAIW*, 341-374.

J. P. M. van der Ploeg, "Zur Literatur- und Stilforschung im Alten Testament," *ThLZ* 100 (1975) 801-814.

R. C. Van Leeuwen, "A Technical-Metallurgical Usage of יצא," *ZAW* 98 (1986) 112-113.

———, "The Day of Yahweh: Theme and Form in Amos 4 and 5" (unpublished M.A. Thesis; Toronto School of Theology, 1975).

———, "Isa 14:12, *Hôlēš 'al gwym* and Gilgamesh XI, 6," *JBL* 99 (1980) 173-184.

———, "Proverbs xxv 27 Once Again," *VT* 36 (1986) 105-114.

F. Vattioni, "Studi sul libro dei Proverbi," *Augustinianum* 12 (1972) 121-168.

J. Vermeylen, "Le Proto-Isaïe et la Sagesse d'Israël," *SAT*, 39-58.

K. von Fritz, "Ziel, Aufgaben und Methoden der klassischen Philologie und Altertumswissenschaft," *Vierteljahrschrift für Literaturwissenschaft und Geistesgeschichte* 33 (1959).

G. von Rad, *Wisdom in Israel* (Nashville and New York: Abingdon, 1972; = *Weisheit in Israel* [Neukirchen-Vluyn: Neukirchener, 1970).

N. A. Waldman, "A Note on Excessive Speech and Falsehood," *JQR* 67 (1976-77) 142-45.

M. Weinfeld, "The Counsel of the 'Elders' to Rehoboam and its Implications," *Maarav* 3 (1982) 27-53.

M. Weiss, "Die Methode der 'Total-Interpretation,'" *VTSup* 22 (1972) 88-112.

M. L. West, *Hesiod: Works and Days* (Oxford: Clarendon, 1978).

C. Westermann, "Weisheit im Sprichwort," *Schalom: Studien zu Glaube und Geschichte Israels* (A. Jepsen Festschrift; Arbeiten zur Theologie I/46; K. H. Bernhardt; Stuttgart; Calwer; 1971) 73-85.

R. Wellek and A. Warren, *Theory of Literature*[3] (New York: Harcourt, Brace and World, 1962).

K. W. Whitelam, *The Just King: Monarchical and Judicial Authority in Ancient Israel* (Sheffield: JSOT Press, 1979).

J. G. Williams, "The Power of Form: a Study of Biblical Proverbs," *Semeia* 17 (1980) 35-58.

R. J. Williams, "'A People Come Out of Egypt' An Egyptologist Looks at the Old Testament," *VTSup* 28 (1975) 231-252.

———, "The Sages of Ancient Egypt in the Light of Recent Scholarship," *JAOS* 101 (1981) 1-19.

J. A. Wilson, *The Culture of Ancient Egypt* (Chicago: University of Chicago, 1951).

R. N. Whybray, "Yahweh-sayings and their Contexts in Proverbs, 10, 1-22,16," *SAT,* 153-165.

H. W. Wolf, *Anthropology of the Old Testament* (Philadelphia: Fortress, 1974).

A. Wolters, "*Sôpîyyâ* (Prov 31:27) as Hymnic Participle and Play on *sophia,*" *JBL* 104 (1985) 577-587.

A. G. Wright, "'For Everything There is a Season': The Structure and Meaning of the Fourteen Opposites (Ecclesiastes 3, 2-8)," *De la Tôrah au Messie... Mélanges Henri Cazelles* (ed. J. Doré, P. Grelot, M. Carrez; Paris: Desclée, 1981) 321-328.

W. Zimmerli, "Das Buch Kohelet—Traktat oder Sentenzensammlung?" *VT* 24 (1974) 221-230.

——, "Ort und Grenze der Weisheit im Rahmen der alttestamentlichen Theologie," *SPOA*, 121-137 (= "The Place and Limit of the Wisdom in the Framework of the Old Testament Theology *SJT* 17 [1964] 146-158 = *SAIW*, 314-326).

——. "Zur Struktur der alten Weisheit," *ZAW* 51 (1933) 177-204 (= "Concerning the Structure of Old Testament Wisdom," *SAIW*, 175-207).

Index to Scripture and Other Ancient Works and Authors

Bible and Apocrypha

Genesis	
18:17	75
18:25	75
29:3, 8, 10	122
37:2	58
45:13	101

Exodus	
15	75
20:16	85
28:2, 40	139
32:24	78
35:22	88

Leviticus	
20:17	58

Numbers	
13:32	58
14:36, 37	58

Deuteronomy	
1:16, 17	58
1:27	111
5:16	97
5:20	85
13:15	77
19:18	85
27:16	97
28:35	97
29:29	69, 75

Joshua	
10:18	122

Judges	
5:4–5	75
5:20–21	75
8:2	48, 51
11:10	58
11:11	82
17:6	104
21:25	104

1 Samuel	
2:30	97
6:5	97
12:16–18	99
16:17	51
18:13	77
18:25–29	81
20:2	76
20:12	76
20:14–17	82
20:18	81
20:23	82
24:14	51
25	93, 142
25:42	142
30:15	101

2 Samuel	
3:10	78
4:11	79
7:13	78
7:16	78
11:1	59
12:1–4	105, 138
12:23	133

14:16–17	58, 76, 77	23:9	97
14:20	76	28:1, 3–4	139
15:1–6	83	28:8	97
15:2–7	81	28:23–29	133
15:3	58	29:24	111
16:12	93	37:27	136
19:27	76	39	135
		40:2	59
1 Kings		40:6–7	136, 140
1–2	78, 80	40:20	85
2:6	80	40:28	76
2:9	80	45:18	78
2:12	78, 80	51:12	136
2:45	78	54:16	78
2:46	79	56:10–12	97
3:9	58	58:13	82
3:11	58	62:3	139
3:28	76		
10:3	77	Jeremiah	
11:33	104	2:8	137
11:38	104	2:25	59
12:1–20	102	3:15	138
12:4	97	6:27–30	77
12:7	82	9:22–23	68
12:9–11, 14	97	14:10	59
21:13	85	10:21	136
		13:18	139
2 Kings		18:20	122
4:10	68	18:22	122
4:27	75	20:7–8	59
19:26	136	22:15–16	138
20	135	23:1–6	137
		23:5	138
Isaiah		23:5–6	73, 137
1:21–26	77	23:12	113
3:5	97	23:26	119
5:16–17	138	25:27	97
5:21	105	25:34, 36	137
8:10	82	26:16–19	135
9:1–6	78	30:21	73
9:6	78	31:35–37	75
11:1–5	78	40:4	47
14:12	87	48:26	97
16:5	78	50:6	137
16:14	97		
19:14	97		

INDEX

Ezekiel	
16:12	139
22:18–22	78
23:42	139
34	137
34:16	138
34:23	137
36:3	58

Hosea	
4:7	97
10:4	82
14:10	97

Amos	
1:3–2:3	96, 98, 118
5:10	83
8:5	120

Jonah	
3:7	107

Micah	
3:12	134–135
6:12	120

Nahum	
2:2	59
3:18	137

Habbakuk	
2:16	97

Zechariah	
5:1–4	102
9:16–17	139
10:1–5	140
11:4–15	143
13:7	143

Malachi	
1:6	101

Psalms	
4:3	101
5:10–11	113
7:16–17	122
8:6	81
9:5	78
9:5–6	78
9:10	112
9:16–17	122
10:18	112
11:4–5	78
16:5	78
18:15	59
19:8–11	124
21:6	101
21:8–14	79
28:3–4	121
29:2	81
31:14	58
32:9	102
33:1	99
35:5–6	113
37:2	136
45:7–8	79
46	134
48	134
55:15	124
64:7	76
68:2	59
69:5	56
72	75, 79, 140
72:4	112
72:1–4, 12–14	76
74:21	112
78:70–72	138
81:6	60
82	75, 79
84	134
87	134
89:5	78
89:15	78
89:37–38	78
89:40	134
90:5	136
93–97	75
93:1–2	78
93:1	85
93:2	78
93:5	99

94:5-6	112	28:28	75
96:8-9	81	29:16	76, 77
96:10	78, 85	31:35	58
97:2	78	32:11	77
103	136	34:24	76
103:19	78	36:26	76
104:5	78, 85	40:2	97
104:35	75		
106:25	111	Proverbs	
109:2	120	1:15	59
109:3	91	3:5	104, 105
110:1	73	3:7	103, 104, 105
112:6-7	85	3:23	59
115:15-16	74	3:35	97, 101
119	116	4:9	139
119:60	47	6:6	108
119:101	59	6:6-11	107
119:18	120	6:10-12	140
120:2	120	6:8	133
120:3-4	59	6:19	84, 85
122:5	78	7:11	59
129:6	136	7:21	113
131	86	8:15-16	142
133	124	8:18	86, 142
135-136	75	9:3	143
144:6	59	9:9	45
145:3	76	10-15	6, 46
145:5	81	10:1-22:16	6, 9
145:12	81	10:4-5	108, 110
147:1	99	10:5	133
		10:6	97
Job		10:8	97
5:4	112	10:10	97
5:9	76	10:11	97
8:10	76	10:12	112
8:12	136	10:13	102
9:33	83	10:18	58, 93, 112
11:7	75	10:20	78
13:8-9	77	10:26	85, 108
19:2	112	11:2	97
28	75	11:16	86, 101
28:3	75	11:21	79
28:11	75	11:22	51
28:20-21	75	12:3	85
28:27	75	12:4	139
		12:9	97

12:10–11	133, 138	18:8		111
12:15	104	18:12		86, 101
12:17	85, 120	18:13		56
12:28	123	18:16		83
13:17	68, 84	18:17	46, 76, 77, 80
13:17–21	84	19:1		95
13:18	97	19:5		85
13:23	46	19:6		83
14:4	133	19:10		99
14:5	85	19:21		69
14:25	85	19:29		102
14:28	81, 139	20:1		98, 99
14:32	113	20:3		63, 86, 101
14:34	58	20:4		108
15:1	51	20:5		76
15:8	102	20:8		79
15:23	59	20:9		109
15:28–22:16	81	20:12		83
15:31	83	20:14		109
15:33	86, 101	20:26		59, 79
16:1	69, 103	20:28 (LXX)		78
16:1–15	73	20:29		102, 139
16:2	103	21:1		69, 76, 105
16:9	69	21:2		104
16:12	78, 79	21:9		60
16:21	124	21:13		122
16:24	124	21:14		83
16:27–28	118	21:19		68
16:27–29	112	21:27		102
16:28	111	21:28		58
16:31	102, 139	21:30–31		69, 106
16:32	95	22:1		95
16–22:16	6	22:4		86
17:1	95	22:10		85
17:3	78	22:13		108, 109
17:6	139	22:17		140
17:7	99	22:22		112
17:10	102	22:29		109
17:15	80	23:8		97
17:17–18	101	23:29–35		140
17:26	80	23:35		98
18:2	76	24:1–22		140
18:4	76	24:13–14		124
18:6	102	24:21–22		73

24:23	99, 140	25:16-17	43, 53, 62, 64, 66, 69, 71-72, 73, 84, 85, 86
24:23-25	79	25:16-27	70
24:27	133	25:17	72, 85, 124
24:28	82	25:17-21	72, 84
24:30-31	133	25:18	59, 72, 84, 88, 119
24:30-34	107, 140	25:18-20	68, 73, 84, 113
24:33-34	140	25:18-24	84
25	46, 116	25:19	60, 85
25-27	18, 44, 79, 81, 131, 142	25:20	73, 85, 124
25-29	6, 9	25:21-22	60, 62, 71-72, 85
25:1	6, 22, 37, 79, 134	25:22	44
25:2	21, 22, 68-69, 70, 71, 73, 75, 77, 103, 105	25:23	124
25:2-3	63, 73-77, 85, 86, 104, 106	25:23-24	85
25:2-5	64, 79, 119	25:24	46, 60, 68, 95, 109
25:2-15	83	25:25	60, 65, 85, 101
25:2-27	21-28, 36, 39, 44, 56-86, 71, 101, 119	25:25-26	65
25:3	76, 90	25:26	68, 71, 79, 85, 86
25:4	56, 78, 82	25:27	21, 22, 60, 64, 68, 70, 71-72, 73, 81, 85-86
25:4-5	40, 53, 62-63, 66, 69, 73-77, 85, 86	25:28	70, 86
25:5	71-72, 75, 78, 79, 80, 85	26:1	22, 68, 81, 90, 101, 102, 105, 133
25:5-6	83	26:1-3	90-93, 99, 102, 113, 119
25:6	63	26:1-12	18, 30, 36, 39, 46, 48, 66, 70, 73, 87-106, 120, 124
25:6-7	114	26:2	58, 90-91, 102
25:6-10	62, 63, 76, 80-82, 83, 84	26:3	87, 91-92, 102
25:7	45, 63	26:4-5	18, 30, 43, 73, 102-106
25:7c-8	58	26:5	105
25:7c-10	117, 119	2:6	68, 108
25:8	56, 63, 72, 84	2:6-7	97
25:9	63, 72, 73, 84	26:6-9	113
25:9-10	57	26:6-12	94, 104, 120
25:10	83	26:7	18, 30, 104
25:11-12	82-83	26:8	101, 105
25:11-15	82	26:9	18, 30, 104
25:11	59, 73	26:9-11	98, 113
25:12	59, 90	26:12	94-95, 101, 104, 106, 108, 109, 123
25:13	53, 59, 60, 65, 68, 73, 101, 133	26:13-15	113
25:13-14	65, 83	26:13-16	36, 39, 73, 88, 107-110, 119
25:14	68	26:3	109
25:15	59, 69, 83, 112	26:16	95, 105, 108
25:16	22, 59, 70, 71, 85, 97	26:17	73, 82, 120

INDEX

26:17-19	119	28:25-26	104
26:17-28	36, 39, 111-122	29:2	71, 101, 109
26:18	59, 88	29:5	113
26:20	115	29:7	71, 138
26:20-23	112	29:12	101
26:23	111	29:14	78
26:24-25	114	29:16	71
26:25	44	29:17	71
26:28	112, 122	29:23	81, 86, 101
27:1-2	73, 128	30:8	141
27:1-22	36, 39, 123-129, 142	31:1-9	140, 142
27:2	81, 101, 123	31:1-29	71
27:3	73	31:10-31	140-143
27:3-4	128	31:15	136, 141, 142
27:4	127	31:16	133
27:5-6	128	31:27	143
27:8	82	Ruth	
26:9	124, 128	2:8	22, 23, 142
27:10	73, 128	3:2	142
27:11	45		
27:11-12	128	Qoheleth	
27:13-14	128	1:13	74
27:14	85	3:2-8	46
27:15-16	128	3:11	74
27:16	73	4:9	95
27:17	51, 73	4:13	101
27:17-18	128	7:23-25	74
27:18	101, 133	7:24	75
27:19	46, 73	8:16-17	74
27:19-20	128	10:5-7	101
27:20	73	10:8	122
27:21	78	11:1	76
27:21-22	128	Lamentations	
27:22	63, 73, 102	3:34	112
27:23	73, 137-138		
27:23-27	36, 39, 131-143	Daniel	
27:24	73, 133-134, 139	2:14	107
27:27	73, 141-142	6:24-25	122
28:1	71	1 Chronicles	
28:8	104	16:29	81
28:11	105	16:30	85
28:12	71	17:12	78
28:18	77	17:14	78
28:19	138	22:10	78

Canticles		25:27	99
1:5	99	27:25	122
2:14	99	27:27	122
4:3	99	27:29	122
6:4	99	28:17	112
		28:21	99
2 Esdras		33:24	102
4	86	37:29-30	59
Judith		Wisdom (Sap Sal)	
8:5	68	9:16	75
Sirach		11:16	122
1:1-3	75		
3:6-12	97	Matthew	
3:21-22	86	6:11	141
3:21-24	86	13:52	39
7:4-7	81, 86	23:6	81
10:18	99	23:25-28	121
10:23-24	101	Mark	
10:27-31	101	4:3-8	133
11:1-6	86		
11:4	75	Luke	
14:2	58	14:7-11	81
14:3	99	Romans	
15:9	99	9:20-23	78
15:9-10	104		
16:21-22	75, 102	1 Corinthians	
20:23	99	11:7	139
21:20	104	James	
22:6	85	2:1-7	81

Other Ancient Authors and Works

Akkadian:
"Counsels of Pessimism"	132-133
"Counsels of Wisdom"	82, 101
"Dialogue of Pessimism"	103
"Gilgamesh"	87, 102
Hammurabi, Codex	79, 137

Aramaic:
Ahiqar   18, 73, 82, 97, 102, 112, 133

Egyptian:
Ankhsheshonq	18, 81, 99, 101, 102, 105
Hardjedef	132
Hekanakhte	133
Hori	18
Merikare	79
Papyrus démotique Louvre 2414	19
Papyrus Insinger	19, 98, 102, 104
Ptahhotep	27, 81, 83, 100
"Satire of Trades"	83
Sehetepibre	22

Greek:

Aristotle	132
Hesiod	17, 132, 133
Menander the Egyptian	82
Sophocles. *Oedipus Rex*	76
Theophrastus	132

Hebrew and NorthWest Semitic:

Aboth 1:9	77
"Gezer Calendar"	133
Karatepe Inscription	79
Sanhedrin	
3:7	77
4:1	77
4:4	81
4:5	77
6:1	77
Yavneh Yam Ostracon	58

Latin:

Ambrose	29
Augustine	29
Cato	132
Jerome	60

Sumerian:

"Farmer's Almanac"	133
Lipit-Ishtar	137
Proverbial Sayings	91

www.ingramcontent.com/pod-product-compliance
Lightning Source LLC
Chambersburg PA
CBHW032256150426
43195CB00008BA/478